Welcome to the EVERYTHING® series!

These handy, accessible books give you all you need to tackle a difficult project, gain a new hobby, comprehend a fascinating topic, prepare for an exam, or even brush up on something you learned back in school but have since forgotten.

You can read an *EVERYTHING®* book from cover to cover or just pick out the information you want from our four useful boxes: e-facts, e-ssentials, e-alerts, and e-questions. We literally give you everything you need to know on the subject, but throw in a lot of fun stuff along the way, too.

We now have well over 100 *EVERYTHING®* books in print, spanning such wide-ranging topics as weddings, pregnancy, wine, learning guitar, one-pot cooking, managing people, and so much more. When you're done reading them all, you can finally say you know *EVERYTHING®*!

FACTS
Important sound bytes of information

ESSENTIALS
Quick handy tips

ALERT
Urgent warnings

QUESTIONS?
Solutions to common problems

THE
EVERYTHING
Series

Dear Reader,

Over the years I've made many knits and many knitting mistakes. There have been lots of UFOs (Un-Finished Objects) and unraveling along the way. Painful learning experiences, yes, but the best kind—the kind that teach you about yourself. I've discovered that the part of knitting I enjoy most (aside from knitting as meditation) is playing with textures and colors of yarn. I love experimenting with combinations until I find those that make me smile. So these days I follow simple patterns. My time and effort go into what I consider the fun part: making a wearable work of art.

Some people feel that "fun" and "art" are no excuse for a sloppy sleeve or a badly made buttonhole. That may be true, but it's still your sleeve and your buttonhole. You made the sweater, with all its faults, and you can choose to take pride in it, or you can pull it undone and begin again. I believe knitting today is a craft of self-expression. I believe that your goal should not be to become an expert in all aspects of knitting (unless that's what you want to achieve) but to make something that's truly a reflection of you.

I hope you enjoy knitting and find, as I have, that happiness is homemade.

Jane Eldershaw

THE
EVERYTHING®
KNITTING BOOK

Simple instructions for creating
beautiful handmade items for your
family and friends

Jane Eldershaw

Adams Media Corporation
Avon, Massachusetts

EDITORIAL
Publishing Director: Gary M. Krebs
Managing Editor: Kate McBride
Copy Chief: Laura MacLaughlin
Acquisitions Editor: Bethany Brown
Development Editor: Christel A. Shea
Production Editor: Khrysti Nazzaro

PRODUCTION
Production Director: Susan Beale
Production Manager: Michelle Roy Kelly
Series Designer: Daria Perreault
Cover Design: Paul Beatrice and Frank Rivera
Layout and Graphics: Brooke Camfield,
Colleen Cunningham, Rachael Eiben,
Michelle Roy Kelly, and Daria Perreault

An Everything® Series Book.
Everything® and everything.com® are registered trademarks of F+W Publications, Inc.

Published by Adams Media, an F+W Publications Company
57 Littlefield Street, Avon, MA 02322 U.S.A.
www.adamsmedia.com

ISBN: 1-58062-727-7
Printed in the United States of America.

J I H G F E D

Library of Congress Cataloging-in-Publication Data
Eldershaw, Jane.
The everything knitting book / Jane Eldershaw.
    p.   cm.   — (Everything series)
            ISBN 1-58062-727-7
        I. Title. II. Series.
TT820 .E53   2002
746.43'2—dc21   2002009411

This publication is designed to provide accurate and authoritative information with regard to the subject matter covered. It is sold with the understanding that the publisher is not engaged in rendering legal, accounting, or other professional advice. If legal advice or other expert assistance is required, the services of a competent professional person should be sought.
—From a *Declaration of Principles* jointly adopted by a Committee of the American Bar Association and a Committee of Publishers and Associations

Cover illustrations by Barry Littmann.
Interior illustrations by Eric Andrews.
Interior stitch samples on pages 75–78, 143–145, 152,
177, 205, 206, and 246 knitted by Christel Shea.
Interior photographs by Scott Watrous and Brooke Camfield.
Special thanks to Sophie Cathro, Scott Watrous, Daria Perreault,
Frank Rivera, and Michelle Kelly for assisting with photography.

This book is available at quantity discounts for bulk purchases.
For information, call 1-800-872-5627.

Visit the entire Everything® series at *www.everything.com*

Contents

Dedication

With thanks and gratitude to my favorite knitters (or would-be knitters): Sheree Bykofsky, Megan Buckley, Anna Clark, Marguerite Smith, Dee Anne Dyke, Gaynor Kaad, Elisabeth MacIntyre, and Julie Walker.

Acknowledgments

With thanks and gratitude to Ed Hamrick of Caron Yarns, Rowena Hart of Ashford Handicrafts, Rob Delmont of Skacel Yarns, Susan Druding of Crystal Palace Yarns, and Catherine Blythe of Spinrite Yarns.

Introduction

KNITTING IS both a creative and a therapeutic endeavor, a way of engaging the fingers in useful work while enabling the mind to wander where it will. Once you've mastered this repetitive, physical activity, you will find it's easy to allow your mind to become calm, to reflect—perhaps even to meditate. Knitting is such a perfect way to unwind that the finished product can seem like just a bonus. Not only is knitting soothing while you're doing it, but you get a satisfying feeling of accomplishment when you successfully complete your project.

The Everything® Knitting Book is your key to the world of those who make things with their hands. From the first moment you pick up those simple-looking sticks, to the time you tie off your last pom-pom, you can rely on this book to walk you through cables, colors, and caring for your creation.

Practice the basics of knitting and the various stitches. Learn to read patterns, and even design your own. Using the variety of methods we describe and illustrate, you'll gain an understanding of why some stitches are better than others for creating certain looks. Do you want a lacy collar or a sturdy ribbed hem? Fringe or sequins? Are you creating a delicate baby sweater set, or are you working with a heavy Irish wool?

In addition to clearly explaining the fundamentals of knitting, from choosing your yarn to selecting the right needles, *The Everything® Knitting Book* teaches you how to finish and decorate your projects. We even give you some information on crocheting and how it can be used to enhance your knitted work.

Once you've mastered the most basic of stitches, you can make a sweater that fits perfectly—one that takes into account your own personal physical quirks, like narrow shoulders or a long waist. Make something that fits *you*—whether it gently forgives a growing waistline or has a high turtleneck to hide your own turtle neck. With a bit of practice, you will be able to make something exactly the way you want it—a rare pleasure, these days, and so unlike the rest of life!

A variety of knitted items will keep you warm anytime

hat knitted by Sophie Cathro; scarf knitted by Colleen Cunningham; sweater knitted by Alice Cathro

If you feel guilty watching TV, try picking up your needles when you tune in. Carry your project with you on car trips, into waiting rooms, or to the kids' soccer practice—when you have your knitting along, any downtime can be productive.

Remember, also, that you're carrying on a fine tradition that's been around for thousands of years. If your grandmother or mother knitted, you are continuing a beautiful family custom. That makes you a link from your family's past to its future. Our resource list includes books and Web sites, as well as guilds and associations. As a hobby, knitting is as social as it is creative. Look into resources in your area for clubs or classes to fit your schedule.

Best of all, knitting is a guilt-free indulgence—one of those rare pastimes that makes you feel good but that isn't dishonest, illegal, or fattening. *The Everything® Knitting Book* has all the information you need to go from novice to natural in no time. Pull up a chair, get comfortable, and put your mind, spirit, and fingers to work.

Chapter 1
Why People Knit

Knitting is as simple and magical as the games children play with string. Just by manipulating strands of yarn, you transform a continuous thread into a piece of fabric. Knitting is a simple, everyday magic that all sorts of people have performed for centuries, in many parts of the world—and it's something you can learn to do, too!

The Basics of Knitting

Knitted fabric is made of loops of thread that interlock row by row. The number of loops in each row determines the width of the fabric. Using needles to pull more yarn through the loops of each row, the knitter continues to build upon the stitches of the preceding row. With each new row, a little more fabric grows from the needles. The knitter shapes this fabric by decreasing or increasing the number of stitches in different areas, according to a pattern. Enough pieces of the right shapes will eventually produce a piece of clothing, a toy, an afghan, or some other unique, handcrafted item.

Don't be intimidated by the complex patterns and intricate stitches you'll see in yarn store displays. The basic knitting stitches are really very easy. As with any new skill, once you know the fundamentals, learning more complicated variations is less intimidating.

Once you learn how to hold your yarn and needles and how to form the knit and purl stitches, the most important skill is turning out even, regular fabric. Knitting evenly is basically a matter of making all your stitches the same size, or with a uniform *tension* or *gauge count*.

FACTS

Knitters even knit sweaters for penguins! At the first sign of an environmental threat, volunteers clothe the miniature breed that lives in the waters in and around South Australia, Tasmania, and New Zealand in handmade sweaters—and constantly need more because the tiny garments are only used once. E-mail the Phillip Island Penguin Parade at ✎*penguins@penguins.org.au* for more information.

As with any craft, you must get a grasp of the basics before you attempt to create anything too ambitious. In other words, allow yourself time to learn how to knit. When you learn to cook, you are prepared for the possibility that your first soufflé might collapse. It's the same with any craft: explore how it's done, become more proficient, and in the process discover which aspect of it appeals to you most.

Who Knits?

According to ✍ *www.WorldKnit.com*, there are 24 million active knitters and crocheters in the United States alone. What kind of people are they?

In the past, knitters may have been the humorous middle-aged ladies that the movies and cartoons depict: portly matrons in shapeless garments of their own manufacture, relentlessly pressing unwanted gifts of grotesquely oversized sweaters on hapless recipients. But this character is a fading memory. Today's knitters include teenagers who knit themselves sexy lacy T-shirts, artists who use knitting needles to make imaginative and often witty objects and wall hangings, and environmentalists who knit sweaters for penguins.

Knitters are men and women from all walks of life. Knitting can introduce you to whole new worlds and to wonderful friends. Why not start a local knitting circle and share the pleasure of creating? The differences among the members' background, aesthetics, and interests will stimulate and inspire the whole group.

Knitting is the perfect hobby for anyone who seems to spend a lot of time waiting around. Anyone who needs to be "present" and aware of what's happening around them can still be gainfully employed doing something for himself or herself.

ESSENTIALS

The best knitters form stitches almost exactly the same size every time. Knitting evenly makes everything easier—from following a pattern, to putting the final pieces together. Imagine trying to assemble a sweater with two different-sized sleeves!

Many knitters love the individuality of handcrafted products. Some want to be part of the back-to-basics, keep-it-simple movement. Still others just long to do something personal and creative with their hands after sitting in front of a computer all day.

Most of all, people who knit create with both their hands and their hearts. Sure, they could buy presents for friends, but it gives them so much more pleasure to make something with love. Many knitters make garments for people they've never met, unborn babies and people in need. Giving is a generous, humanitarian trait that people who knit seem to share. From the thousands who responded to the soldiers' needs for warm clothes in the trenches during World War I to the thousands who knit for others today, knitters help make the world a warmer, cozier place.

A Brief History of Knitting

Few knitted garments from ancient times have survived. Besides being well used, they were made of common materials that disintegrated over time. The craft itself, being a minor and domestic one, only recently captured the interest of many historians.

Nevertheless, we know that hand knitting has been practiced for thousands of years. Knitted socks have been discovered in Egyptian tombs that date from between three and six centuries B.C. The craft probably spread from the Arab countries along the trade routes. It's likely most of the folk-knitting traditions of Europe and Asia originated from techniques the Moors brought to Spain in the eighth century A.D.

Spreading Trends

By the ninth century, knitting had spread via the sea trade routes to the islands off the coast of Scotland. Aran and Fair Isle aren't just the names of knitting styles; they are the names of the places where those styles started. Legend has it that a ship from the Spanish Armada was wrecked off the island Fair Isle in 1558. The sailors were wearing brightly colored sweaters with Catholic symbols knitted in, which the islanders adapted. Whether this actually happened or not, the craftspeople living on Fair Isle created a distinctive and beautiful style of knitting characterized by striped bands containing crosses, lozenges and stars, among other symbols.

Other remote fishing villages of eastern Scotland, northeastern England, and Cornwall developed unique styles, too—no doubt for practical reasons. Fishermen going out to sea in freezing conditions need warm sweaters. A stitch that creates a thick pad of wool—such as the thick cables in Aran-style knitting or the extra wool used in multicolored Fair Isle patterns—makes a much warmer sweater than a plain stitch. Often, the traditional designs use these thicker decorative stitches over the chest area.

FACTS

Each fishing village once had its own knitting patterns, in much the same way that the Scottish clans had individual tartans. Patterns were passed down through generations, described and shown rather than written down. These designs were so localized that, it is said, at one time it was possible to identify a drowned fisherman's home by the style of his sweater (or, to use the old style English word, gansey).

By the Middle Ages, knitted clothing was common throughout Western Europe. Knitting and hosiery guilds, or craft groups, were formed to teach male apprentices how to make caps, stockings, and gloves. ("Flat" knitting is a recent trend—knitting was originally done on four needles to make tubular garments, like hosiery.) By the sixteenth century, hand knitting was an important industry. Britain, with its many varieties of sheep and superior wool production, exported worsted (or yarn) stockings, and the art of making fine metal knitting needles was perfected. Even Shakespeare mentions knitting in his plays—in *The Taming of the Shrew*, servants wear "garters of an indifferent knit."

The Start of Modern Knitting

During the reign of Queen Elizabeth I, William Lee, a clergyman, invented the first knitting machine in England.

The story is that Lee presented the queen with a pair of wool stockings. Perhaps afraid that the new invention would endanger the hand-knitted woolen clothing industry, she asked him to try to make silk stockings, which at that time were a Spanish import. Lee succeeded, but the queen still refused to grant him a patent.

Lee took his manufacturing operations to France—a country notorious for those unique knitting characters, the *tricoteuses*, women who sat by the guillotine during the French Revolution. Charles Dickens made them famous in his novel *A Tale of Two Cities*: "All the women knitted. They knitted worthless things; but the mechanical work was a mechanical substitute for eating and drinking. . . . Darkness encompassed them . . . where they were to sit, knitting, knitting, counting dropping heads."

Until about the mid-1800s, only the lower classes knitted. Poor children learned how to knit at age four and were encouraged to knit in groups, singing knitting songs to help them keep a uniform and quick pace.

In the nineteenth century, the Industrial Revolution mechanized knitting machines and the hand-knitting trade declined. Then, of course, it became a genteel pastime for fashionable ladies. Even the young Queen Victoria knitted. Yarn manufacturers started printing knitting pattern books to help sell their wares.

Knitting reached its height of popularity in England during World War I, when uniform items were in short supply. Queen Mary issued an appeal for woolens. Sheet music, posters, postcards, and patriotic knitting books urged both men and women to do their part in the war effort. So they knitted nonstop—in trains, restaurants, and the theatre—producing thousands of khaki-colored socks, vests, mitts, and a headdress known as a balaclava helmet that covered the ears and neck.

Knitting on the Runway

The Edwardians rejected Victorian formality after World War I, and a more relaxed style of dress came into fashion. Pastimes like golf and motoring became popular, too, and sports pullovers and cardigans made of knitted fabrics were comfortable to wear while doing them. When the Prince of Wales wore a Fair Isle sweater while golfing in Scotland in 1922, he started a fashion that both sexes adopted.

Coco Chanel was one of the first couturiers to enthuse over knitted garments. In the 1920s, she wore striped French fisherman's sweaters, and her knitted suits were popular in the 1950s. In 1920, Italian Elsa

Schiaparelli designed a sweater with a *trompe l'oeil* bow on the front that would not look dated today.

In the 1960s, knitting machines became more efficient, making available a greater choice of knitted fabrics. Synthetic yarns made easy fitting, casual, jersey clothes like Mary Quant's "Ginger Group Collection" ubiquitous. Then came the 1970s, with the movement towards all things natural—natural fibers, ethnic styles, and hands-on crafts like crochet. Today, as life becomes more and more technological and fast-paced, there's a renewed interest in knitting and crocheting by hand.

Knitting as Art

Design your own style of clothing

knitted by Ann MacLaughlin

Now that computer-controlled knitting machines can mass-produce the most complicated patterns mechanically, hand knitting has become a personalized art. Designers are using all sorts of new and exciting materials, including yarns made from suede, rags, plastic sheeting, and fur. In Florence, Italy, a semiannual trade fair, called Pitti Filati, is dedicated just to yarns.

The whole area of textile art is becoming more and more popular, with a growing trend toward combining freestyle knitting, crochet, and embroidery to create wall hangings, three-dimensional objects, and one-of-a-kind wearable art. As young craftspeople take up the ancient art of spinning, they add to the variety of available materials by using unusual fibers from all-but-forgotten breeds of goats and sheep.

High Fashion

Innovative designers like Kaffe Fassett, whose book *Glorious Knitting* (Ebury Press, 1999) was a huge success, have rejuvenated the craft and made knitting a whole new art form. His intricate patterns use dozens of complicated color designs. But they produce sweaters with such exuberant mixtures of bold and bright colors, patterns, textures, and styles that knitters attempt them anyway.

Many celebrities have collected Kaffe's unique designs, including Barbra Streisand, Lauren Bacall, John Schlesinger, Ali McGraw, Irene Worth, Shirley Maclaine, Helen Frankenthaler, Alan Bergman, and H.R.H. Princess Michael of Kent.

In 1988, the Victoria and Albert Museum hosted a retrospective exhibition of Kaffe's work, making him the first living textile artist to have a one-man show at the museum.

Museum Quality

Other art galleries have begun taking knitted pictures and sculpture seriously, too. In 1997, The Gallery at Harmony Hall Regional Center, in Fort Washington, Maryland, held a show entitled "Breaking Patterns: Contemporary Hand Knitting in the United States." The exhibit presented knitted objects as art, in much the same way sculptures and paintings are customarily displayed and promoted.

FACTS

Diana, Princess of Wales, furthered the popularity of picture knits by wearing these distinctive sweaters. One was a gift from Australia that featured a koala on the front. Jenny Kee, the artist, was one of the first designers to produce hand knits that were also works of art.

Today, many artists are exploiting the possibilities of yarn texture, stitch structure, and color in knitting. Oliver Herring, a German-born artist, knits shiny, opaque, three-dimensional objects from common plastic transparent tape and sometimes strips of silver Mylar. Freddie Robins, an artist who finds knitted textiles a powerful medium for self-expression, designs surreal garments. Her sweaters might sprout three arms or feature floor-sweeping sleeves, and her other work includes witty "tree cozies" and "log cozies." Her work has been shown in Sotheby's London galleries.

Who would have guessed that the beginning of the twenty-first century would see such a renaissance in the textile arts? Never has there been a more interesting time to explore all the creative possibilities knitting has to offer.

Simplify Your Knitting Experience

If knitting is so easy, why do some people lose patience and abandon their knitting projects halfway through? Here are some ways around the most common pitfalls:

- **Don't rush.** For your first attempts, take a ball of strong wool—real wool is elastic and easy to work with—and any size pair of needles (the large sizes are often easier for beginners to handle). Knit a square, strip, or oblong just for the sake of knitting. Then unravel the piece and start again. Do this over and over.
- **Experiment.** Try different combinations of purl and knit stitches. With every practice square you knit, your tension or gauge will be stabilizing. In fact, what you are really doing is practicing making gauge swatches. You will learn whether you are a loose or a tight knitter, a helpful thing to know before you start a real pattern.

ALERT

Until you've had a bit of practice making things, find a beginner's project and follow the pattern exactly. Make the gauge swatch with exactly the yarn and needles indicated. If your swatch is bigger or smaller than it should be, adjust needle size accordingly.

- **Read the directions.** The first thing to do is to read the directions all the way through before you even pick your needles. Make sure everything is clear and that you understand all the stitches and directions. If there's something you can't grasp, get help from books or knitting experts (someone at your yarn shop, for example, or an experienced knitter friend) before you begin. Don't wait until you've bought the yarn to discover that a pattern is too hard to follow.

- **Help yourself.** Take a few minutes before you begin, to make your pattern user-friendly. Enlarge and photocopy the pattern, then put it into a format that is easy to follow. Some knitters glue each row of the instructions to index cards so they can flip from one card to another. Some copy out the instructions into a notebook, writing them in a more easy-to-follow format. The main thing is to have a method that makes it easier to remember where you are in the pattern.

- **Know the lingo.** At first, reading a knitting pattern is like trying to read a foreign language—and because many patterns are from other countries, sometimes you are! Be aware of your pattern's origin. This book uses both British and American terms, such as the British "tension" for the American "gauge count," to help you become familiar with both.

Reading patterns will become easier with time. Once you've followed a few, the abbreviations and the way instructions are written will all start to make sense. It's important to start with a simple pattern so you don't get discouraged. Many patterns are coded for different levels of ability, so look for one that matches your expertise.

Other Considerations

Keep a vision of the finished product in mind. When you make a fitted garment, you should have an idea of the shapes you are making. Beginners who blindly try to follow the "slip-ones" and "knit-two-togethers" without seeing the big picture can make all sorts of mistakes. If you understand why you are decreasing—to shape an armhole, for example—you'll know whether the fabric is making the right shape and be able to correct any problems that arise.

QUESTIONS?

What if you love a pattern but it seems too difficult?
See if there's a child's version you can make first. Knitting on a smaller scale is more manageable, and there are fewer stitches to unravel when something goes wrong!

It's also important to know yourself, your temperament, and your abilities. For example, if you like working through complicated crossword puzzles, and you can't rest until they're finished, a plain garment in stockinette fabric will probably bore you. You need to find a pattern complicated enough to keep you interested. If, on the other hand, you are an impatient person with a short attention span, go for big needles and big knits. Keep in mind your own idiosyncrasies. If you know your tension is uneven, and some of your stitches are bigger than others, you can hide the flaws with a nubbly, textured wool, or you can make a lacy scarf, which is all holes and cobwebby fabric.

ESSENTIALS Be tolerant of a few flaws. Don't let your perfectionist tendencies get out of hand! A machine can knit a garment perfectly, but what you are creating is a work of art, with unique characteristics.

If you're upset at the way a project seems to be turning out, leave the knitting for a few days and then look at it again. Ask yourself if you, or the person you're knitting it for, would wear it as is. If the sleeves aren't attached properly or your necklines turned out lumpy, the garment is going to look more hands-at-home than high fashion. If you know you wouldn't be happy wearing the garment, cut your losses and rip it out. Fix what's bothering you, or use the yarn to make something easier.

Better to end up with something you'll use than something that will sit in your closet forever, making you feel resentful whenever you catch sight of it. The trick to completing your knitting happily is to know the limits of your mechanical skills and to match the project to your personality.

Don't be afraid to ask for help or suggestions. Enthusiastic knitters who run their own shops are usually happy to find patterns for wool you like, send away for special items, or query manufacturers for more of a particular dye lot when you've run out. If they have time, some will also help you understand where you've gone wrong with a pattern if you take your knitting in to show them. Naturally, they'll be more eager to help if you are considerate. Call ahead, and try to time your visit for a quiet time, like mid-week. Don't arrive just before closing time, and leave the kids at home.

Think Ahead

Although you won't appreciate this advice until after you've completed your first few projects, it's important to keep track of what you make, right from the beginning. Keep a notebook or binder, complete with swatches of the yarn you used and a label from the yarn with washing instructions. Write down whom the garment was for, how you visualized it, any difficulties you had, and how it turned out. If possible, take a photograph of the finished product.

FACTS

Most knitters find that the repetitive nature of the craft is no strain on their hands. In fact, knitting can be a good exercise. This is especially true if you use light circular needles, so that your hands aren't carrying the entire weight of the wool, and if you take frequent breaks.

Record the amount of yarn the project took, how much you had left over, and any changes you made in the pattern or size. You can also note the yarn tension and needle size you used. These notes will help you figure out, generally, how much yarn you use on different garments for different people. The next time a few balls of beautiful yarn catch your eye, you'll know what you'll be able to knit with them. Your "knitting book" will be a great reminder of the yarns you enjoyed using as well as those that were disappointing when they were knitted up. If you include your tension gauge sample, you'll have even more information.

When you're planning a new project, think about the who and the why of it, as well as the how and the what. In other words, try to make something special each time you knit. Whether you decide to make a blanket for a friend's new baby, or a glorious jacket in exotic yarn as a treat to yourself, the loving feelings that initiate a project can also elevate it to a work of art.

CHAPTER 2
Yarn

Yarn is the generic word for any spun fiber, whether it comes from a plant (such as cotton, flax, or linen) or an animal (silk, wool, angora, or mohair), or it is man made (like polyester and acrylic fibers). When it comes to the art of knitting, however, yarn is a fundamental element. Choosing the best yarn for your pattern is critical to your success.

Yarn for Knitting

When you start a project, you'll find that you have both practical and creative yarn choices. You must weigh the advantages and disadvantages of the different yarns available, keeping in mind the purpose of what you're making. Your main decision concerns fiber content and care of the finished garment—for example, wool is warm, but must be hand washed.

Man-Made Fibers

Instead of wool, you may choose a man-made fiber, such as Acrilan, Orlon, or Nylon. These polyester and acrylic yarns became popular after the 1950s. They're still usually cheaper than wool. Acrylic is good for people who are allergic to wool or for garments that are mothproof or easy to wash. Baby and children's clothes are washed (and dirtied) frequently, so synthetic yarns might be your best choice.

However, acrylics tend to pill—get little balls of fiber on their surface— and are not as elastic as wool or as forgiving to knit with. They also don't breathe like wool does, so they're not as good as keeping you warm and dry, and they seem to stain easily. Sometimes a blend of both is a good compromise.

Plant Fibers

Yarns made from plants—cotton, linen, ramie, sisal, hemp, jute, raffia, and flax—are usually stiffer and less elastic than yarn spun from animal hair. They also slide less easily over knitting needles. Because the fibers have no give, you may find them difficult to knit with. Garments made with cotton often need to be hand washed, and they tend to stretch out of shape after a while. This is especially true with ribbing: always knit ribbing in cotton on smaller needles to help prevent saggy, stretched-out cuffs. Follow the washing directions carefully to reduce stretching and prevent running, or bleeding, colors. If you are going to use a light color and a dark color together, be sure to do a washing test first.

Fibers from Animals

Silk is made from fibers unraveled from the silkworm's cocoon. Silk yarn is strong and shiny. Because it is so slippery, though, a heavy silk hand-knit can slide out of shape easily. Loosely twisted silk yarns tend to pill, and silk disintegrates more quickly than other yarns when exposed to sunlight. Yarns blended from silk and other fibers often prove more satisfactory for knitting than pure silk yarn.

Wool is ideal for knitting because its elasticity forgives uneven tension—if your stitches vary from tight to loose, using wool can help even this out somewhat. Sometimes children find wool itchy, but the many different breeds of sheep produce wool of varying softness.

FACTS

Aran is a type of wool as well as a style of sweater. It is less processed than other wool. Its natural oils are not stripped out, making it very waterproof. Aran wool comes in natural, creamy colors.

Shetland wool comes from sheep on the Shetland Islands. It is a good, fine wool for featherweight lace knitting. Lopi yarn is from an Icelandic breed of sheep, which produce long, soft wool good for knitting outdoor wear. Merino is one of the best all-round varieties of wool.

Cashmere and mohair come from goats; mohair is the fuzzier of the two. Both are expensive and luxurious. Before knitting a pattern in mohair, keep in mind that some people find it scratches against the skin. The yarn tangles very easily, too. It can be a headache to unravel if you are following a complicated pattern and keep making mistakes. (Some knitters say that putting mohair in the freezer for an hour or so makes it easier to pick apart.)

Cashmere yarn is luxuriously soft, but it's rare and expensive. Cashmere garments can get matted if they are washed in water that's too hot. For hand knitting, cashmere is often spun with wool to make a stronger and cheaper yarn.

Angora yarn comes from albino angora rabbits. Rabbit hair is short and slippery and difficult to spin, so it's usually mixed with other fibers.

Pure angora is expensive, very fluffy, and it tends to shed—some people are allergic to it. Angora needs to be washed carefully and should never be dry-cleaned with heat.

Alpaca yarn comes from the alpaca, an animal like a llama. It is heavier and less elastic than wool. Alpaca garments easily stretch out of shape, but they wear well. When knitted, it is very soft and slightly hairy, which some people find irritates the skin. Alpaca usually comes in natural shades: beige, grays, and browns.

Ply, Thickness, and Weight

Although there is no universal standard in the way yarns are manufactured, there are universally accepted terms to indicate the thickness of a yarn, such as DK, or double knit. Yarns from different makers, however, differ in thickness and in length. One company's double knit may be of a completely different thickness than another company's.

Manufacturers make many types of yarn and give them all sorts of creative names to help sell their products. These clever names don't always give an indication of the yarn's thickness.

Confused? It's safest to buy exactly what a pattern calls for, especially when you're starting out. Even experienced knitters can easily miscalculate the amounts they need if they are substituting. There's no harm at all in substituting if you can achieve the right gauge count with a different yarn. Read on for more information.

Ply—especially when linked with a number, such as *2-ply*—looks as if it should refer to a yarn's thickness. In practice, though, ply just signifies how many strands of spun yarn were put together to make a particular yarn. Untwist a section of yarn and you will be able to count the ply. Two-ply yarn, for example, is made up of two threads, or strands, twisted together to make a thicker strand. One manufacturer's 2-ply can be much thicker, or thinner, than another's.

Alternately, in Europe, ply is more of a reference to weight. An 8-ply yarn (which may be made up of three strands) is similar to a sport weight yarn.

Various ply, thickness, yarns, and weight

scarf knitted by Daria Perreault

Weight

The five general terms that indicate different weights of yarns go from the most delicate, *baby yarn*, to the heftiest, *extra bulky*. There is also a very fine 2-ply, or lace-weight yarn, but it is usually used for making lace with a crochet hook.

Baby yarns, also called fingering weight yarns, are very fine. In Europe they are called 3-, 4-, or 5-ply. These yarns are softly twisted and lightweight. They are suitable for delicate garments, such as shawls and socks, and baby clothes. Fingering yarns usually knit at a gauge of 7 or 8 stitches to the inch on smaller-sized needles. Of course, these gauge numbers are just general guidelines—every manufacturer's yarn is slightly different.

Sport weight yarns, also called double knit or DK weight, make lightweight adult clothes. They knit up to 5 or 6 stitches to the inch on number 6 needles. In Europe, this weight is often called 8-ply.

Worsted weight is a good all-purpose yarn. The gauge is usually 4 stitches to the inch on a number 6 to a number 9 needle. There is also a heavy worsted weight, which is a bit thicker. In Europe, worsted weight is equal to 10-ply or Aran weight.

Chunky knit, or bulky, yarns are extra thick and good for outdoor garments. They knit up quickly at 3 stitches to the inch on a number 10 or 11 needle. In Europe, this is called 12-ply yarn.

Extra bulky, also called super bulky or chunky, is the thickest category. These yarns knit at a gauge of 2–2½ stitches to the inch on number 13 needles or larger. You can finish a garment made in extra bulky in a few hours. The European equivalent is 14-ply.

If necessary, you can sometimes turn a lighter yarn into a thicker one by using two strands at once. But, as always, checking gauge is the only way to be sure you are using the right weight of yarn. The following chart gives approximate equivalents.

YARN WEIGHT CONVERSIONS

Two strands fingering weight (4-ply)	One strand sport weight (8-ply)
Two strands sport weight (8-ply)	One strand worsted weight (10-ply)
Two strands worsted weight	One strand bulky weight
Three strands worsted weight	One strand extra bulky weight

Texture and Color Combinations

You'll find that some terms on yarn labels refer to the yarn's type, not its weight. For example, crepe yarns are lightweight with a crinkly surface that comes from being more tightly twisted than other yarns. Ultimately, then, they produce a smoother fabric.

Other textures include boucle and chenille. Boucle, or poodle yarn, has irregular loops and a lumpy surface that gives knits a spongy look. Chenille is not spun like most yarns. The deep pile is applied to a central core, which gives the knits a distinctive, velvety look. In general, textured yarns can be difficult to work with. They are not recommended for beginners.

If you'd like to add some variety to your early projects, your best bet is to experiment with color. You can use separate colors to make stripes or contrasting hems and cuffs. Or you can look for yarns that are, themselves, multicolored. Tweed yarns are strands of different colors twisted into one yarn, creating subtle multicolored effects when they are knitted up. Similarly, heathers include flecks of similar or complementary colors, giving the finished yarn great depth.

ESSENTIALS

Variegated yarns are a good choice for beginning knitters who want variety in their work but who aren't at the level of working multiple yarns. Variegated yarn also hides uneven and twisted stitches better than solid colors.

Ombre and variegated yarns are dyed with a sequence of several different colors repeated along the strand. The length of each color varies slightly so that as you knit, the colors form a pattern on the finished item.

Next time you have an afternoon free, spend some time in your local yarn shop or craft store. Most shops have a dizzying array of options, and the better stores have some samples knitted up already. It's one thing to like the balls of yarn stacked in bins—it's quite another to get a real idea of how your yarn will come together in a finished item.

Buying Yarn

Yarn comes in balls, skeins, and cones. A skein is usually bigger but thinner than a ball and often contains more yarn. Cones, usually sold for use with knitting machines, hold more yarn than a skein or ball. The yarn is wound around a cardboard cone shape. Always wash your gauge swatch when using yarns manufactured specifically for machines. They are often given a waxy coating to tame down any loose threads that might catch on the internal parts of a knitting machine.

ESSENTIALS

Always buy the best yarn you can afford. When you are choosing or matching colors, look at the yarn in daylight. A store's fluorescent lights can distort hues.

On a budget? You may find quality yarns for cheaper prices at thrift shops—you can even harvest yarn by unraveling hand-knit sweaters you find there.

Craft shops often have specials on discontinued wool and odd balls. Or, if you knit for charity, put up a notice at your church asking for donations of leftover yarn from finished or abandoned knitting or crochet projects. Many people sell their yarn stashes on online auction sites like ✑*www.eBay.com,* too.

If you are willing to experiment, you can use unconventional threads as yarn—anything long and flexible enough can be knitted. String from the hardware shop can make hammocks or tote bags. Some people knit with ribbon, raffia, or strips cut from fabric or plastic sheeting.

Varied yarn types and textures

knitted by sophie Cathro (l) and Christel Shea (r)

Read the Label

Yarn labels contain all sorts of useful information

TO START:
First pull left (←) yarn end free from inside of skein. Then, slowly pull right (→) yarn end and continue working with it.

POUR COMMENCER:
Premièrement, enlevez le bout du fil gauche (←) de l'intérieur de la balle, puiz tirez lentement le bout du fil droit (→) et continuez a travailler avec celui-ci.

PARA EMPEZAR:
Primero jale la punta izquierda (←) del estambre desde el centro de la madeja. Despunes, lentamente jale la punta derecha (→) y continue trabajandolo asi.

WORSTED WEIGHT • 4 PLY / BRINS / CABOS

NO NAME YARN

SUPER SAVER

NO DYE LOT

NET WT 8 oz | POIDS NET 225 g | PESO NETO 225 g

MACHINE WASHABLE AND DURABLE	LAVABLE ET SECHABLE A LA MACHINE	SE PUEDE LAVAR Y SECAR A MAQUINA
100% ACRYLIC	100% ACRYLIQUE	100% ACRILICO
Mothproof Colorfast Shrink-Proof	Antimites Bon Teint Ne Rétrécit Pas	Antipolilla No Destiñe No Encoje
CARE INSTRUCTIONS ON REVERSE SIDE OF LABEL	MODE D'ENTRETIEN AU VERSO DE L'ÉTIQUETTE	INSTRUCCIONES PARA EL CUIDADO AL REVES DE LA ETIQUETA

Before you buy any yarn, always read the information on the paper label (around a ball of yarn) or on the tag (attached to a skein). The label tells you what kind of yarn it is, how you should care for the finished garment, and how much yarn there is to a ball. Some labels even have free patterns printed inside.

The label will also carry the dye lot number. Even natural-colored wool that doesn't look dyed goes through chemical processes and has dye lot numbers. There's usually also a number for the color: ordering is safer when you can refer to the color by number instead of by name. Be careful not to confuse the two.

Yarns are dyed in batches. Because balls from different dye lots may vary slightly in tone, it's very important to always buy enough yarn in one dye lot to finish your project. Even though the yarns of a different dye lot may look the same in a skein, subtle variations of color can show up in the finished knit. If you worry about buying too much, see if you can return "unopened" skeins.

Color maven Kaffe Fassett takes a completely different view—he welcomes subtle color variations and thinks the more colors in a sweater, the better. Indeed, if you do end up with skeins of different dye lots, make it a feature. Change balls every few rows, so the fabric will look variegated by design, or use different dye lots for different sections of the knitting. If you use the odd dye lot yarn on the ribbing or collar, for example, the change of stitch and needle size minimizes the color difference.

Using Yarn

Start by pulling out the end of the yarn from inside the ball or skein. Poke two fingers in and extract a little hank of yarn if you can't find the tail. By pulling the yarn from the inside out, the ball won't roll about as much, and there's less chance of the yarn getting tangled and dirty.

If you have a very loose yarn, you might want to purchase what's known as a "yarn bra," a mesh bag to hold the yarn ball together. Things around your home, however, will work just as well; you can use an old sock, a length of nylon pantyhose, or resealable plastic bags of appropriate sizes. Close the bag almost completely shut, leaving a small gap for the strand of yarn. These ideas also help prevent tangling if you are using several different colors of wool.

At Loose Ends

When you see that you don't have enough yarn on a dwindling ball to complete a new row, leave the end of the yarn loose and start the next row with the new ball. Start using the new yarn at an edge that will be joined to another and become a seam—darning in loose ends neatly is difficult at an edge that will show. When you come to sew up the garment you can retie the ends neatly and darn them into the fabric, or you can use the longer ones to sew up the seams.

Unless the knitting pattern tells you to, never knot the beginning of a new ball to the end of the previous ball in the middle of the row. The knot will make a lump that can work its way to the right side of the fabric, even though you've tied it on the wrong side.

If there is a fault in the yarn—a knot or lumpy section that's not meant to be there, or a length of too-thin or badly-dyed yarn—cut it out and discard that section. Start again where the normal quality resumes.

Although it's not the best option, splicing the yarn ends together is another alternative. Splicing works best with busy patterns, or fluffy yarns, which will hide the thickened fabric.

To splice your ends together, unravel about 3 inches at the end of the old ball of yarn. Do the same with 3 inches at the beginning of the new ball. Twist the strands from the two ends together between your palms so they make an invisible join. (Moistening your hands can help.)

An alternative method of splicing is to use a tapestry needle. Thread the new yarn on the needle. With the point of the needle about 4 inches from the end of the old yarn, insert it into and through the old yarn for about 2 inches, weaving the two together. Unthread the needle and thread it with the end of the old yarn. Insert it into the new yarn and pull it through in the same way. Cut off the ends if they stick out. Again, rolling this section between damp palms can help smooth it.

How Much Is Enough?

Often, you reach the end of a row and find only a few feet of yarn left in the ball you're using. You know you shouldn't knot yarn in the middle of a row, but how can you tell if you have enough to complete another row?

Put your knitting down on a flat surface, then lay the yarn across the fabric. If you're working in a smooth stitch like stockinette, you should have enough to knit one row if your yarn reaches at least four times across the width. Allow an extra width or two for a heavily textured fabric.

QUESTIONS?

How can I tell if there enough for one row?
Make a loose slipknot halfway along the yarn you have left. Work one row. If you haven't reached the knot by the end of the row, you know you have enough yarn to work another row.

If you do happen to run out of yarn in the middle of a row, it's worthwhile to unravel back to the beginning of the row and start again with a new ball. Some knitters try to splice the two yarns to make an invisible join, but this method always creates a weak link that can easily become unraveled when you use or wash the fabric.

Amount of Yarn You'll Need

Yarns are mainly labeled by weight, not by length of the thread. Because the density of dye can affect the yarn's weight, you cannot trust any two skeins to have the same length of thread, even though they may weigh the same.

Some yarn wrappers give the length of the yarn they enclose, and you can do rough calculations using those figures.

For a basic pullover or cardigan, using smooth yarns and lightly textured or plain knitting, you'd need about 600–700 yards for babies, 800–1,500 yards for children, 1,400–1,600 yards for a woman, and 1,700–2,400 yards for a man. (You'd need more yarn if you were using Aran or heavily cabled patterns or if using two or more colors.)

 SSENTIALS

If you have a metric pattern, you may need to convert grams to ounces. Use the following formula 100 grams = 3.52 ounces. Most metric-labeled yarns are sold in 50-gram balls. Two 50-gram balls equal about 3½ ounces.

The safest plan is to buy exactly the type and amount of yarn your pattern recommends. This will be measured in number of skeins. If you plan on substituting a different yarn, take note of the following guidelines:

1. Use a similar type and weight of yarn.

First of all, be sure to use the same *type* of yarn indicated. A pattern designed for a chenille yarn will be completely different if it's made with a smooth cotton fiber. The weight must be similar, too. If the pattern calls for sport weight, don't try to use fingering weight yarn.

If you are unfamiliar with the yarn the pattern calls for, your yarn vendor should know. If you do find someone who knows something about the yarn, ask them for the weight category it belongs to, the yardage per ball, and the fiber content of the yarn.

A thick sweater with vertical highlights

knitted by Judith MacInnes

If your searching turns up nothing, you can get an idea of the weight of a yarn by the gauge mentioned in the pattern. Compare the number of stitches to the inch in the pattern with the number of stitches to the inch of the categories listed earlier in this chapter. For example, if the suggested gauge is 4 stitches to the inch, then you can safely assume that you are working with a worsted weight yarn.

2. Figure out the yardage of the original yarn.

Once you've found a similar type of yarn, the second step is to figure out how much you'll need. If the pattern calls for ten skeins of the original yarn, you might try getting that many balls of the new yarn, but that isn't a very accurate method of substitution. It's better to go by yardage and to compare the length-per-ounce with the original yarn.

Most knitting patterns published in magazines and books today include the required yardage. If they don't, the same research methods you used to determine yarn type will help you find its yardage, too. The amount of yarn in two skeins of the same weight can vary a lot. Therefore, length is a more useful indicator than the weight of a ball.

3. Use math to work out the amount of yarn you'll need.

Take the number of skeins required for each color in the pattern you want to use, being sure to use the amount called for in the size you plan to make. Multiply by the number of yards (or meters) per ball or skein of that yarn.

For example, if a pattern requires ten balls of yarn, and each ball is made up of 200 yards (182 meters), you would multiply 200 by ten to get 2,000 yards (or 1,820 meters). That's the total yardage the pattern requires.

To figure out how many balls of the new yarn you'll need, find the length of each new ball or skein. Yardage should be printed on the yarn wrapper. Divide the total yardage the pattern requires by the yardage of your new yarn.

Try to work completely and consistently in either meters or yards to avoid confusion.

Do You Have Enough Yarn?

To find out how many square inches of fabric you will get per skein, knit up one ball and measure the resulting fabric. For example, one ball knitted up might make a 15" × 5" piece of fabric. That ball produces 75 square inches of fabric.

Using the schematic drawings in your pattern, determine the surface area of the fabric you want to make. If you are making a vest, for example, and the front and back of each side measures approximately 15" × 18", that's 270 square inches apiece. Divide that by 75, the number of square inches one ball of your yarn will produce, and you've found that it will take 3.6 balls for each side. (Round it up to four, totaling eight balls to make the vest.)

Remember that ribs and fancy stitches usually take more yarn than plain areas, so it's a good idea to overestimate. Most stores will let you return unused skeins.

Here's where the knitting notes you've kept will come in handy, too. After making a couple of sweaters for yourself, you'll know about how much of a particular weight of wool it takes to complete a sweater in your size. If you know the weights and yardage you used, you'll be able to work out what amount of other weights of yarn you'd need for a garment of the same size. (And if you see a few balls of yarn on sale, you'll know whether there's enough to make a whole sweater or not!)

CHAPTER 3
Needles and Tools

In its most basic form, knitting requires only needles and yarn. The most common needles come in straight pairs, but there are other tools you should know about, especially circular and double-pointed needles for making tubular fabric, hooks for cables, and bobbins for multicolored patterns. As projects become more complicated, these accessories will make your life easier.

Types of Knitting Needles

Most knitters have a favorite among the three most popular types of needles: pairs, circular, or double-pointed. Although each has its advantages, and each works best for certain types of knitting, you won't know which you prefer until you've tried them all.

Straight Needles

Straight needles are the needles beginners most commonly use. They work best for making flat pieces of fabric to be stitched together later. They have points at one end and knobs at the other to hold the stitches on. Straight needles are usually 10 to 16 inches long. The length varies so you can choose needles that are long enough to hold your stitches comfortably. As you work on different projects with different yarns, you'll probably end up with many pairs.

Circular Needles

Circular needles—usually two short pointed needles joined by a length of flexible nylon—are for knitting large, tubular, seamless items like sweaters. With these needles, you can never come to the end of a row: you aren't knitting in rows, you're knitting round and round in circles. To knit stockinette (also known as stocking stitch) you don't have to alternate purl with knit rows. Just keep doing knit stitches: You're always working on the "right" side.

ALERT

Be sure that the joint between needle and cord is smooth. If it isn't, the stitches will catch on it, which is extremely annoying. Check for this with any circular needles you buy, whether they are kits of interchangeable needles or single units.

The cord that joins the two needle ends varies in length from 6 to 40 inches. Your pattern should specify the length you need. With straight needles, the length isn't absolutely critical unless you have too many stitches on too short a needle. But if the cord on circular needles is too long, your knitting might not be able to stretch from the end of one needle to the other.

Circular needles are also good for knitting flat fabric. Circulars are usually lighter in weight than pairs, and since most of the stitches are held on the joining cord, the weight of the fabric is not on the needles. The work is distributed more evenly between your hands, so they tire less. Circulars also hold more stitches. The stitches don't slide off as easily when they're in your bag, and you don't keep losing the free needle.

QUESTIONS?

Do I really need lots of different types of needles?
Since each project you do will probably call for at least two different sizes of needles, you'll eventually acquire many different pairs. Don't throw out old needles, even if you find others you prefer to use. They will always come in handy for holding stitches, parking pieces of knitting you have temporarily abandoned, or for picking up stitches prior to unraveling.

New circular needles are often tightly wound in their package, making them very curly and difficult to work with. To relax out the cord, soak in hot tap water for about five minutes. Then hold the cord out taut until it cools. Another method you can use is to drape them over the shade of a lit lamp. The heat from the light bulb will have the same effect as the hot water. Be careful not to leave the needles hanging too long, or they will scorch.

You can find circular needle kits that have separate points and strings. Simply choose the needle size and length of cord you need. These kits work well and provide options for most projects.

Double-Pointed Needles

Some tubular items have such a small diameter that even the smallest circular needles wouldn't work. Socks, mittens, and turtlenecks require double-pointed needles. Double-pointed needles may be called by their initials, *dpns.*

Needles and knitting accessories

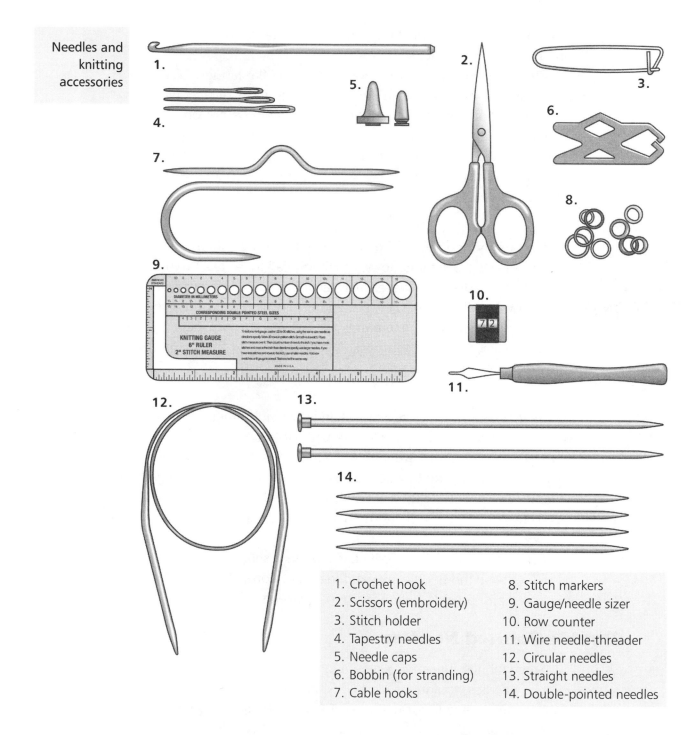

1. Crochet hook
2. Scissors (embroidery)
3. Stitch holder
4. Tapestry needles
5. Needle caps
6. Bobbin (for stranding)
7. Cable hooks
8. Stitch markers
9. Gauge/needle sizer
10. Row counter
11. Wire needle-threader
12. Circular needles
13. Straight needles
14. Double-pointed needles

Double-pointed needles are available in sets of four or five. (American manufacturers sell them in sets of four, European manufacturers in sets of five.) Because the needles are pointed on each end, you can work round and round in circles, the way you do with circular needles. One needle is always free to work the stitches, which are evenly distributed on the remaining needles. When the stitches are divided among only three needles, you create sharp angles in your work and stretch the stitches at each end of the needle. This stretching forms "ladders," a line of loose stitches running down the fabric. To keep your stitches even, use a marker to note the beginning of your row, and every so often redistribute the stitches among the needles.

Double-pointed needles come in all the same materials as regular straight needles; they also come in various lengths, to hold a lot of stitches or only a few. Most are between 4 and 9 inches long. Before you invest too much in very short needles, try them out. Needles shorter than 5 inches may tend to dig into your hands while you're using them.

Needle Materials

Needles have been made out of all sorts of materials over the years, from ivory to steel. Today they are most commonly available in aluminum, plastic, wood, and bamboo. You can still find shops and Web sites that sell rare, antique, and handmade needles.

ESSENTIALS

Experiment with various types of needles made from different materials. You will find there is a difference. Just as finding a pen you love makes writing easier, finding needles that are a joy to use can make knitting that much more of a pleasure.

Don't get carried away with fancy, impractical needles—it's not just about how cute they look. As tools, needles affect the way you knit. For example, steel needles are heavy and can tire your arms. Wooden and bamboo knitting needles are light and feel pleasant in the hands, but their rough surface tends to catch at yarn fibers.

The needles' shape, too, affects the speed and efficiency of your knitting. Needles can be long and tapered at the tip or short and stubby; some have sharp points, others are blunt. You should try them all to find the style you prefer. If you often need to knit 3 or 4 stitches together, for example, you'll want a sharper point. If you are using a thick, nubbly yarn, you'll want a blunter point that won't pierce and split the fibers. If possible, test the needles you want to buy with the yarn you'll be using.

Keep in mind these other considerations:

- Thinner sizes of bamboo needles can break easily.
- Wooden needles can be costly, especially if they are made from exotic woods.
- Colored needles that are in contrast to the color of the yarn make stitches easier to see.
- Aluminum or nickel-plated needles are inexpensive and smooth, but some knitters find them too cold and rigid.

This ribbed hat is perfect for children or adults

knitted by Sophie Cathro

Arthritic knitters often prefer flexible plastic needles or those made from casein, a protein in cow's milk. Casein needles are light and flexible and come in bright colors. They are also static resistant, so yarn doesn't stick to them. They may be difficult to find in shops, but they're available on the Internet.

Needle Sizes

Needle sizing can be confusing, so be patient until you figure it out. Always check where a pattern was printed before you buy the needles it recommends—metric European sizes are different, and some old knitting books still use the English Imperial sizes. British needles use a higher numbers for thinner needles; American needles are sized the other way around. (European needles sometimes have their equivalent U.S. sizes, but not always.)

One useful tool is a gauge card, or needle-sizer. A needle gauge card has holes in graduated sizes. If you find a marked needle, but you are unsure of its origin, fit it through the holes until you find a match. This tool is useful for unmarked needles or for plastic needles whose numbers have worn off. Some gauge cards are multipurpose. They offer needle-size conversions, as well as markings to measure your knitting gauge. Shop around to find the card that best suits your needs.

For a complete list of needle sizes and conversions, refer to Appendix B.

Other Accessories

So, you've chosen your yarn and your needles. What else do you need? Not much, really. As with any craft or hobby, the market is full of tools and gadgets that will make your life easier. Most things you won't need until you're working on complicated projects, and even then you'll be able to find creative alternatives. However, a few basics are necessary, even (and especially) for beginners.

Scissors—Never break yarn by pulling. Yanking stretches and distorts your work. Get in the habit of always carrying a small pair of scissors with your knitting. Folding scissors are ideal, as they won't snag (or cut!) the yarn while sitting in your bag.

Crochet hook—Crochet hooks have many uses in knitting. For instance, they are the best tools for rescuing dropped stitches. (See Chapter 20 for more on crocheting.)

Tape measure—Occasionally, you'll need to check your gauge and measure your work. A small ruler is okay for checking gauge, but a tape measure is better for measuring large areas of work.

Tapestry needle—A needle with a large eye and blunt point, a tapestry (or embroidery) needle is useful for weaving in ends. It's also good for picking up whole stitches when sewing pieces together. The needle's large eye holds yarn easily without shredding the fibers.

Yarn stores are full of all sorts of useful accessories. Row counters, for instance, sit at the end of straight needles to keep a tally of the number of rows knitted. Some knitting needle gauges check needle sizes. Other gadgets hold and mark your stitches, to designate the various parts of your work, and to help you keep track of where you are in your pattern.

ESSENTIALS

Keep your knitting and accessories together! Buy specially made knitting baskets or bags from your craft shop, or improvise with any compartmentalized plastic container. Those sold as fishing tackle or toolboxes or as toiletries bags work well.

It's not necessary to buy these things until you need them. In fact, many can be easily improvised by using items you probably already have. Safety pins work well as stitch holders, for example, as do twist ties that come with garbage bags. And regular plastic drinking straws can be snipped up to make stitch markers that slip onto smaller needles. Some knitters use washers from their tool kits as markers. Bobby pins can double as markers or cable needles; they can also be used to capture a dropped stitch before it runs too much. Corks or small plastic caps will protect the points of your needles from damage while you're not knitting—they'll also prevent your needle points from causing damage.

CHAPTER 4

Getting Comfortable

T here you are at the doctor's office, the train station, or the Laundromat. You're minding your own business, trying to count and keep your rhythm. Knit, knit, purl. Knit, knit, purl. From across the way, you feel the eyes watching you. One row, two rows, and here it comes: "You know, you're doing that the wrong way."

Different Ways to Hold the Needles

In almost every country, different regions have developed and passed down unique ways of holding the needles and manipulating the yarn. You could say that every country has its own method of knitting.

In some countries, such as Greece and Turkey, the yarn is looped around the knitter's neck, or clipped with a hook to her clothing, to get an even tension. In Portugal, the yarn is carried on the left thumb and needles are held horizontally. In some parts of Britain, the right needle is held in a sheath attached to the body.

In the United States, two methods of knitting in are most common: the Continental, and the English (or American) styles. The basic difference between the two is which hand holds the yarn. This chapter details instructions for these two methods.

Although any method will feel awkward in the beginning, keep trying. It doesn't matter whether you're right- or left-handed, each hand does some of the work. Your main consideration is to regulate the tension and flow of yarn and to control the needles and yarn at all times.

In both methods, one normally grips the needles the same way—as one would a knife, so the needles are under the palm of each hand. If you find that difficult, you can hold the needles any way that is comfortable and will produce even stitches. In some countries, knitters hold the right needle like a pen, or tucked under the arm. Experiment as much as you need with the positioning of your hands and the yarn in order to establish your own knitting preferences.

Different Ways to Hold the Yarn

When you carry the yarn in your right hand, and throw it around the working needle to make a stitch, you are using the *English* method.

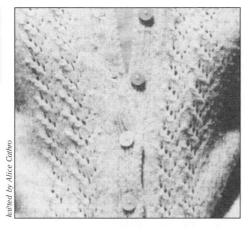

Cardigan
with open
work detail

knitted by Alice Cathro

When your left hand holds the wool and you move your working needle to grab the wool to make a stitch, you are using the *Continental* method. (This name is misleading: Knitters in many European countries do not hold their yarn in their left hands.) The Continental method is a bit more like crocheting. If you already know how to crochet, you may prefer to start this way.

The instructions for both methods will become clearer when you actually start knitting. If you understand the pros and cons of each method you'll be motivated to start learning—and keep practicing—the version that makes most sense to you.

The Continental Method

Advocates say this method is faster because the yarn is closer to the needles and therefore requires less movement. Less movement means more efficient knitting, as well as less chance of repetitive strain injury.

When you start working with two colors it's a help to be familiar with the Continental method because you can hold one color in each hand. The yarns don't tangle and neither color has to be dropped to pick up the other.

However, beginners usually find that holding the working yarn in the left hand is more complicated, so their work is much smoother with the English method.

To knit in the Continental method, hold both needles like knives, under the palm. On the left hand, the thumb and middle finger control the point of the needle while the index finger passes the yarn around the right needle tip. Hold the left-hand needle relatively steady; the right needle should be doing most of the work.

The right needle, meanwhile, picks up new stitches. The direction in which the right needle enters the stitches on the left determines what kind of new stitch you create.

The
Continental
method of
knitting

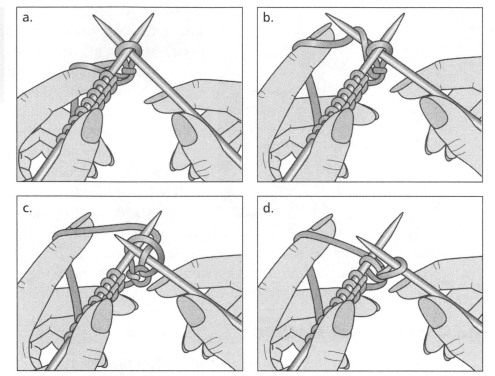

The English Method

To knit in the English method, hold both needles like knives, under your palms. Control the working yarn with your right hand, while your left thumb and index finger control the left needle tip.

FACTS

If you research the history of knitting, you'll know that there is no need to feel self-conscious if you knit using a different method. The only thing that matters is whether you produce neat fabric comfortably. When deciding which method you will knit with, go with the way that works best for you.

When it comes to manipulating the yarn, most English method knitters move their entire right hand to bring the working yarn to, and around, the point of the right needle. That's the time-consuming part of this method. If you can adopt part of the Continental technique and use your index finger to hold the yarn taut, bring it to the needle point, then wrap the yarn around, you'll be more efficient. As with any technique, this takes practice!

The English method of knitting

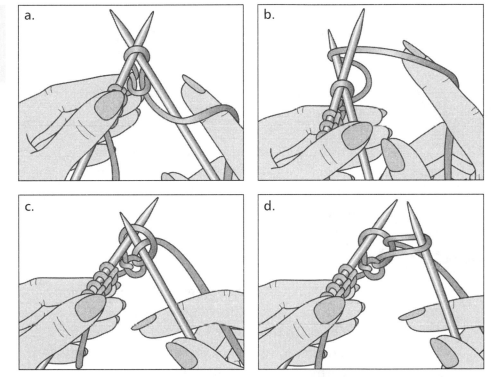

Controlling Tension

Whether you choose to work the yarn with your left hand (Continental) or your right hand (English), you will need to control the tension of your working yarn to maintain even stitches. Some people wrap the yarn around either the index or little finger of the working hand; others use the crook of the little finger to create the yarn tension.

To wrap the yarn around the little finger, pass the yarn under and then around the little finger, over the ring finger, under the middle finger and over the index finger. The index finger holds the yarn taut while forming new stitches on the right needle.

Alternate ways of holding the wool to create tension

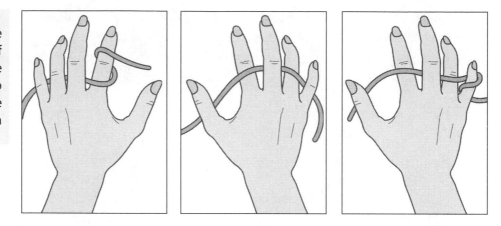

To keep the yarn taut with the crook of the little finger, pass the yarn under the little finger, over the ring finger, under the middle finger and over the index finger. Again, the index finger holds the yarn up so the right needle tip can scoop it up.

Casting On

Now that you know a little bit about the two knitting methods, you're probably anxious to get started. But before you can knit, you have to get a first row of stitches on your needle. *Casting on* is the process of producing a foundation row of stitches on your knitting needle so you can begin your garment. This step must be done properly because the first row helps to determine the tension of your knitting. It's important that both the size and tension of the stitches are consistent.

SSENTIALS

Beginners have a tendency to hold the needles too tightly, especially when casting on, which makes the whole process more difficult. Keep your hands, arms, and shoulders relaxed.

For practice, use a worsted weight wool yarn. Worsted is an easy weight to start with, and wool has a certain amount of natural elasticity. Size 10 wooden needles are also good for your first session. Wooden needles won't slip out of the stitches as easily, and the stitches themselves will be large enough for you to see what you're doing.

There are many different methods of casting on. Most are just slight variations of each other with different names. The methods can give a different look to the beginning of your knitted piece. They can also differ in the amount of elasticity and firmness they give the finished hem. Although there is no need for the beginner to learn five or six different methods of making stitches, you should be aware that it's possible to create different effects by the way you cast on. Don't make the mistake of sticking with the first method you learn and using it for everything. After you've covered the basics and move on to create your own hand-knitted garments, choose the casting-on method that will give you the look and firmness you want.

Making a Slipknot

How to make a slipknot

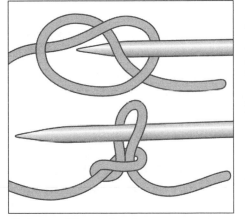

A slipknot is the basis of all casting-on techniques. It is the starting point for almost everything you will knit or crochet.

To make slipknot, take a ball of yarn and pull the working end out from the center (see page 22).

Make a loop in the yarn, then draw some of the yarn from the ball side through the loop. The part you've brought through is the slipknot. Place the loop on an empty needle and pull the yarn's tail end to tighten it.

Thumb and Single-Needle Casting On

Most beginners find casting on one of the more difficult parts of knitting. The easiest method to start with is the thumb and single-needle method. Once you have that first row on the needle, knitting gets easier. You can practice making knit and purl stitches and then learn the more difficult methods of casting on later.

Take the needle with the single slipknot on it in your right hand.

Take the yarn that leads to the ball, the working yarn, in your left hand and slip it over your thumb. Hold the rest of the yarn down with the other fingers. Your hands should be crossed so that your left hand with the thumb sticking up and the yarn wrapped around it is on your right and the right hand with the needle in it is on your left.

The thumb and single-needle method of casting on

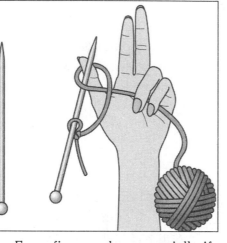

Put the tip of the right needle under the loop of yarn on your left thumb. Slip your thumb out, leaving the stitch on the needle. Loop your left thumb around the yarn again, and repeat until you have the desired number of stitches.

If you are doing this the right way, there will be a ridge along the bottom of the stitches. If you are doing it the wrong way, you'll just have spiraled the wool around the needle.

For a firmer edge, especially if you are using cotton or some other non-elastic yarn, lift the loop off your thumb with your forefinger and give it an extra turn before putting it on to the needle.

The simple thumb method makes a loose edge, unsuitable for quality work, but it is fine for practicing, or for any project where the edge is covered by decoration, such as fringe.

The Double Cast-On

The double cast-on (also called long-tail or "Y" cast-on) uses two strands of yarn to make a stitch. You are actually casting on as well as working the first row of knit stitches at the same time. Therefore, when you've completed casting on, you already have the first right-side row. The double cast-on produces a simple yet firm edge that is satisfactory for most garments.

Before you begin, look at your pattern to find out how many stitches you'll be casting on. Allow about an inch for every stitch, plus a few inches more for a tail. Pull out enough yarn to cast on the number of stitches called for. (Some people like to use the tail to sew up seams.) The length you pull out is a rough estimate—make it a generous estimate to be sure you have enough. Make a slipknot in the yarn at the distance you have measured out. For example, if you need 20 stitches, allow 20 inches for the stitches plus about 6 for the tail—measure 26 inches from the end of the yarn and make a slipknot there.

QUESTIONS?

What can you do if you cast on too tightly?
If you tend to cast on tightly, use a larger needle for this step then resume the proper size for the rest of the knitting. Again, keep experimenting until you find what works.

Put the slipknot on an empty knitting needle and pull the yarn to tighten. Hold the needle with the slipknot in your right hand.

Drape the tail end of the yarn around your left thumb, and the yarn leading to the ball around your left index finger. Wrap the last three fingers of your left hand around the rest of the two strands of yarn.

With your right hand, insert the tip of the needle up through the left-hand side of the loop on your thumb. Move the tip of the needle to the right and over the yarn on your index finger to pick up the stitch from the right-hand side of the yarn. (In other words, bring the needle up from under on the left, then over, and up from under on the right.)

The double cast-on method (also called long-tail or "Y" cast on)

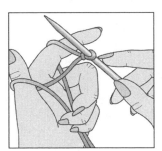
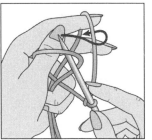
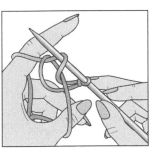

The needle will almost automatically come back down through the loop on your thumb. Slip your thumb out and gently pull the short end of the yarn to tighten the stitch. The yarn from the index finger should end up on the needle as a stitch; the loop from your thumb will end up forming the knit row along the bottom of the needle. Repeat until you've made all your stitches.

The Two-Needle Method of Casting On

The two-needle method is one of the most common because you form the cast-on row almost like you do when knitting. However, it is difficult to control the tension when you're still learning, giving you an uneven, ragged edge. Be patient, and continue practicing this method when you're doing your gauge swatches. You'll get the hang of it!

Make a slipknot with a 6-inch tail, and put it on an empty knitting needle. Hold this needle in your left hand, and the empty needle in your right. Insert the tip of the right-hand needle into the bottom of the slipknot, under the left needle.

The two-needle method of casting on

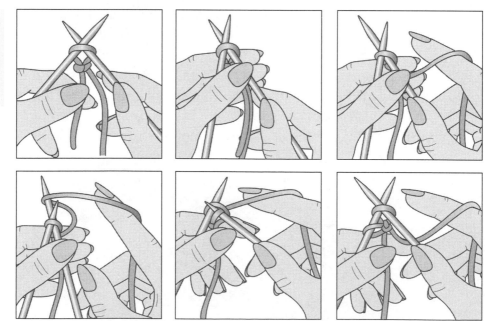

Take the working yarn and wind it over and around the right hand needle. Use the tip of the right needle to draw the yarn back through the slipknot stitch. You now have a stitch on each needle. Slip the newly made stitch from the right needle back onto the left needle.

Pull the yarn gently so that the stitches fit around the needle.

Continue making new loops in this way until you have made the number of stitches your pattern calls for.

Common Mistakes When Casting On

Casting on is one of the most difficult parts of learning to knit—don't worry if you don't find it easy to do. For some knitters, the hard part is just getting those first stitches onto the needles. For others, it's the first row after casting on that they have trouble with.

Keep with it! Once there's a bit of fabric on the needles, you can see what's happening, and the next rows are almost always easier. The following hints may help:

- Casting on too tightly makes it difficult to push the needle through the stitch and pull a loop of yarn back to work the first row. To remedy this, try not to pull the yarn too tightly after casting on each stitch. You can also cast on using a large needle, and then switch on the next row to the correct size. If your stitches are too loose, try a different casting-on method, or cast on with a smaller needle then switch up to the right size on the next row.
- If casting on is causing you a tremendous amount of difficulty at the very beginning, ask for help. After you've practiced making stitches, you can go back and figure out casting on. However, once you are doing your first project, decline assistance. Everyone knits with a different tension; letting someone else knit a few rows might show up as an obvious patch of looser or tighter stitches in the fabric.
- If you must stop knitting in the middle of a row, bring both needles together so the points and ends are beside each other. Slide the stitches away from the needle points. When you pick up the

knitting later, remember that the working yarn is leading off the right-hand needle.

- Beginners often want to know which is the right side of their work after they have cast on. If you used the single-needle methods, you are on the wrong side. If you used the double-needle method, you are on the right side. That's because the double-needle method works both the casting on and the first row together.
- Knitters usually end up becoming very partial to one way of casting on. Try the different methods until you get an edge that you like. If you like one side of your first row better than the other, you can simply use the side you like best and call that the right side.

ESSENTIALS

Never put your knitting away in the middle of a row, if you can help it. Doing so will stretch the yarn and create gaps in your knitting. And don't stab the needles through the knitted fabric or the ball of yarn, you could pierce the yarn and weaken it, causing split stitches later.

Experiment with different casting on methods now, before you get involved in actual projects. Gauge swatches are the perfect time to test different techniques (see Chapter 5). You will see how different methods of casting on create different edges, and you'll see them in the context of real fabric. Then you'll be able to decide what works best for you. As you proceed, keep in mind that knitting is an art *and* a craft—it should be a fun, creative, and unique personal experience.

CHAPTER 5
Beginning to Knit

Two stitches form the foundation of most knitted fabrics: *knit* (or plain) and *purl*. There are thousands of complicated and fancy stitches, but almost all of them are different combinations of knit and purl. Therefore, these are the two stitches you must learn to knit first. When you begin practicing them, you will understand how the size of the fabric you make will vary according to your gauge.

The Knit Stitch

The basic principle of the knit stitch is to drag some of the working yarn through the loops already on your needle, one by one to the end of the row. The right needle approaches the stitch from the front left to back right, picking up yarn in back, and pulling it forward. Try holding the yarn in both your right and left hands to find which method is the most comfortable for you.

First we'll outline the way to make a knit stitch holding your yarn in the right hand, then the left.

Knit Stitch with the Yarn on the Right

Keep your row of cast-on stitches close to the tip of the needle but not so close that the stitches slip off the end. Hold the needle in your left hand and take the empty needle in your right hand.

You will use your left thumb and index finger to manipulate the stitches on the left needle and your right thumb and middle finger to manipulate the right needle and the working yarn.

Insert the tip of the empty right needle into bottom of the first stitch. The tip of the right needle goes under the left needle, and the working yarn that leads to the ball should be behind the needles.

Hold the working yarn in your right hand in whatever manner gives you the most control. To revisit different methods of holding the yarn, refer to Chapter 4.

*Use your right forefinger to bring the yarn around and over the right needle so it is between the two needles.

Now use the tip of the right needle to bring the yarn through the first stitch. Making sure the new loop stays on the right-hand needle, draw the right needle away and gently slip the stitch off the left-hand needle to complete it.

You now have 1 stitch on the right needle. All the rest are still on the left needle.

Repeat this process from * until all the stitches from the left needle are on the right. You have completed your first row of knitting!

Now, move the needle full of stitches to your left hand, take up the empty needle in your right, and begin a new row.

Working your needles for the knit stitch (continental method)

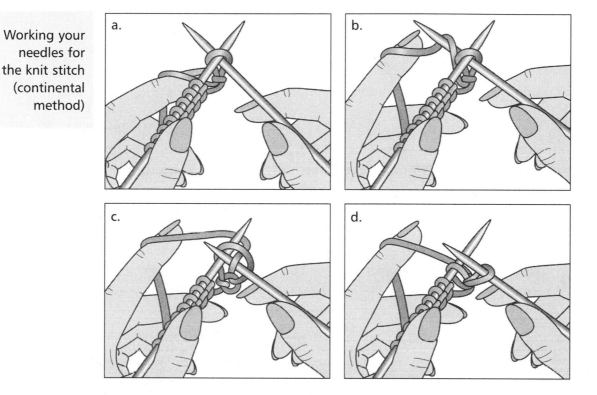

Knit Stitch with the Yarn on the Left

Keep your row of cast-on stitches close to the tip of the needle but not so close that the stitches slip off the end. Hold the needle in your left hand and take the empty needle in your right hand.

You will use your left thumb and middle finger to manipulate the left needle and the working yarn, and your thumb and index finger to manipulate the right needle.

Insert the tip of the empty right needle into bottom of the first stitch. The tip of the right needle goes under the left needle, and the working yarn that leads to the ball should be on the back side of the needles.

*Use your left forefinger to bring the yarn over and around the right needle so it is between the two needles.

There's a children's rhyme to help you remember the sequence the first few times you do the knit stitch:

Under the fence,
Catch the sheep,
Back we come,
Off we leap.

With the tip of the right needle, bring the yarn through the first stitch. Making sure the new loop stays on the right-hand needle, draw the right needle away and gently slip the stitch off the left-hand needle to complete it.

You now have 1 stitch on the right needle. All the rest are still on the left needle.

Repeat this process from * until all the stitches from the left needle are on the right. You have completed your first row of knitting!

Now, move the needle full of stitches to your left hand, take up the empty needle in your right, and begin a new row.

Most patterns, including some in this book, use abbreviations for knit (K) and purl (P), among other things. Some abbreviations are included in the instructions that follow, but you can also refer to Appendix A for a complete listing.

Garter Stitch

If you make a piece of fabric by knitting all the rows in knit stitch, you are making a fabric in what's called garter stitch. Both sides of the knitted fabric look the same, with ridges, so either side can be the right or wrong side. Garter stitch uses more yarn than stockinette (described later), the more popular knitting fabric type, and is thicker and springier. It doesn't tend to curl as stockinette does. The common abbreviation for garter stitch is *g. st*. If garter stitch were written in the typical pattern format it would look like the following illustration.

GARTER STITCH

Cast on any number of stitches.
1st row: Knit (K) every stitch.
2nd row: K every stitch.
Repeat these 2 rows.

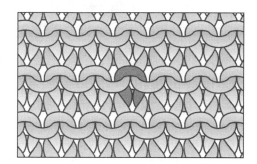

The Purl Stitch

After the knit stitch, the purl stitch is the next most important stitch to master. Together with the knit stitch, it forms the basis for most other knitting stitches, especially the basics: stockinette, rib, and moss (or seed) stitches. The purl stitch differs from the knit stitch in that the needle enters the stitch from the opposite direction (back right to front left) and the yarn is kept to the front of the work, not the back.

Purl Stitch with the Yarn on the Left

Keep your row of cast-on stitches close to the tip of the needle but not so close that the stitches slip off the end. Hold the needle in your left hand, and take the empty needle in your right hand.

You will use your left thumb and index finger to manipulate the stitches on the left needle and your right thumb and middle finger to manipulate the right needle and the working yarn.

Insert the tip of the empty right-hand needle into the first stitch on the left needle at the back (and bottom) of the loop. The tip of the right needle should be on your side of the left needle, going from the right rear toward the left front. The working yarn will be at the front, on your side of the needles.

*Holding the yarn in your left hand, use your left index finger to bring the yarn up and over the right needle so it is between the two needles.

Now, bring the yarn through to the back using the tip of the right needle. Make sure the new loop stays on the right-hand needle, and draw the needle away to gently slip the first stitch off the left-hand needle and complete the stitch.

You now have 1 stitch on the right needle. All the rest are still on the left needle.

Repeat the process from * until all the stitches from the left needle are on the right needle. You have completed your first row of purl stitch!

Now, move the needle full of stitches to your left hand, take up the empty needle in your right, and begin a new row.

Purl stitch
with the yarn
on the left

Purl Stitch with the Yarn on the Right

Keep your row of cast-on stitches close to the tip of the needle but not so close that the stitches slip off the end. Hold the needle in your left hand and take the empty needle in your right hand.

As you practice knitting, remember two things: 1. Keep your row of cast-on stitches close to the tip of the needle but not so close that the stitches slip off the end. 2. The "old" stitches are on the needle in your left hand; "new" stitches are on the needle on your right.

You will use your left thumb and index finger to manipulate the stitches on the left needle and your right thumb and middle finger to manipulate the right needle and the working yarn.

Insert the tip of the empty right-hand needle into the first stitch on the left needle at the back (and bottom) of the loop. The tip of the right needle should be on your side of the left needle, going from the right rear toward the left front. The working yarn will be at the front, on your side of the needles.

*Holding the yarn in your right hand, use your right forefinger to bring the yarn up and over the right needle so it is between the two needles.

Now, bring the yarn through to the back using the tip of the right needle. Make sure the new loop stays on the right-hand needle, and draw the needle away to gently slip the first stitch off the left-hand needle and complete the stitch.

You now have 1 stitch on the right needle. All the rest are still on the left needle.

Repeat the process from * until all the stitches from the left needle are on the right needle. You have completed your first row of purl stitch!

Now, move the needle full of stitches to your left hand, take up the empty needle in your right, and begin a new row.

Purl stitch with the yarn on the right

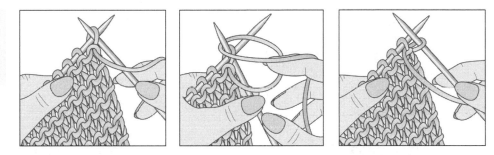

Stockinette Stitch

Stockinette (or stocking) *stitch*, also called plain knitting, is made by knitting and purling in alternate rows. Stockinette fabric is one of the most common fabrics used in knitting patterns. It's a simple knit to show off fancy yarns and colored designs, it's not too bulky, and it drapes well.

The drawback to stocking stitch is its tendency to curl. Because one side of the fabric is more compact than the other, it will roll upon itself. Stockinette works better for sweaters or sewn items than it does for scarves and other open-edged projects.

Stockinette always has a right (smooth) side and a wrong (ridged) side. The ridged side of stockinette looks similar to garter stitch (see figure on page 51). When a garment is made in stockinette and the ridged side is considered the right side, the stitch is called *reverse stockinette.*

Because stockinette produces such a smooth fabric, any irregularities in tension from one stitch to another will be apparent. If you work your purl rows tighter or looser than your knit rows, you will also get an uneven look. This is easily remedied, though, by knitting tubular fabric on circular needles. That way you never have to do a purl row, you just go round and round in knit.

If stockinette stitch were written in the typical pattern format it would look like this:

STOCKINETTE (STOCKING) STITCH

Cast on any number of stitches.
1st row: Knit (K) every stitch.
2nd row: Purl (P) every stitch.
Repeat these 2 rows.

Stockinette (stocking) stitch, and reverse stockinette

Tension or Gauge

The principal behind tension, or gauge, is not hard to understand. When you knit with thick yarn on big needles you get big stitches—only a few stitches per inch of knitted fabric. When you knit with very fine yarn with thin needles you get tiny stitches—and there'll be a lot more of them per inch.

It's also logical that when you knit very tightly you will get more stitches to the inch, whereas knitting loosely will yield you fewer. These three variables—yarn thickness, needle size, and personal tendency to knit loosely or tightly—determine the size of the piece of fabric you make whenever you pick up needles and yarn.

Understanding this, you can see why it's important to figure out whether your knitting corresponds with the pattern designer's assumptions about your knitting.

A *gauge swatch* is the test sample you do to check whether your knitting is looser or tighter than the pattern requires. To create a gauge swatch, knit a square of fabric, then count the number of stitches you get to the inch. Compare this number to the gauge listed in your pattern to see if they match. The pattern's sizing is based on a certain gauge; if yours is different, you will end up with a garment that is either too big or too small.

ESSENTIALS Every pattern begins with the gauge notation, sometimes called a stitch measurement or tension note. If your test swatch does not match this notation, try to correct the problem by adjusting your tension. You can also switch to a size smaller or larger needles.

If a pattern says "Gauge: 8 sts = 2 inches over St st," it means that your gauge is correct if 8 of your stitches in stockinette measure 2 inches. If the pattern is written using metric measurement, do all your measuring in metric too. Trying to convert from centimeters to inches is just inviting mistakes. If you are using a European pattern, make sure you are using the right size needles, whether metric or not. The table in Appendix B should help figure this out. If the tension or gauge swatch produces a different number of stitches, you must change the size of the needles you use until you, too, get 8 stitches over a 2-inch-wide area of knitting.

How to Make a Gauge Swatch

In the example given above, the pattern asked you to measure a 2-inch sample. To get a true measure of your knitting, though, your test square must be a little larger than 2 inches, because the stitches at the sides of a piece of knitting tend to be looser than the ones in the middle. The bigger your sample, the more accurate your calculations will be.

If you are using an unevenly textured yarn that varies along its length between skinny and thick, slubby patches, you'll need to make an even bigger swatch. In this case, take five different readings, which will probably vary, and calculate the average (by adding them together and dividing by five).

Use the needle size specified in the pattern. If no stitch style is mentioned, use stockinette. Some knitters begin and end their squares with a stitch like moss or garter stitch, and do a few stitches on each side in that pattern, too, to help keep the swatch flat, but you don't have to.

QUESTIONS?

Do you need to wash the swatch to test for shrinkage?
Some advocate measuring, then washing and drying the swatch before measuring again. Washing the swatch is not necessary at this stage unless the pattern requires it or if you know you are working with a yarn that will shrink.

When you've made an approximate square shape, cast off. Smooth the panel onto a flat surface such as an ironing board or a padded tabletop. Pin the square down, if necessary, but don't stretch it.

Rather than just placing the measuring tape on the knitting, take two pins, and mark the beginning and end of the specified number of stitches. Then measure the distance between the pins. If you find it difficult to count the V-shaped stitches in stockinette, turn the knitting over and count the bumps on the other side. You can also mark out the required measurement and count the number of stitches between the pins.

Check your gauge in several different places, all of them away from the edge of the sample. Taking several measurements will give you a good representative reading. It will also indicate whether your tension is consistent (even if it's not accurate).

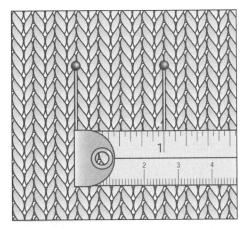

Measuring
a tension
square

Getting too many stitches to the inch? Try using needles a size larger. Getting too few? Use the next size down. Switching knitting needles is usually easier and less frustrating than attempting to alter your knitting style.

Don't forget: When you find the correct size needle to use for the main part of the garment, you'll need to find the right size needles for the ribbing, too. For example, let's say your pattern calls for the body of the garment to be worked in number 9 needles and the rib in number 7. If your swatch gauge tells you that you should use number 10 needles for the main part, you will need to use number 8 for the rib.

ESSENTIALS

Remember that when it comes to gauge, as little as half a stitch matters. Multiplied over a whole sweater, that half stitch will be the difference between a hand-knit that fits perfectly and one that isn't quite right.

As an added precaution, you may want to check your gauge after you've knitted about 4 or 5 inches of the actual project, just to be sure you're maintaining the gauge. Measure the fabric flat and off the needle for best results.

At this early stage, not too much work will be lost if you have to unravel and start again with different size needles.

Sometimes pattern instructions will give gauge measurements for both stitch and row counts. If you can't get both in sync, just work on making your stitch gauge work—you can always adjust the number of rows to make the garment longer or shorter as needed.

Gauge Testing Is a Tool

As you do more and more knitting, your gauge will stabilize. You'll learn whether you tend to knit loosely or tightly, and you'll often be able to predict whether you should knit a garment on smaller or larger needles.

Even so, you should still do a gauge swatch for each project. Gauge is more than how tightly or loosely you knit. It's also determined by the structure of the stitch, the degree of give (elasticity) in the yarn, and how it settles down after the knitting is finished.

ESSENTIALS

Gauge is a great tool when you want to get creative with yarn. It is your key to knowing how much yarn you will need for any project. All you have to do is work up a square in the yarn you want to use, and see if it works for your pattern.

Making a gauge square is also a great opportunity to test-drive your project. The first few rows might show that the variegated yarn you've chosen doesn't knit up as well as you'd anticipated or that it picks up lint like crazy. You may learn that a fancy stitch in the pattern is incredibly difficult to do or that the fibers from the blue yarn shed onto the white. Most of these problems are easier to address when you catch them early on.

The best thing to with knitting swatches is to store them with the details of all your knitting projects. Your project file or binder will help you remember the different things you've made, how they turned out, and whether you want to use the yarn again. You will also always have some spare yarn available if you need it to mend a garment, and you'll know where to find it!

CHAPTER 6

Edges, Rib Stitch, and Casting Off

J ust as different casting-on methods produce different edges, varying your stitches at the ends of the rows—or the piece—can produce a variety of side and top edges. Read on to learn various selvage and binding techniques and to understand how each is appropriate for certain effects.

Selvages: Special Side Stitches

If you've done any dressmaking, you may recall that the side edges of a piece of fabric are called *selvages*. When you make a knitted piece of fabric, you have the same thing. Usually, you sew selvages together to make up the finished garment. Your job will be much easier if the edges are finished in such a way that they are easy to join. Some patterns, then, tell you to knit the first and last stitches of your rows in a selvage stitch—to prepare the edge for a neat seam when you sew two edges together.

ESSENTIALS

Placing a marker just before or after the selvage stitches will remind you to do them, if they are not indicated in the pattern you are using. Just pass the marker from one needle to another as you work a row.

Selvage stitches are especially useful when you are knitting a lacy fabric with large stitches or patterned holes that make it difficult to sew seams. Working selvages is not always necessary, especially if you are knitting a basic, solid stitch like stockinette. Usually, however, you'll get a more professional look if you use a selvage.

Different selvage stitches serve different purposes. They can create a neat edge if one part of a garment won't be sewn to another, or they can create loops that make it easy to pick up stitches at the finished edge.

SLIP STITCH, OR CHAIN EDGE

The *slip-stitch selvage* is useful when you will be joining seams with a *backstitch*. It's also handy when you need loops for picking up stitches or adding crochet edgings.

Slip the first stitch of each row from the left needle to the right, and

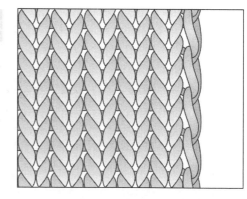

work all the other stitches normally. On the right (front) side, slip the first stitch *knitwise* (K-wise) then follow the pattern to the end of the row. On a wrong-side row, slip the first stitch *purlwise* (P-wise) then follow the pattern to the end of the row.

 ## CHAIN EDGE FOR GARTER STITCH

If you are knitting in garter stitch, this selvage produces a neat chain edge:
On every row: Slip one P-wise, take working yarn to back, then knit to the end of the row.

What does "slipping a stitch" mean?
Slipping a stitch means transferring a stitch from the left to the right needle without creating a new stitch. Knit- or purlwise refers to the direction in which the right needle takes the slipped stitch. Knitwise means the right needle enters from the left front of the stitch; purlwise refers to the right rear.

 ## GARTER STITCH SELVAGE FOR STOCKINETTE

This selvage worked on stockinette helps prevent curling. It makes a neat row of bumps, or seeds, which make a handy guide when sewing seams.
Knit rows: Knit normally.
Purl rows: Knit first and last stitches.

 ## DOUBLE GARTER SELVAGE

If you are not sewing your stockinette fabric together, you will need some edge to keep the fabric from curling. The double garter creates a firm, even selvage, suitable for open or unadorned edges.
Every row: Slip one K-wise, K1; K2 at end of row.

Rib Stitches for Cuffs and Hems

A rib stitch (also known as ribbing) is often used for a cuff or waistband because it makes a fitted, elastic fabric that grips snugly and springs back into shape when stretched. Rib patterns made by alternating knit and purl stitches on the same row, making vertical ridges.

ALERT

Remember that with any rib stitch, the stitches you purled on the previous row are knit stitches on the following row. Keep this in mind: Knit into the flat stitches, purl into the bumps.

The most common rib is a single rib, in which you knit one then purl one until the end of the row. This rib has the most crosswise elasticity. If you work a pattern with a greater series of knit and purl stitches, the resulting fabric will be less clingy.

SINGLE RIB STITCH

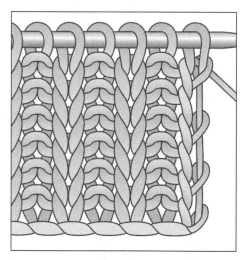

Cast on an even number of stitches.
First row: *P1, K1, repeat from
* to end.
2nd row: *K1, P1, repeat from
* to end.
Repeat these 2 rows.

Always bring the yarn between the needles, not over the top of a needle, or you will create extra stitches by mistake.

When knitting rib patterns, you continually move the yarn to and fro as you alternate between knit and purl stitches. The extra distance the yarn travels means that ribbing uses more yarn and takes longer to do than stockinette or garter stitches.

There are many different kinds of ribs, all variations on the single rib stitch (also called one-by-one rib). Ribbing can be a combination of any number of knit and purl stitches in series, whether two by two (K2, P2), three by two (K3, P2), or so on.

ESSENTIALS   Doing a rib requires a lot of manipulation, which may lead to a looser gauge because the tension is more difficult to control. Patterns generally call for ribbing to be done on needles two sizes smaller than the rest of a garment to keep the ribbing a bit tighter.

Single rib stitch pulls in the tightest. If you prefer the look of a looser waistband, cast on using a larger needle or work a double or triple rib. Again, experiment and practice, and know that every piece of knitting is unique!

DOUBLE RIB

Cast on a number of stitches that is a multiple of 4, plus 2.
1st row (right side): K2, *P2, K2; rep from * to the end of the row.
2nd row: P2, *K2, P2; repeat from * to the end of the row.
Repeat these 2 rows.

CASTING ON IN RIB

For a consistent look to your band of ribbing, try casting on in rib.
Make a slip knot and place it on the left needle. Insert the right needle purlwise. Purl a stitch and slip to left needle (taking care not to twist the stitch).
*Insert your right needle knitwise between the last 2 stitches, and knit a stitch. Slip the new stitch to your left needle.
Insert right needle purlwise between the last 2 stitches, and purl a stitch. Slip the new stitch to left needle.
Repeat from * for the required number of stitches.

KNIT 2 PURL 1 RIB

Cast on a number of stitches that is a multiple of 3, plus 2.
1st row (right side): K2, *P1, K2; repeat from * to the end of the row.
2nd row: P2, *K1, P2; repeat from * to the end of the row.
Repeat these 2 rows.

When binding off in rib, it's important to remember to knit the knit stitches and purl the purl stitches as if you were continuing to rib. This keeps the bound-off edge of the fabric elastic.

Binding or Casting Off

Binding off, also known as *casting off*, is how you finish your knit fabric so you can take it off the needle. When you bind off, you secure the stitch loops so the fabric cannot unravel.

Unless your pattern directs you differently, you should work each stitch you are binding off the same way you would work it if you were not binding off. If you are working in ribbing, you must bind off in rib—knit the knit stitches and purl the purl stitches as you come to them, and pass the old stitch over the new stitch as usual. So, if you were working in a single rib stitch, you would knit the first stitch, purl the second stitch, then pass the first stitch over the second. Knit the next stitch, and pass the old stitch over the new one. Purl the next stitch, and so on.

There are two rules to remember when binding off. First, always bind off using the same stitch you've been working in. Second, always bind off loosely.

Similarly, if you are working in seed stitch you must bind off in seed stitch. If you are working in stockinette, you must bind off in the stitch of whichever row you are on (preferably on a knit row). Pattern directions almost always call for casting off to be done this way. The usual abbreviation is *BO* in the pattern.

Always bind off loosely to ensure that the bound-off row doesn't pull in the fabric you've been knitting. The binding should have the same tension as the rest of the fabric and as much give as the body of garment. This is especially important when working necklines—the wearer must be able to get his or her head through the opening!

If you are casting off too tightly, try a larger size needle to get the right tension. If you have trouble getting a relaxed tension, another option is to try the suspended, or elastic, method of casting off. This method enlarges the stitches by keeping them on the left needle while you work the next stitch. In a pinch, you can also simply loosen each working stitch by hand, one at a time, as you finish.

Basic Binding Off

The basic method of binding off

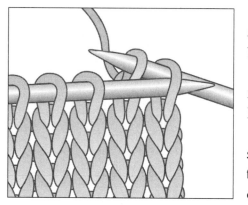

Follow these steps to bind off a piece of fabric completely in the basic method:

Work the first 2 stitches of the row in pattern. You should now have 2 stitches on your right needle.

Insert the left needle into the stitch farthest to the right. Lift it over the stitch just worked and completely off the needle, letting it fall between the needles. Don't pull the yarn at all! Remember, you are binding off loosely.

Work the next stitch on the left needle.

Again, you have 2 stitches on the right needle. Insert your left needle tip into the first stitch on the right needle; lift it over the second stitch and completely off the needle. Repeat until just one stitch remains on the right-hand needle (and there are none on the left-hand needle).

Cut the yarn from the ball (about 6 to 8 inches away from your knitting) and pull this tail through the loop of the last stitch. Pull the last stitch tight, creating a firm knot to prevent unraveling. If you are going to sew a seam on the bound-off edge, you can leave a length of yarn long to sew the seam with. Otherwise, use a tapestry needle (see Chapter 3) or a crochet hook to weave the yarn in and out of a row of stitches on the back of the knitting so that it will not show.

ALERT

If your pattern tells you to bind off only a few stitches, say, at the neckline or under the arm, be sure you've counted the number of bound-off stitches correctly. You only count as bound-off those stitches you actually lift over another stitch and drop off the end of the needle.

When binding off, you work 2 stitches to bind off 1 stitch. If, for example, the directions read "K9, bind off the next 4 sts, K9 . . . ," you must knit 9 stitches, then knit 2 more stitches before starting to bind off. Bind off four times. After the 4 stitches have been bound off, the last stitch remaining on the right-hand needle counts as the first stitch of the next nine in pattern.

You may need to bind off stitches in groups, over several rows, to achieve a curved cast-off finish. You may get jagged "stair steps" instead of a smooth curve. To make the edge a bit neater, slip the first stitch of a group when you bind off.

Suspended or Elastic Binding Off

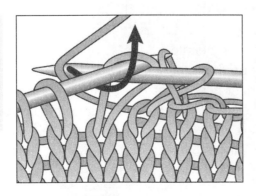

The suspended or elastic method of binding off

The elastic bind-off is similar to basic binding off. It enlarges the cast-off stitch in the process, meaning you don't have to use larger needles to get a loosely bound-off edge.

Work the first 2 stitches of the row.

Insert the left needle into the stitch you knitted first, on the right needle, and lift it over the second stitch. Instead of dropping it between the needles, as you would for a basic bind off, keep it on the left needle.

Now, work the second stitch on the left needle as you normally would. As you slip this new stitch off the left needle, the lifted stitch will drop, and you will have 2 stitches on the right needle. Use the left tip to lift the first stitch onto the left needle. Again, work the second stitch on the left needle, and continue binding off until just one stitch remains on the right hand needle (leaving none on the left needle).

Cut the yarn from the ball (about 6 to 8 inches away from the knitting) and pull this tail through the loop of the last stitch. Pull the last stitch tight, creating a firm knot to prevent unraveling.

English Binding Off

The English method produces an edge similar to basic binding-off, but the stitches are more open. Some people find it easier to do.

Work the first 2 stitches together by inserting the needle into both stitches and treating as if they were one. Put this new stitch back on to the left needle.

The English method of binding off uses a common decreasing technique knit two together (K2 tog). Because this method doesn't require pulling stitches over, it's easier to control your tension and bind off loosely.

Work the next 2 stitches together (the one you just slipped back and the next) by inserting the needle into both stitches and treating them as if they were one. Again, put the new stitch back on to the left needle.

Repeat until just 1 stitch remains on the right hand needle (and there are none on the left needle).

Cut the yarn from the ball (about 6 to 8 inches away from the knitting) and pull this tail through the loop of the last stitch. Pull the last stitch tight, creating a firm knot to prevent unraveling.

Invisible (or Tubular) Binding Off

Use the invisible method on regular single rib to make an inconspicuous, flexible finish. You must work very loosely; do not pull the tapestry needle tightly as you would in sewing.

When you reach the last row, unwind the ball of yarn you are working with. Starting at where the working yarn leaves the needles and measure out about four times the width of your piece of knitting. Cut the yarn, and thread the end on to a large, blunt tapestry needle.

Insert the threaded needle knitwise into the first stitch, which should be a knit stitch, and slide the stitch off the left needle.

Insert the needle purlwise into the next knit stitch. Skip the purl stitch that will be next on the left needle. Pull yarn through loosely, but do not drop the stitch.

Now, insert the embroidery needle purlwise into the first stitch on the left needle—the purl stitch that you just skipped—and drop the stitch off the needle.

Take the threaded needle behind the knit stitch (now at the tip of your left needle). Insert it knitwise into the next purl stitch, and draw yarn through.

Repeat until all the stitches have been dropped.

The invisible, or tubular, method of binding off

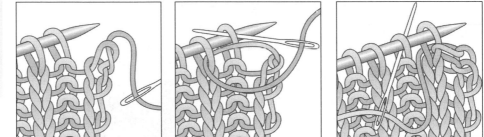

Joining Shoulder Seams Instead of Binding Off

To get a neat, perfectly matched shoulder seam when you are joining the front of a garment to the back—and to avoid sewing yet another seam—follow these directions for casting off matched pieces together.

No matter what the pattern says, do not bind off your shoulder stitches after you've shaped the neck and come to the end of the instructions for the front or back. Leave the shoulder stitches on a needle or holder until both sides are complete, and you are ready to join them together.

For each shoulder, you'll use three needles—all the same size as those you used for the body of the garment. One holds the stitches from the back shoulder and one the stitches from the front shoulder. The third will be your right needle.

ALERT

In order to bind off two pieces of fabric together, especially shoulders, you must have an equal number of stitches on both needles. If you are working with uneven numbers, you'll end up with uneven seams—especially problematic around necklines.

Place the two knitted pieces with right sides facing each other. If the needles are facing opposite directions, slip the stitches from one to an empty needle. Both left needles, then, should face the same way, with the fabrics' right sides together.

Hold the two left needles with the stitches together. Insert the right needle through the first stitch on the front needle and the first stitch on the back needle. Knit the 2 stitches together. Repeat with the second stitches on each needle, then slip the first stitch over the second and drop as you would when doing a basic cast-off.

Continue in this manner until all the shoulder stitches have been bound off. Pull yarn through the last stitch. The result is a slightly ridged seam that is neat and flexible and that won't stretch.

Bind shoulders off together (three-needle bind-off)

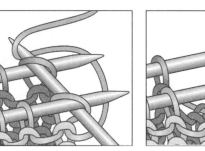  

CHAPTER 7

Variations on the Basic Stitches

The two basic stitches, knit and purl, are just loops until you alternate rows of them and a pattern emerges: they become stockinette. But that's just the beginning of what's possible when you mix and match stitches. Once you start alternating and combining stitches within rows, you create effects that are interesting to touch and look at but that are still simple to do.

Pattern Stitches

You can make a variety of patterns—textures, interlocking cables, and open lacy designs—just using the two stitches you already know. Some patterns use the thousands of different combinations of knit and purl stitches. Others use techniques such as decreasing then replacing the lost stitches.

Such sequences and combinations are called *pattern stitches*. Repeated across a piece of knitting, they will make up a knitted fabric with a specific texture. The minimum number of stitches that a complete motif requires in a row is a *stitch multiple*. The minimum number of rows that one complete motif requires is the *repeat*.

This chapter gives you some examples of easy pattern stitches to incorporate into your first projects. Using the concepts of multiples and repeats, you can mix complementary stitch patterns to vary textures or show off beautiful yarn. Consider making a stitch sampler for a pillow cover just to get some practice.

Choosing a Stitch

It's easy to fall in love with a stitch pattern, but be sure you can use it for the project you have in mind. Just as there are rules to observe when substituting yarns, there are things to take into account when exchanging one stitch for another.

A basic sweater made with a stitch different from the one specified in the garment pattern will look like a completely different sweater. If you also change the color and yarn type, you'll produce a new style as well.

Most importantly, you should only use fancy stitches with smooth wool or cotton yarns. Very fuzzy yarns and highly textured yarns hide the pattern. In general, save novelty yarns, like boucle and poodle yarns, to work in a stockinette pattern. It's also true that different yarns work better with different types of stitches. Soft, light yarns, for example, are better with lacy stitches, and tightly twisted yarns are better with small, textured stitches. The search for the right yarn and stitch combination is yet one more reason to work a gauge swatch.

The stitch should be appropriate to the garment, too. Close, dense stitches are best suited to outdoor wear; open stitches work well for light indoor garments. Choose reversible stitches, which make a fabric that looks identical on both sides, for items like shawls that have no "wrong" side.

Stitch Multiples

To know how to substitute one stitch pattern for another, you have to understand how stitch patterns are made up of stitch multiples. To take a very basic example, in a knit 1, purl 1 rib, the stitch pattern is made up of just 2 stitches, repeated over and over. That pattern, then, has a multiple of 2. A more complex stitch pattern will have a longer stitch multiple.

Another factor in a pattern's complexity is how many rows make up a repeat. A design that has a 30-row repeat, even if the multiple is not difficult, needs to be followed carefully. Multiples that take only 2 rows to form a pattern can be easily memorized and easily worked.

QUESTIONS?

Is it possible to use patterns with different multiples?
Just do the math to make sure your new stitch will fit. The number of stitches in the new multiple must divide evenly into the number of stitches you cast on. Remaining stitches can be balanced at either end of the row.

Directions for stitch patterns will tell you at the beginning what the multiple is. They may be written something like "multiple of 8 sts plus 2." This means you can use this stitch pattern with garment patterns that call for you to cast on any number that is two more than a number divisible by eight: 16 (+2), 32 (+2), 96 (+2), etc. The "plus 2" stitches make the pattern begin and end properly and are balanced at each end of the row. Extra stitches are usually hidden in the seams at each side of the fabric. You should also divide any remaining pattern stitches between each end if you are substituting one stitch pattern for another.

In a garment pattern that uses a stitch pattern, you can tell a multiple because the instructions for it will usually start with an asterisk (*) and end with a semicolon (;) or will be contained within brackets. You'll then be asked to repeat the stitch pattern "from * across" the row. Count the number of stitches to be repeated across the row (the stitch multiple) plus the end stitches. If you find a different stitch pattern with the same stitch multiple, you can substitute one for the other. If the new stitch fits into the garment pattern the way the old one did, you shouldn't have to make any other adjustments.

Stitch patterns are classified according to structure, that is, depending on the way they are created. Lacy patterns use *yarn overs* and *slip stitches. Cable stitches* twist or carry stitches. *Ribs* are combinations of knit and purl stitches aligned in vertical rows. Each stitch has its own decorative and practical use.

Simple Textures

The most basic stitch patterns are simple combinations of knit and purl stitches that add texture for visual interest and also to keep the fabric from curling. Stockinette fabric has a natural tendency to scroll inward, but stitches made from a more or less equal combination of knit and purl are much more stable. Such patterns are often interchangeable; an item designed in one pattern can usually be made in another.

Like rib, seed stitch uses up more yarn than a stockinette fabric. Because most people also work seed stitch with a looser tension than stockinette, you might consider using smaller needles.

Seed and Moss Stitches

Single seed stitch is one of the most basic texture stitches. Like a simple rib, it consists of alternate knit and purl stitches. In a seed stitch, however, the stitches are worked alternately. A stitch that has been knitted on one side of the fabric will also be knitted on the other; a stitch that has been purled on one side will be purled on the other. So, unlike a rib, which has vertical rows of identical stitches, seed stitch results in an all-over textured pattern. The fabric is also reversible, so both sides of the work are identical.

Moss stitch has all the same characteristics of seed stitch, but creates a looser fabric. Rather than alternating the K1, P1 pattern every row, it alternates every 2 rows. The fabric is still reversible and doesn't curl.

Because they don't curl, seed and moss stitches also create an effective, stable border for garments made in stockinette. Ribs are also stable, but they gather the fabric (as in cuffs and waistbands), a look you may not always want.

SEED STITCH

Cast on an even number of stitches.
1st row: *K1, P1; Repeat from * to end of row. (Read: Knit 1 stitch, purl 1 stitch alternately across the entire row.)
2nd row: *P1, K1; Repeat from * to end of row.
These 2 rows form the repeat of the pattern.

DOUBLE SEED STITCH

Cast on a number of stitches that is a multiple of 4.
1st row: *K2, P2; Repeat from * to end of row.
2nd row: *P2, K2; Repeat from * to end of row.
These 2 rows form the repeat of the pattern.

BROKEN RIB

Cast on an even number of stitches.
1st row: Knit to the end of the row.
2nd row: *P1, K1; Repeat from* to the end of the row.
These 2 rows form the repeat of the pattern.

 ## SLIP-STITCH RIB

Cast on a number of stitches that is a multiple of 5, plus 6.
1st row (right side): P2, K2, *P3, K2; Repeat from * to last 2 stitches, P2.
2nd row: K2, P2, *K1, slip 1, K1, P2; Repeat from * to last 2 stitches, K2.
Repeat these 2 rows to form the pattern.

 ## BASKET-WEAVE PATTERN

Cast on a number of stitches that is a multiple of six, plus four.
1st row: (wrong side) K4, *P2, K4; Repeat from * to the end of the row.
2nd row: P4, *K2, P4; Repeat from * to the end of the row.
3rd row: K4, *P2, K4; Repeat from * to the end of the row.
4th row: P4, *K2, P4; Repeat from * to the end of the row.
5th row: K1; P2; *K4, P2; Repeat from * to the end of the row, ending with K1.
6th row: P1, K2, *P4, K2; Repeat from * to the end of the row, ending with P1.
7th row: K1; P2, *K4; P2; Repeat from * to the end of the row, ending with K1.
8th row: P1, K2; *P4, K2; Repeat from * to the end of the row, ending with P1.
These 8 rows form the pattern.

ZIGZAG PATTERN

Cast on a multiple of 15 stitches.
1st row: *P1, K1, P1, K12.
Repeat from * to the end of the row.
2nd row: *P11, K1, P1, K1, P1.
Repeat from * to the end of the row.
3rd row: *K2, P1, K1, P1, K10.
Repeat from * to the end of the row.
4th row: *P9, K1, P1, K1, P3. Repeat from * to the end of the row.
5th row: *K4, P1, K1, P1, K8. Repeat from * to the end of the row.
6th row: *P7, K1, P1, K1, P5. Repeat from * to the end of the row.
7th row: *K6, P1, K1, P1, K6. Repeat from * to the end of the row.
8th row: *P5, K1, P1, K1, P7. Repeat from * to the end of the row.
9th row: *K8, P1, K1, P1, K4. Repeat from * to the end of the row.
10th row: *P3, K1, P1, K1, P9. Repeat from * to the end of the row.
11th row: * K10, P1, K1, P1, K2. Repeat from * to the end of the row.
12th row: *P1, K1, P1, K1, P11. Repeat from * to the end of the row.
13th row: *K12, P1, K1, P1. Repeat from * to the end of the row.
14th row: *P1, K1, P1, K1, P11. Repeat from * to the end of the row.
15th row: * K10, P1, K1, P1, K2. Repeat from * to the end of the row.
16th row: *P3, K1, P1, K1, P9. Repeat from * to the end of the row.
17th row: *K8, P1, K1, P1, K4. Repeat from * to the end of the row.
18th row: *P5, K1, P1, K1, P7. Repeat from * to the end of the row.
19th row: *K6, P1, K1, P1, K6. Repeat from * to the end of the row.
20th row: *P7, K1, P1, K1, P5. Repeat from * to the end of the row.
21st row: *K4, P1, K1, P1, K8. Repeat from * to the end of the row.
22nd row: *P9, K1, P1, K1, P3. Repeat from * to the end of the row.
23rd row: *K2, P1, K1, P1, K10. Repeat from * to the end of the row.
24th row: P11, K1, P1, K1, P1. Repeat from * to the end of the row.
These 24 rows form the repeat of the pattern.

DIAMOND PATTERN

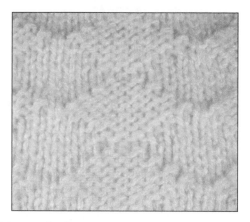

This stitch is reversible (that is, it looks the same on the front and back).

Cast on a multiple of 8 stitches.

1st row: *P1; K7; Repeat from * to end of row.

2nd row: K1, *P5, K2; Repeat from * to end of row.

3rd row: P3, * K3, P2; Repeat from * to end of row.

4th row: K3, * P1, K4; Repeat from * to end of row.

5th row: Purl entire row.

6th row: K3, * P1, K4; Repeat from * to end of row.

7th row: P3, * K3, P2; Repeat from * to end of row.

8th row: K1, *P5, K2, Repeat from * to end of row.

These 8 rows form the repeat of the pattern.

RIDGE PATTERN

Cast on an even number of stitches.

1st row: K to end of row.

2nd row: *K2 tog. Repeat from * to end of row.

3rd row: K into front and back of each stitch.

4th row: P to end of row.

These 4 rows form the repeat of the pattern.

Practice with a purpose. Try these stitch patterns before you use them for a garment, but make squares big enough for some kind of use. Dishcloths, pillow covers, doll blankets—even squares for a patchwork afghan—will make use of your work and let you practice without needing to be perfect.

CHAPTER 8

Increasing, Decreasing, and Picking Up Stitches

I ncreasing and decreasing the number of stitches on your needles gives you a way of shaping a piece as you make it. Picking up stitches lets you build on to bound edges. Some methods add a decorative element while others are strictly functional. Mastering these techniques will enable you to give your fabric the form you want.

Increasing Stitches

You change the shape of your fabric by changing the number of stitches on the needle. To make the fabric wider, you *increase* the number of stitches; to taper it, you *decrease*. For example, working 2 stitches together at the end of every row will decrease the number of stitches on your needle pretty quickly. It will also make a sharp, 45-degree angle there. Working 2 stitches together at the end of every other row, however, will give a subtler angle. Once you know how to shape your knitting, you can adapt commercial knitting patterns and start designing your own garments.

Decreasing creates a noticeable line because the remaining stitches are pulled to the right or the left where one is missing. The pattern you are using will tell you how to make the kind of increasing and decreasing stitches it requires, but knowing about the different kinds helps you understand what you're doing.

ALERT

If possible, and depending on the pattern you are using, do all decreasing and increasing not in the first or last stitch of a row, but in the second or third stitch in from the edge. That way, the selvage will still be smooth for sewing or picking up stitches.

In knitting patterns, the most common abbreviations for increasing by a single stitch are *inc. 1* or *inc 1 st*. There are three basic methods of increasing, each of which creates a slightly different decorative effect. How do you know which to use? It depends on the look you want. In some fabrics or garments, it looks better to accentuate the shaping, while in others it doesn't.

Yarn-Forward Increase

The easiest way to make a new stitch is to simply put a loop of yarn over the needle. This type of increase can be indicated in patterns by several different terms, most often *yarn over* or *make one* (see Appendix A for abbreviations). Yarn forward *(YFWD)* or yarn back *(YBK)* will bring the yarn over the needle in a certain direction depending on the stitch you are working. You may also see yarn 'round needle *(YRN)*, or yarn over needle *(YO)*. YRN tends to be used in British patterns. You'll find YO in patterns published in the United States.

SSENTIALS

As with many handcrafts, knitting has several terms for the same instruction. When using a new pattern or book, refer to the abbreviation key to become familiar with the terms you'll need to recognize. In time, you'll know all the versions!

The new loops from these increase methods are worked as normal stitches on the following row, and they do leave a slight hole in your fabric—not necessarily a bad thing. Some methods of increasing take advantage of the holes to create a lacy effect or an eyelet pattern along the line of increasing. Chapter 15 has more information on making lacy stitches using yarn-forward (or yarn-over) increases.

Making a yarn-forward increase

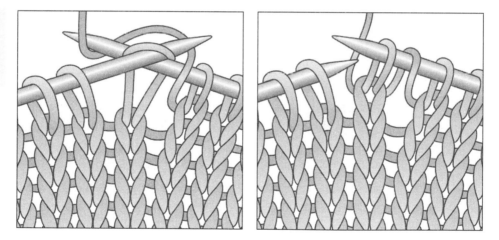

Raised-Strand Increase

A much less visible method of increasing is *raising* the strand that lies between the stitches on the left and right needles and placing it on the left needle as a stitch (facing the same direction as the other stitches). Knitting into the back of this strand will twist it while making an added stitch. (If you don't twist the stitch, it will form a hole.)

Making a raised-strand increase

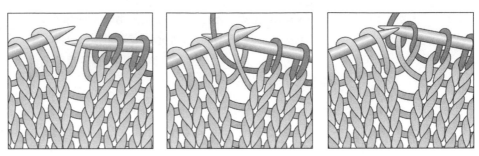

Lifted Increase

Lifted increase

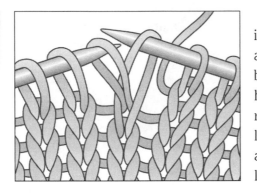

Lifted increases are also less visible than a yarn over. To create an additional stitch, knit into the stitch below the next stitch on your left hand needle. In essence, you are re-knitting into a stitch from your last row. Lifted and raised increases are subtle, and preserve the smooth look of your knitted fabric.

Bar Increase

The most usual method of increasing one stitch is to work into a stitch twice. Knit the stitch, then, without slipping the last loop off the needle, knit into the back of the same stitch. When you slip the original stitch off the left-hand needle, you'll have 2 stitches on the right needle made from one original stitch! This method produces a little bar in the fabric at the base of the new stitch, which is easy to see when you are counting rows between increases.

Decreasing Stitches

As with increase methods, different methods of eliminating stitches create different visual effects, depending on which stitches lie on top of others and in which direction they cover them.

The easiest way to decrease is to knit 2 stitches together. To do this, insert the right needle through 2 stitches on the left needle, instead of the usual one, and then knit or purl them together. Pull the yarn through both stitches, as if they were 1 stitch. (In a pattern, this is abbreviated as *k2tog* or *p2tog.*)

Knitting 2
stitches
together

Knitting 2
stitches
together
through
the back

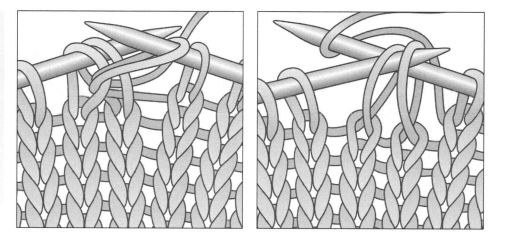

While this is the easiest decrease method, you won't want to use it all the time. It creates a decrease line that slopes to the right, and sometimes you'll want one that slopes to the left. For example, say you are shaping the front of a raglan-sleeved sweater, which tapers in on both sides. You would make a left-sloping decrease on the right side, and a right-sloping decrease on the left side.

ESSENTIALS

The general rule is that the direction of the decreased stitch should follow the angle at the edge of the fabric. Therefore, if the fabric slopes to the left then the decrease should, also.

Most decreasing stitches are made on the right side of the work. The beginning of the row should have left-slanted decreases, and the end of the row should have right-slanted decreases. The decreases, then, will follow the line of the edges.

Left-Slanting Decreases

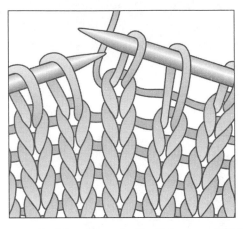

Working a slip one, slip one, knit two together decrease

The most usual left-slanting decrease is "slip 1, slip 1, knit 2 together," abbreviated *ssk*. To work this, you slip 1 stitch (K-wise) onto the right needle without knitting it. Slip the next stitch the same way. Put both stitches back onto the left needle (now twisted), then knit them together.

A variation on the ssk decrease is "slip 1, knit 1, pass slipped stitch over," abbreviated *sl1, K1, psso*. This means you slip the first stitch, knit the next stitch, then bring the slipped stitch over the knitted stitch as you would if you were binding off.

Right-Slanting Decreases

Given that many decreases are worked in pairs, you need to know how to do right-slanted decreases as well. For the ssk decrease at the beginning of the row, you simply knit 2 together (*K2 tog*) toward the end of the row.

To K2 tog, use the same technique you learned for the English method of binding off. Simply insert the right needle into 2 stitches at once, and create 1 new stitch.

Making decreases and increases somewhere in the row other than the edge will create three-dimensional shaping, creating the equivalent of darts and gathering in dressmaking.

If your left decrease was a sl1, K1, psso, perform the opposite combination at the end of the row to create a right decrease. Knit 1 stitch, and return it to the left needle. Using the right tip, bring the second stitch over the one you've just returned. In essence, you are slipping a stitch in reverse. Although these instructions tell you *how* to create a stitch, your patterns will specify where and when you should do them to be sure that the direction of the decreases are even on either side of your fabric.

Working a knit 2 together right decrease

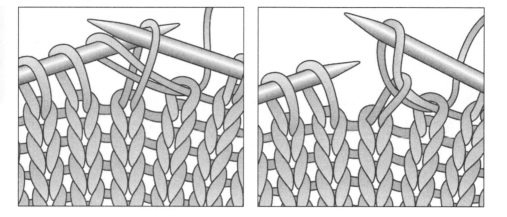

Picking Up Stitches

Patterns often tell you to pick up stitches along a neckline or armhole so you can add a rib border to finish the garment. Picking up stitches is also an easy way to finish a neckline, add a collar, or complete button and buttonhole plackets without having to knit a separate piece of fabric and sew it on. Done properly, picking up stitches creates a neater, more professional effect than sewing.

ALERT

The tricky part of this technique is picking up the right number of stitches at evenly spaced intervals. Picking up too many stitches makes the ribbing buckle; picking up too few will make the ribbing too tight. Aim to give the picked up stitches the same spacing as those that were knitted.

Across a horizontal row, you can pick up every stitch. On a vertical edge, however, you'll have more rows per inch than stitches. You'll have to use another guide for picking up the stitches. Picking up a stitch for every row will give you too many, while picking up a stitch from every second row might give you too few.

Knitting patterns usually tell you to pick up a certain number of stitches, but they don't detail from where along the neckline or armhole you should take them. Remember, too, that if you have changed the length of a piece of knitting to make it fit better, you will probably need to pick up a different number of stitches than what the pattern indicates. In this instance, it's better to ignore the pattern and go with what looks right.

If you do intend to pick up the number of stitches the instructions give, you will work out a method for distributing the stitches evenly. One way is to divide the length of fabric edge where stitches are to be picked up. Mark the halfway point, then halve it again to find the quarter and three-quarter divisions. Mark these points with some sort of clip or device—safety pins work well. Divide the number of stitches equally between these sections.

An alternate method is to pick up every possible stitch along the edge of the neckline or armhole so that you leave no gaps. Then, on the next row, knit or purl 2 together at evenly spaced intervals to get down to the number of stitches the pattern requires.

Some knitters have devised formulas, such as picking up 1 stitch to every 3 rows, depending on the tension of the rows and the stitch that will be finishing the edge. If the stitches you pick up will be worked in rib on a small needle, sometimes the stitches and row tension will be almost equal.

ALERT

Watch out for gaps! You will see whether you are leaving holes as you go. Remedy the situation by releasing the stitch you've just taken up and picking one up from another place to see if that works better.

A more exact method is to work out what your gauge is in ribbing. When you know the number of stitches per inch, multiply it by the length of the area you will be picking up from. That's the number of stitches you should pick up. For example, say the schematic drawing on your pattern shows that a band for buttons needs to be 12 inches long, and you know you knit in rib at 5 stitches per inch. You multiply 5 (your gauge in ribbing) by 12 (the length of the band) to get 60—that's the number of stitches you should pick up.

To find out sooner rather than later that a neckline doesn't look right, stop and check after you've picked up the stitches and worked a couple of rows of rib. Use a tapestry needle to thread the stitches onto a long piece of ribbon, and tie the ends of the ribbon loosely. That way, you can try on the sweater and get an idea of how the finished garment will look before you've gone too far.

How to Pick Up Stitches

To pick up stitches from a cast-off edge, hold the knitted fabric in your left hand with the right side facing you. If the rib will be worked in rows, use one of a pair of needles. If it will be worked in rounds, use a set of double-pointed needles. Select knitting needles two sizes smaller than the size you used to make the fabric.

ESSENTIALS

If you will be using a different color for the new edge or collar, pick up the stitches with the original color, then switch to the new color on the first row. This will help disguise the join and give a neat appearance.

Insert the point of the right needle under the edge stitch, from front to back and under both loops. Be sure to go through a whole stitch, not just one side of it. Wind the yarn around the needle and draw the yarn through as though you're knitting a stitch. Proceed from right to left until you've covered the whole area. Do not split stitches (that is, accidentally draw yarn between the ply of the yarn).

After your picking-up row, the first row will be on the wrong side. If done in rib, the first row should be worked with as tight a tension as possible. This will avoid gaps and make a neat join with the main part of the sweater. Use the needle size called for in the pattern.

To pick up stitches from a side edge, hold the knitted fabric in your left hand with the right side facing you. Insert the point of the right needle between the first and second stitches of the row (that is, one complete stitch from the edge). Be sure to go through a selvage edge knot and not just one side of a stitch. Wind the yarn around the needle and draw the yarn through as though you were knitting a stitch. Proceed from right to left.

Picking up stitches from a cast-off edge of knitted fabric

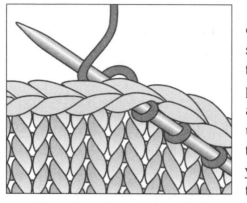

You may find it easier to use a crochet hook to pick up the stitches. Again, use a smaller size than what you used for the main part of the garment. Insert the hook as you would a knitting needle, but use the hook to pull a loop of yarn through, then place the loop on your needle (remembering to use the size called for in the pattern).

Although this process takes time, it's worth doing right. Start again if you don't like your results after the first few rows. Ask for help, or try a different technique until you're satisfied with the results.

CHAPTER 9
Following Knitting Patterns

Knitting projects all begin with a plan—a pattern. The pattern may be a chart or graph, or line-by-line instructions. The usual kind of line-by-line pattern, bristling with abbreviations, can be intimidating to a beginner, but if you know what to expect, you can proceed confidently. Like reading a recipe, translating patterns is just a matter of knowing the language.

Different Types of Patterns

Knitting patterns describe how to create a knitted item one piece of fabric at a time and how to put it together. A comprehensive pattern should include a photo or drawing of the finished garment, a list of required materials, a description of the gauge necessary to make the item the right size, a list of all abbreviations used, and stitch pattern instructions, if necessary.

Good patterns also show diagrams or schematic drawings of each finished section with overall measurements marked, so you can see at a glance what your goal is.

ESSENTIALS

By checking your knitting measurements against the diagrams, you'll know that your finished garment will be the right size. That way you won't have any unpleasant surprises. Check regularly to catch problems before it's too late!

There are two main types of patterns: line-by-line, and chart or diagram patterns. When using the line-by-line knitting pattern, it's necessary to work out what the abbreviations mean; with the chart pattern, you have to interpret symbols. Some people find it easier to work with words, others with pictures, but try both types at least once. When you know what type of instructions you prefer, look for those patterns. (If you hate both types, look for one of the "plain English" books of knitting patterns now available in bookstores.)

Read the Chart

Chart patterns are printed on a squared grid. Each row of squares is numbered at the side to represent a row of knitting. You start at the bottom, reading from right to left for knit rows and left to right for purl rows. If you are working from a chart designed for circular needles, all rounds are read from right to left.

Each square represents a stitch. Symbols in the squares indicate the kind of stitch to work. Designs for knitting in different colors are usually in chart form and are easier to follow than written instructions would be. Stitch patterns for fabric stitches can be either line-by-line or in chart format.

FACTS

Companies that make and sell yarn also produce patterns, so naturally they want you to buy their yarn to make the pattern they've provided. It is possible to use different yarns if you know how to work the right substitution.

The more information a pattern gives, the more useful it will be. A really helpful pattern will not only tell you how many balls of yarn various sizes require, it will also tell you how much one ball weighs and the length of yarn in a ball (the yardage). If you want to substitute yarns, this information is a big help.

Shop Around

Yarn shops sell patterns and yarn, but you can also shop online—where you can find free patterns—or in bookshops or homemaker magazines. Once you know what you're looking for, you'll discover the multitude of patterns available for knitters of all levels.

Some patterns, or pattern books, offer several versions of one pattern. If you find a basic pattern you like, see what adjustments might create a whole new look!

Before Beginning a Pattern

Reading a recipe right through to the end before you begin cooking can save you from unpleasant surprises and extra shopping trips. Reading a knitting pattern ahead of time can do the same. Several factors deserve special attention right from the beginning. While cooking may take an afternoon, some knitting projects can take months. Ensure a successful experience by being prepared!

Check Your Sizes

Don't rely on the photograph on the cover of a pattern for sizing—the model could be wearing a larger or smaller size than normal. Only by working with actual measurements will you know if a garment is going to be tight fitting or loose.

Check whether the pattern is in inches or centimeters, and stick with that method of measurement, using whichever type of measuring tape is necessary. Trying to translate measurements from inches to centimeters is asking for trouble.

Schematic diagram with fabric measurements

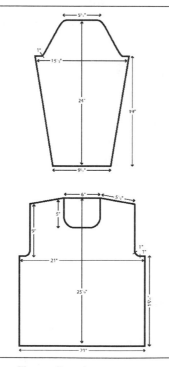

The pattern will give a range of possible sizes for the garment, with the smallest size written first and the others in square brackets after it: 6 [8, 10, 12, 14]. In the pattern text, any different instructions are provided for the range of sizes in the same order and manner—with the smallest first and the rest in square brackets. When only one number is given for a certain instruction, it applies to all sizes.

Remember that when a pattern says that the smallest size is for a "34-inch bust," that means your size, not the size of the garment. Most patterns have some extra inches of *ease* added in—allowing for the difference between a person's measurements and the measurements of the finished garment.

For a fitted garment, a minimum of 4 inches of ease is usually allowed in the bust. For a nonfitted garment, such as a sweater with drop sleeves, a minimum of 8 inches of ease is generally allowed. But the amount of ease varies with the yarn used: a finer yarn can make a tighter-fitting garment than a bulky yarn.

Even if a pattern doesn't provide schematic diagrams—and many of the older patterns don't—it will give chest measurements and length for each size. Measure the person you are going to fit and determine if these are correct.

ESSENTIALS

An excellent way to check measurements is to work from a favorite garment similar to the one you are making. The ease is already accounted for, so if you match what you are making to something you own that fits you well, you can be confident you'll get a great fit.

You can sketch your own schematic diagrams to make sure that the pieces the pattern asks you to construct will make the size sweater you want. Check the width of the front, for example, by dividing the number of stitches the pattern asks you to cast on for the front by the gauge. If you cast on 75 stitches at a gauge of 5 stitches to the inch, your fabric will be 15 inches wide. Mark this on a rough sketch of the garment. Continue reading through the pattern, working out the key measurements for the rest of the pieces.

Use graph paper to make a more accurate diagram, with each square representing a stitch. Because a stitch is wider than it is long, this won't give you a realistic idea of the shape of each piece, but it can help you follow the pattern. (Craft stores carry knitting graph paper if you do want to make really accurate diagrams.)

Check Your Tension

You've worked out what sizes you'll get if you follow the knitting instructions in the pattern gauge. Now you have to be sure you are actually knitting in that gauge so the pieces you make will be the right size. As you learned in the section on gauge calculations, test your gauge and decide which size needles to use before you start.

Have Your Supplies

Make sure you've checked the "materials required" section of the pattern and that you have everything you need to complete the garment: all the yarn (plus one), the right needles, and any buttons and finishing accessories. Have something to count rows with—even if it's just a safety pin at every tenth row. Put another pin at the row where you start decreasing: it'll be easier to count the rows from that point. Tapestry needles and crochet hooks have a million uses, so try to keep one of each in your knitting bag.

Don't forget to work your gauge in the stitch the pattern calls for. There can be a big difference in tension between stockinette and a fancy lacy stitch.

Making Patterns Easier to Read

For most people, the most difficult part of working a knitting pattern is making sense of the instructions. Most patterns use abbreviations to keep from taking up too many sheets of paper. Each company has its own writing style, but most use recognized knitting abbreviations and explain any that are unusual. (For a list of common abbreviations, see Appendix A.)

ESSENTIALS

Read right through the pattern before you even pick your needles to make sure everything is clear. Study it until you understand any special stitch instructions, and check that all the abbreviations are explained somewhere in the pattern.

Find a way to make your pattern user-friendly. Enlarge and photocopy the pattern, then enclose it in a plastic sleeve and use a waxy pencil to make notes to yourself and keep your place. Or use a highlighter to cross off rows on a photocopy in a way that still lets you see what's written underneath.

Even if you only use large sticky notes to mark your place when you put your work aside, it will help.

Lastly, if your pattern comes from Europe, check that you are using the right size American needles, that you have enough ounces of yarn if the weight is given in grams, and that all the instructions are clear. Try to convert as little as possible from metric to inches, if you have to at all, because it's frustrating trying to work out exact equivalents. If the pattern is written using centimeters, get a centimeter ruler for measuring.

Understanding the Repetition Conventions

Several phrases have particular meanings when they are used in patterns. Reading through the pattern first will get you used to the designer's approach, but you should be familiar with a few standard instructions.

For example, when the pattern says, "work the stitches as they appear" or "work the stitches as presented," you should purl the purl stitches and knit the knit stitches (as in ribbing, or stockinette).

Once the stitch or design repeat has been given, rather than printing the same instructions over and over again, instructions may simply say, "work in pattern." To do this, keep working the instructions exactly as they are listed, carefully keeping track of your stitches and rows. Use stitch markers if necessary, and keep notes on the number of the repeats and rows you've completed.

When repeating anything, it's important to make sure you are doing it the correct number of times. It can take perseverance to decipher a pattern's instructions regarding the number of repetitions.

"Work even until . . ." means work without increasing or decreasing. Counting your stitches periodically will help you ensure that you haven't dropped or picked up any stitches by mistake.

When a pattern tells you to "end with a wrong-side row," it means that you complete a wrong-side row before starting the next instruction in your pattern. Similarly, "end with a right-side row" means that the last row you work should be with the right side facing you. In stockinette, for example, you would work a knit row, then stop and follow the next instructions.

Repeating Rows

Some instructions for repetitions can be complicated. If math is not your strong suit, pattern instructions might read like a word problem with no solution. Trying to process all the steps at once can intimidate beginning knitters, but the following examples should help you make sense of some common abbreviations.

dec 1 st every 4th row three times, then every 8th row three times.
To work this instruction you would decrease 1 stitch on rows 1, 5, and 9, then decrease 1 stitch on rows 17, 25, and 33.

Rows 24 to 42: Repeat rows 4 to 8 consecutively, ending with row 7.
To do this, look back at the instructions for rows 4, 5, 6, 7, and 8. Work them in order three more times, which brings you to row 38. Then work just rows 4, 5, 6, and 7 again. This last repeat of row 7 will be row 42.

When dealing with repeating rows—especially with complicated stitch patterns—it will be worth your while to list out the corresponding rows, at least until you find your rhythm. You will also find that after knitting several inches "in pattern," the pattern itself becomes clear, making it easier to follow.

Asterisks and Parentheses

Either by themselves or in combination, asterisks and parentheses indicate a sequence of stitches. These sequences are called multiples when they complete one segment of a pattern stitch horizontally. In a line-by-line pattern, asterisks signal the beginning of a sequence, which may be referred to if the sequence continues across the row. In some patterns, the sequence is set off with asterisks at both the beginning and the end of the sequence.

*K2, P2; rep from * to end. Knit 2, purl 2, then repeat this sequence until the end of the row. In this example, the sequence is a multiple of 4 stitches.

K1, *P2, K2, P1; rep from *, K1. This sequence instructs you to knit 1 stitch, then purl 2, knit 2, and purl 1 across the entire row. At the last stitch, knit 1.

inc, K5, P 1; repeat between * 2 more times. If this were written out, it would read: inc, K5, P1, inc, K5, P1, inc, K5, P1. When a pattern says, "rep between * two more times," it means that after you work the instructions once, you repeat whatever instructions are between the asterisks two *more* times (three repeats in all).

(K1, P1) twice. Parentheses enclose instructions to be worked the number of times specified immediately following the parentheses. In this example, work the actual instructions twice, for a total of 4 stitches.

ESSENTIALS

Take it slow when trying to figure out complicated pattern instructions. Work out the sequence from one comma or semicolon to the next, and be careful to work a stitch or row the number of times stated. Going one stitch at a time, you will be able to make sense of it all.

*K4, (yo, dec, K2) 4 times; repeat from * 3 more times. To make things more confusing, this instruction uses asterisks and parentheses in combination. Again, take the pattern apart. Working from the asterisk, you would first knit 4 stitches. You would then work the following sequence four times: the yarn-over increase, then the decrease, and the 2 knit stitches. Repeat the sequence three times for a total of four repeats.

[K1, P1, *K1, (P2 tog, K1) 2 times, P1; repeat from *, K1, P1]; repeat between [ ]. To work these instructions, work the first 3 stitches, then the instructions in parentheses twice, then the purl stitch, then the entire instructions from the *, followed by the next 2 stitches. Then go back to the first bracket and repeat the entire sequence to the last bracket.

Row 14: Repeat Row 4. A pattern will often tell you to repeat an entire row (or round). In this case, you must look back at the instructions for row 4 and repeat them for row 14.

Parentheses sometimes indicate garment sizes and provide additional information to clarify instructions. Square brackets can be used in the same way as parentheses, but are usually used in combination with them to make instructions clearer.

Reading Stitch Pattern Charts

Many people find it easier to interpret charts for stitches rather than figuring out the multiple repeats between the brackets and asterisks of line-by-line patterns. On a stitch pattern chart, each stitch is indicated by a symbol. You read the chart the same way as the knitting is done, from the bottom upwards. Remember that you are looking at a diagram of how the knitting appears on its right side.

QUESTIONS?

Is there a good way to conveniently hold the knitting pattern?
Try a music stand, if you have one in your home. A magnetic board with a magnetic ruler is another good option. You want your pattern out of the way of your knitting, but still close enough to see.

For example, the symbol for stockinette is a short vertical line. That symbol means that the stitch must be knit on the right side and purled on the wrong side—basic stockinette stitch. If the design is to be knitted in stockinette, odd-numbered rows represent knit rows and even-numbered

Reversible
blanket with
diamond
pattern

knitted by Judith MacInnes

rows represent purl. If the design is worked in another stitch, the odd-numbered rows represent the right side of the fabric and the even-numbered rows the wrong side. Sometimes the pattern prints the right-side rows darker than wrong-side rows to make it easier to distinguish between the two. Rows are usually numbered at the beginning of the row they are for. Thus, row 9 will be indicated on the right side of the diagram, but not the left. This means row 9, an odd-numbered row, is worked from right to left.

Sometimes on knitting charts you will see empty spaces left where stitches have been decreased or not made yet. Where "no stitch" is indicated (sometimes shown with shaded spaces), work just the stitches of the chart, skipping the "no stitch" spaces.

ESSENTIALS

On a stitch pattern chart, each square represents a stitch and each horizontal line represents a row of knitting. You work from the bottom up and remember that right-side rows are read from right to left, and wrong-side rows are read from left to right.

If the graph is on squared paper, your knitting will not be in proportion. A stitch is wider than it is long, making it more horizontal than square, but the designer of the chart should have allowed for this.

Charts that accommodate different garment sizes may have more than one set of edge stitches. Read the instructions carefully to find out which set you should be using.

With charts, as with line-by-line knitting instructions, it's essential to keep track of where you are. A ruler placed just above the row you are working on can help. You want to be able to see the area you have just worked, so you can check to see that you are working a stitch into the right one on the previous row.

CHAPTER 10
Finishing and Caring for Knits

Y ou've finished the knitting part of a project, but there's still the finishing to be done! Finishing can involve anything from darning in the loose ends and blocking the knitted pieces to sewing up the seams and adding buttons. Proper finishing—attending to the details—makes a hand-knit item look well made.

Preparing the Knitted Pieces

After all that knitting, it can be frustrating to find that you have at least another hour's work to do to make your item presentable. Even so, don't rush this part. Put the same effort into making up a garment that you did in working the stitches and following the pattern. Your finish work shows. It's worth taking the time to get it right. A bulky or uneven seam can detract from pretty stitches, an unusual design, and the hard work that went into making the fabric.

Holding a piece of knitting up to the light is how commercial knitting factories check for flaws. Do the same with your fabric for one last check for dropped stitches or mistakes.

Before you start the finishing processes, lay out the knitting on a table and place the pieces that go together against each other to check that each edge is the right length to join up with its matching edge. Make sure that the back and front are the same length and that the sleeves match each other.

Darning in the Yarn Ends

Tidy up the wrong side of the work before you sew the pieces together. A tapestry needle is best for darning or weaving in any loose ends of yarn, although some people find it easier to use a crochet hook. If you've changed colors at the end of rows, work the ends into the selvage or the seaming.

Some detailing come after you've finished knitting but before you start the finish work. Appliqués, embroidery, or pockets are easiest to add now, while the pieces are still flat.

To darn in the ends, thread them into the tapestry needle. Insert the needle vertically into an adjacent stitch and pull the yarn through. Don't work too tightly; keep the tension of your sewing consistent with the knitted stitches in the fabric itself. Some people try to split the stitches with their needle for a more secure darn—this also hides the ends better, too.

Pull the yarn end through 3 or 4 stitches in this way, then go diagonally in two directions, then backward. Cut off the excess yarn, leaving about a ½-inch tail to prevent the woven-in yarn from escaping the weave over the course of wearing or washing.

Weaving in the ends is also a good time to catch any loose stitches that are pulling away from each other and creating holes.

Blocking

Blocking is the process of flattening knitted pieces to the right shape and size before you assemble them. Blocking evens out the tension of the knitting slightly and gives it a crisp look.

There are two preferred blocking methods: pressing with an iron or moistening the fabric. Wool and natural fiber yarns can be pressed. Synthetic yarns, or knitted pieces with a lot of heavily textured areas, block better if they are moistened. Pressing can squash raised stitches, ruining their effect. It is also best not to block a garment that has a lot of ribbing.

Blocking with Moisture

The easiest way to block with moisture is to use a spray bottle, the kind used for misting plants. Empty misters are available at just about any store that sells house wares. If you choose to recycle one you already own, be sure it is clean. Chemicals or solutions left in the bottle could damage your knitting.

ALERT

Before you apply moisture to a fabric, read the yarn label for its recommendations on blocking, washing, and pressing. Different yarns need different methods of blocking. If the yarn wrapper says, "Do not block," or "Do not press," you must skip this step.

Use a large flat surface, such as a padded table top, for pinning the pieces of the garment. You can buy blocking boards or simply work on whatever's available: the ironing board if it is big enough, or on the floor with a towel under the knitting. You can make your own blocking board from a piece of foam core, available at art supply stores. You'll need a piece big enough to spread out the largest piece of knitting you've done and thick enough to support pins easily.

Smooth one piece of knitted fabric at a time on to your blocking board. Place pins (nonrusting) at regular intervals all around the edges of the knitting. Gently shape the knitting as needed to straighten edges or ease curves into a smooth arc. The lines of stitches should be straight horizontally and vertically. Do not stretch out the ribbing.

QUESTIONS?

What if the yarn label does not include blocking instructions?
If you have no information from the yarn label, use moisture to block. It's simple, safe for all yarns, and generally gives good results.

When the pieces are pinned out, spray them lightly and evenly with water from the spray bottle and then leave them to dry.

An alternate wetting method is to soak a bath towel in water, wring it out, then spread it over the knitting. After an hour or so remove the towel, shape the knitting and pin it in place, then leave the pieces to dry.

Blocking with Heat

Pinned fabric for blocking

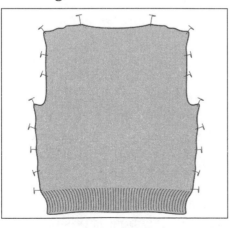

If you use an iron to do your blocking, read any ironing directions or symbols on the yarn wrapper. If you used the yarn your pattern recommends, check the pattern for information on pressing. You can also press the gauge swatch to see how the yarn reacts to heat.

Some yarns, such as mohair and synthetics, cannot be pressed. Others can take only low heat. The yarn wrapper should tell you which heat setting to use and whether the fabric should be pressed over a damp or dry cloth. Natural fibers such as wool, cotton, and linen are usually pressed through a damp cloth; synthetic blends take a cool iron over a dry cloth.

Pin the pieces as you would for blocking with moisture. With the iron at the appropriate setting, gently *press* the fabric by raising and lowering the iron over one small section at a time. This method applies heat to set the stitches without flattening or dragging the knitting. This procedure is time consuming and requires a gentle hand—pressing too heavily takes the life out of knitted fabrics.

Joining Seams

When you are ready to sew up the sweater, consult the pattern for the order in the pieces should be sewn. Usually the shoulders come first, then the side seams, then the sleeves get set in. The neckband or collar finishing comes last.

If the pattern doesn't go into details about constructing the garment, think through the process before you begin. For example, think how you'd prefer to work the neck of a turtleneck sweater. You could do it on two needles and have a seam. In this case you'd sew up only one shoulder before picking up the stitches to work the neck. If you'd prefer a seamless turtleneck (the neatest choice), you could work it in the round. In that case, you'd begin by sewing up both shoulders.

ESSENTIALS

For sewing seams, you need a tapestry needle with a large eye and blunt end that won't split the yarn. Whichever stitch you choose, try to make the seam as elastic as the fabric it is joining.

The pattern may also suggest a method for sewing each seam. If it doesn't, consider what you are sewing before choosing a stitch. For example, a backstitch seam will hide lots of loose ends along the selvage successfully. In other places, such as button bands or collars where the seam must be very flat, you should choose invisible seaming.

Pin or baste pieces together before you begin sewing. Keep checking as you sew. to be sure you're not inadvertently stretching one side more than the other. Your goal is to end up with an even seam.

Even if you hate sewing, seaming a sweater is not difficult. If possible, sew up the item using the same yarn with which you knit it. If the yarn has a very uneven texture, however, it may not be suitable because it could break at the thinner parts. Choose a similar colored 4-ply yarn or a needlepoint yarn instead. Find a color that matches and a similar fiber that is cleaned in the same way. (Don't, for example, sew up a silk garment with a woolen thread.)

Mattress or Ladder Stitch (Invisible Seaming)

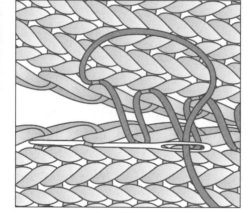

Mattress stitch method for invisible seam

Mattress stitch is an excellent, all-purpose seaming stitch that makes an invisible seam.

To start the mattress stitch, place the two pieces of knitting to be joined on a flat surface, with right sides facing you. Hold the two edges together, matching them row for row. Thread the needle, and beginning at the hem, secure the yarn with a couple of stitches on the back.

Bring the needle to the front between the edge stitch and the second stitch in the first row, going under the horizontal bar between the stitches. Insert the needle into the same place on the opposite piece of fabric. Keeping the needle coming out the front at all times, use a zigzag action, going from side to side, taking up the strands that correspond to those on the other side, making rungs from one piece of knitting to the other. After several stitches, pull the stitches together firmly (but not too tightly), closing the seam as you go. The seam must be the same tension as the rest of the fabric in order to lie neat and flat.

If you are sewing together a ribbed section of knitting with this seaming stitch, make the join correspond with the rib pattern as much as possible. In other words, sew a vertical row of purl stitches next to a vertical row of knit stitches, and aim for a seamless look of continuous rib.

Backstitch Seaming

Sewing a
backstitch
seam

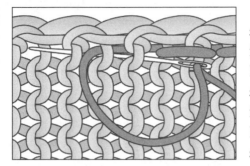

Backstitch seams are sewn 1 stitch in from the edges of the fabric. This method is excellent for hiding messy edges because the seam can be spread and pressed flat. Backstitching is suitable for lightweight yarns, or for sleeve and shoulder seams.

Place the two right sides of the fabric together, matching the rows at the edges. Secure the yarn with a couple of stitches on the back. Then bring the needle to the front 1 stitch beyond the secured thread. Send the needle through to the back just behind where the yarn emerges, and bring it back up 1 knitted stitch ahead. This stitch will always bring the needle through the front of the work the width of 1 stitch ahead of the last stitch.

Make a continuous line of stitches of equal length on the side of the work facing you. On the reverse side the stitches should form a straight but slightly overlapping line.

Don't pull the stitches too tightly. Check after every few stitches that the seam is not too tight in relation to the knitted fabric. If the yarn can be pressed, open the seam and press it carefully with the point of the iron.

Flat Seaming

Sewing a
flat seam

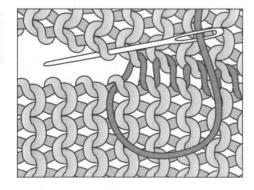

A flat seam is one that is completely flat when opened. Flat seams are the best to use on ribbing.

Place the two pieces together with right sides facing, matching the edges exactly. As you sew this stitch, keep your index finger between the two pieces of fabric. Secure the yarn with a couple of stitches on the back, then pass the needle through 1 edge stitch directly across to the matching stitch on the other side. Along the length of the seam, pass the needle through both layers of knitting, as close to the edge as possible.

Setting in Sleeves

Fitting sleeves into armholes is considered the trickiest part of putting together a sweater, so take your time with this part of the assembly.

Some people prefer to sew the shoulder seams together first. Then they sew the sleeve on to the main body, starting at the armpit and circling around over the shoulder to the armpit on the other side. They sew up the side and sleeve seam last.

Others knitters prefer to set in the sleeve after the shoulder and side seams are finished, when the sleeve itself has been sewn into a tube. The circle of the sleeve is then set into the circle of the armhole. If you choose the latter method, sew in the sleeve in two parts. First sew from the armpit up to the top of the sleeve on one side, then stop and go back to the armpit and sew up the other side of the sleeve. That way you can gather any extra fabric at the top of the shoulder where it looks best.

Adding sleeves can be tricky

hat/scarf knitted by Sophie Cathro; sweater knitted by Alice Cathro

For either method, block the fabric first. Next, fold each sleeve in half along its length. Put a pin at the fold, in the center of the top. This is the point that must meet the shoulder seam. Pin or baste this part before you start sewing, to make sure the two areas fit together neatly.

Place right side to right side, and use a mattress stitch to sew the pieces together. After you've sewn up the garment, give it a final press only if it needs it (and the fiber allows for it).

Once your garment is sewn and pressed, you've arrived at the big moment—trying on your sweater! Don't despair if it doesn't look quite right. You can almost always fix what's wrong by unpicking the sewing, and reassembling the garment.

Caring for Knits

After all the work that goes into making a knitted garment, you don't want to ruin it during washing. You'll be glad you saved a yarn wrapper from your yarn so you can refer to the laundry symbols before washing or pressing.

Your gauge swatch can be useful here, too. If you want to machine wash the item, but you're afraid it might get damaged, do a test run with the gauge swatch. Measure the sample square before you toss it into the machine so you'll be able to see whether any shrinkage occurs.

Knits are ruined by excessive handling and sudden, drastic temperature changes during washing and rinsing. Don't wash in lukewarm water and then rinse in cold, and never wash in very hot water.

Wool garments, especially, need special care. Wool shrinks and becomes matted if it's washed in hot water. Always hand-wash a woolen garment unless the yarn wrapper specifically indicates that machine washing is possible. Use lukewarm water for both washing and rinsing.

Machine Washing Knits

If the yarn wrapper says you can machine wash a garment, look at the symbols and be sure you keep to the recommended temperature. (See the international care symbols in Appendix C.)

Even if a yarn is considered machine-washable, you need to be careful. If you're washing a knit with an especially loose weave, make sure it will not catch on other garments' hooks, eyes, or zippers. For protection, turn the knit inside out before washing and place it in a pillowcase or netted lingerie bag. Such bags will keep the garment self-contained and reduce stretching.

Set the washing machine cycle to the delicate or gentle cycle, and wash in cold or warm water, not hot.

Rinse the garment in warm water, and add fabric softener to the final rinse if desired. At the end of the cycle, promptly take the garment out of the washing machine. It's better to air-dry knits flat instead of in a dryer, to avoid pilling and wearing out the garment prematurely.

FACTS

For extra softness, some knitters wash their knits in a little bit of shampoo, instead of harsh detergent, and add hair conditioner during the second rinse. You can also use less detergent. Knits usually don't need heavy-duty cleaning, and extra soap left in the garment can cause skin irritation.

Air-drying the item on a flat surface also allows you to reshape the garment before it dries—like reblocking. Lay the garment out on a towel or a mesh drying frame, and ease it into shape.

Dry knits away from direct sunlight and radiators.

Hand-Washing Knits

If the instructions on the yarn wrapper recommend hand washing, use lukewarm water and a product made for washing delicate fabrics. There are special neutral soaps you can use, but a little mild dishwashing liquid works well, too.

Let the knitted item stay in the warm, soapy water only a minute, gently squeezing and kneading the fabric to loosen dirt. Knits, particularly woolens, should not be soaked for any length of time.

Rinse the item with tepid water as needed until the water is clear. Some people add a few drops of vinegar to the last rinse when rinsing wool or silk garments to remove any soap and brighten the colors. Others add a little hair conditioner to the final rinse water or glycerin if the wool seems to be very dry. As air-dried fabrics get stiff—especially cotton—you may want to add a little liquid laundry softener.

When you've finished rinsing, fight the urge to wring the fabric even though it holds a lot of water. Twisting a knit vigorously will stretch the fibers. Instead, support the weight of the wet knitting as you lift it out of the water to prevent stretching and sagging. In fact, try not to let any part of the garment hang when it is full of water. The weight will pull it out of shape.

QUESTIONS?

How do degrees Celsius translate to familiar temperatures?
To get an idea of relative temperatures, use this guideline 60°C is the temperature of water from a hot tap, hotter than the hand can bear. 50°C is hot to the hand, 40°C is pleasantly warm to the hand, and 30°C is cool.

Gently press out what water you can against the side of the tub. Then wrap the garment in a towel. If the sweater is not colorfast, use an old towel. If the towel is colored, be sure that it won't transfer its color to the garment. Roll up the towel with the garment inside, hold for a few seconds, and then unwrap. Most of the moisture will now be in the towel. With really heavy knits you may have to repeat this process with more dry towels.

Knits are best dried on a frame covered in mesh that allows the air to circulate. You can also use a clean, dry towel over a frame that allows the air to circulate. Lay your knitted garment out on this, shaping it the way you want it to dry.

ALERT

You should not iron knitted garments, but you can press them if necessary. As in blocking, rest the iron gently on the surface of the knit, then lift. Press on the wrong side of the sweater, using a steam iron. Don't pass the iron back and forth across the fabric as you do when ironing.

If the yarn wrapper recommends dry cleaning your finished garment, be sure to tell the dry cleaner not to press the knit afterward. Ask them to fold it instead of returning it to you on a hanger.

Dealing with Snags

If a thread gets pulled but has not been broken, use a crochet hook to pull the loop to the back of the fabric. It may be possible to work the extra yarn back into the fabric by easing the stitches around the snag. Try to get the stitches to take the yarn back into the places where it was pulled from by easing a little yarn from one stitch to another, working your way along a row.

If the ends are broken, first tie them together into a knot with short ends. The surrounding stitches will be a little more taut because some of the yarn length has been lost. Try to ease this tautness over as wide an area as possible to make it less noticeable.

Darning leaves an obvious patch. Try to avoid darning it wherever possible. Consider embroidering over holes if it's feasible. Needlepoint yarn comes in a wide range of colors and has a texture similar to many knitting yarns.

If you saved remnants of your yarn, a hole can be "invisibly" mended. Otherwise, for just a little extra yarn, look in the side seams for a long tail that might have been sewn in. It will be exactly the right color as the rest of the sweater. To do invisible mending, pick up loose stitches with a small needle from below the hole and knit them together with the stitches they've separated from, incorporating the stitches at the side at the same time.

Dealing with Pilling

When short fibers come loose from knitted fabric and bind together to form small balls of lint on the surface, that's known as pilling.

Some yarns tend to pill more than others do. Tendency to pill depends on the fineness and length of the fibers, the properties of the yarn, and the chemical treatments it has received. Synthetic fibers have a reputation for pilling more than wool, but these days most yarns are modified during manufacture to reduce the problem.

Sweater with textured vertical stripes

knitted by Judith MacInnes

The softer the yarn, and the more friction it is subject to, the more likely it is to pill. To avoid pilling, some people recommend adding a drop of glycerin to the wash water. Others recommend removing the pills as they appear. You can buy special abrasive tools that you stroke over the surface to "defuzz" your knitwear, or you can try using masking tape to pull them off, but both these methods can roughen the surface of the knit. If only a few pills have formed, pluck them off carefully by hand. Whichever method you choose, be gentle with the yarn.

Storing Yarn and Knits

Never hang a sweater. Even on padded hangers, they'll stretch out of shape as the weight of the yarn pulls the fabric and distorts the shoulders. To fold knits with a minimum number of creases, lay the sweater flat on its front. Fold back each side to about one-quarter the width of the sweater. Then fold each sleeve back along its seam to follow the edge of the fold. Finally, fold the sweater in half horizontally. You should have a folded sweater that looks like it belongs on a department store display.

When it comes to storing your knits, tightly sealed containers are probably the best way to guard against insects. Clear or translucent plastic boxes work well—you can tell at a glance what you have stored. It's easier to find containers sized perfectly for convienent under-the-bed storage.

Cedar chest oil vapors destroy small moth larvae, but they do not kill larger ones. If you keep yarn in a cedar chest, lightly sand the cedar wood each season to intensify the cedar oil vapors and deter insect infestation.

Freezing wool to 0°F or –20°C is said to kill moth larvae. However, at the egg and pupa stages, moths are apparently more resistant. If you want to be quite sure yarn is moth-free before storing it, put the yarn in a plastic bag, squeeze out as much air as possible, and keep it in the freezer for about three days. Let the yarn come to room temperature inside the bag before you open it. Then, leave the yarn somewhere hot for several days to allow any moth eggs to hatch or pupae to become moths. Put it back into the freezer to get rid of what develops, and you should have killed any type of moth infestation.

FACTS

Various products are sold as moth preventatives, such as bay leaves, cedar chips, pyrethrum, and naphthalene mothballs. In fact, they just disguise the smell of wool, and eventually their aromas fade. Check items stored this way often to be sure they are still okay.

Keep yarn in a dry place to prevent mildew. Never put away dirty woolens because they attract moths. Make sure knitted items are completely dry after washing and before you store them.

CHAPTER 11

Let the Games Begin

S o you know how to get stitches on the needles, and you know how to get them off. You even have the beginning idea of what to do in between, and after it's all over. You're probably anxious to start a project, but try to keep things simple at first. It's good to test your abilities, but make sure you choose a project you can finish.

Knitting Projects—Where to Start

The easiest items for beginners use a pair of straight needles to create square or oblong shapes. Scarves, dishcloths, potholders, pillows, or even squares joined together into an afghan are all respectable projects that can be as easy or as difficult as you choose.

Simple Squares

If you're up for experimenting, try making the squares without help. Use different yarns or varying stitch combinations to create texture and variety. Your yarn shop may sell beginner patterns for simple bags or hats that are made from squares, too. Even a sweater is easy, if you make an untailored tunic with straight, untapered sleeves.

QUESTIONS?

What if your pattern doesn't have a schematic or outline diagram?
Try to draw your own schematic from the information given. To figure the width, for example, divide the stitch total (at its widest part) by the gauge. If you are directed to cast on 25 stitches, and the gauge is 10 stitches over 2 inches, you would divide 25 by 10 (the gauge) and multiply by two (the gauge measurement). The width in this example would be 5 inches.

Search for patterns that include a schematic diagram of what each finished knitted piece should look like. These blueprints are useful. As you knit, you can measure your work and check the measurements against the diagram. You'll also be able to see at a glance how the article is constructed, which will help you decide whether the project is beyond your abilities. The greater the number of pieces to a garment, the longer and more complex the assembly will be. To begin with, stay away from patterns with lots of small additions like flaps and pockets.

When you've made squares in plain stockinette or garter stitch, try them in more complicated stitch patterns, such as the stitches shown in

Chapter 13 and Chapter 15. You can judge a stitch's degree of difficulty by the size of the *repeat* (or *multiple*). In other words, the shorter a stitch pattern is, the easier it usually is to do.

Baby sweater set: hat, mittens, and collared sweater

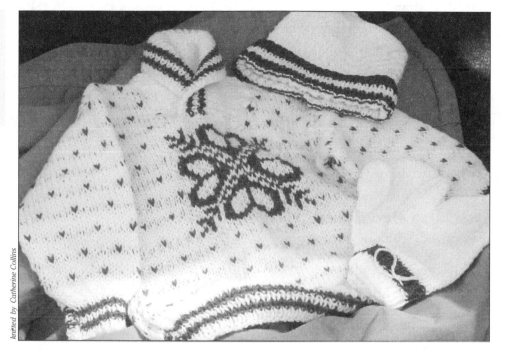

knitted by Catherine Collins

Expanding Your Horizons

When you're comfortable with basic knitting, you can start practicing increases, decreases, and picking up stitches. Then you'll be ready to make a shaped garment, like a vest. It will need a little shaping around the arms and neck, but this is easy to do. You make two different pieces, the back and then the front. When those are done, sew the shoulders and sides together. The pattern will then instruct you to pick up stitches from the armholes and neck so you can kit a ribbed edge to finish the garment neatly.

Baby booties, mittens, and slippers are small items with simple patterns available that you could attempt at this stage.

ALERT

When browsing through patterns, look for the descriptions "super-quick" and "beginner." These patterns should be fast and easy, with easy stitches and shaping and can be constructed from simple shapes that require minimal assembly. Patterns that call for heavy wools and large needles are usually easy patterns to follow.

Sweaters with drop or raglan sleeves are probably best for the beginning knitter. It's easier with these styles to get a neater join. You can tell raglan sleeves because the seam where the sleeve meets the body of the garment runs from the armpit to the neck, rather than over the shoulder.

A cardigan with buttons is a bit more complicated than a sweater because you must do bands for the buttons and buttonholes.

Knitting Proficiency!

Once you are ready to try working on double-pointed needles and have mastered decreasing, you have rounded out most knitting requirements. A cap will be easy, or try a toy like a snake. Make a long tube for the body, increasing at beginning, then decreasing at the end. Give it lots of wild stripes and perhaps decorate it with I-cord (see Appendix D) or sew-on eyes.

ALERT

Remember to think about safety issues when it comes to any toy or knitted project for a baby or toddler. Beware of buttons, ribbons, eyes, and other finishing touches that could pose a choking hazard.

Some people find socks the hardest garments to make. Turning the heel can be tricky. But if you've made all the other projects mentioned here, you should be ready to tackle anything! You might want to make something using two colors, attempt a Fair Isle design, or try cable stitches. You can call yourself an expert knitter when you find making items made with three colors or more a breeze and can tackle anything that has to be carefully fitted. Then you are ready to attempt a pattern translated from another language—or a dog sweater!

Knit and Purl

These patterns produce beautiful items, and require no more than simple knitting and purling. Scarves are so easy to do because you can create any pattern you like using yarn you love. These three versions produce different effects depending upon the stitch combinations you use. The narrow fabric means they work up quickly, too—the ribbed chenille scarf only requires one skein of yarn and can be completed in a weekend!

Simple Scarves

Work this pattern in one of two ways. If you knit every row, producing the garter stitch, you'll have a fabric that lies flat and is moderately ridged on both sides. If you knit and purl alternating rows, your fabric will be smooth on one side, and tightly ridged on the other. It will also curl, so keep the wearer's preferences in mind as you proceed.

MATERIALS: Worsted weight 4-ply: 12 oz. Given the simplicity of the knitting itself, this is the perfect opportunity for you to explore your options with different yarns. Boucle is slightly difficult to work, but produces a gorgeous scarf—no one will know how easy it was!

Size 10 or 11 needles, as you prefer

GAUGE: Gauge will vary, depending upon the yarn and needles you choose, but should fall around 4sts = 1 inch, 6 rows = 1 inch. Finished size should be approximately 8" × 60–70" (as you prefer).

INSTRUCTIONS: Stockinette
Cast on 30 sts.
Row 1: Knit across row.
Row 2: Purl across row
Bind off when scarf is desired length.

INSTRUCTIONS: Garter
Cast on 30 sts.
Knit every row.
Bind off when scarf is desired length.

Girl's Ribbed Chenille Scarf

The following instructions produce a fast and easy scarf, sized for a child. For a wider, or longer scarf, use two skeins of the recommended yarn.

MATERIALS: Chenille yarn: 1 skein (75 yards) produces a 5½" × 42" scarf

Size 11 and 10 straight needles

GAUGE: In 1 × 1 rib, 5 sts = 2 inches

INSTRUCTIONS: Using size 10 needles, cast on 16 stitches in pattern (K1, P1).
Rows 1 and 2: *K1, P1, continue from * across.
Row 3: Knit onto size 11 needle, continue in pattern.
Row 4: Use second size 11 needle, and continue in pattern until you have approximately 2 yards of yarn left.
To finish, continue, in pattern, onto size 10 needle for last 2 rows.
Bind off in pattern.

Textured
scarves

Bouclé scarf
(left)
and Chenille
scarf (right)

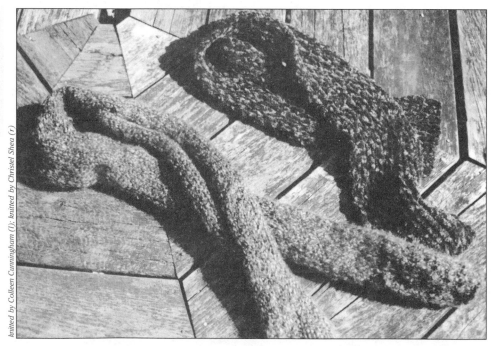

knitted by Colleen Cunningham (l): knitted by Christel Shea (r)

Common Beginner Problems and Frustrations

When you first learn to knit, you will be concentrating solely on getting the stitches made and getting them from one needle to the other without dropping any. Your very first bit of fabric will probably have some loose stitches, and it may look messy. Don't worry about it! Just keep practicing until you are comfortable making knit and purl stitches. When you can make them easily, it's time to look critically at your work and improve the look of the fabric.

- If your fabric looks messy, pay more attention to the size of your stitches. Try to make them all even. Every time you make a stitch, pull the yarn snugly against the right needle before you slip it off the left.
- After uneven tension, the most common mistake beginners make is to twist stitches without realizing it. In a plain stitch, such as stockinette, twisted stitches will distort the fabric. If you drop any stitches as you are knitting, be sure to put them back on the needle the right way round. (To straighten a stitch that is backwards, just take it off the needle and turn it around.)

Dropping stitches will produce a run in your fabric. Keep a crochet hook handy, and refer to page 122 for detailed instructions on how to correct this error.

- Does the whole process seem to be slow? You may be making it more difficult by working too far from the tips of the needles or using needles with very long, very blunt tips. Keep moving the stitches on your left needle up towards the point as you work while also pushing the stitches on the right needle toward the knob end.
- Keep your movements efficient. Moving your whole hand to make each stitch makes unnecessary work. Let your fingers do the work. At first, this will seem more difficult than using the whole hand, but it's much more efficient once you've mastered the technique.

- New knitters often find they've added extra stitches by mistake. You may be mistaking the loopy stitches at the edges of your work for extra stitches. Take a moment at the beginning of each row after you've knitted the first stitch to pull up, not down, on the yarn to tighten it. Pay special attention to make sure you are not working the first stitch twice because it is so big. Do the same at the end of a row, pulling the yarn to tighten the stitch.

- Keep track of your working yarn. It's easy to pick up stitches if the yarn inadvertently gets on the wrong side of the work, or if you don't pull the right needle away far enough to let a finished stitch settle down. If you see holes in the middle of your fabric, you've picked up stitches by mistake.

- Does your knitting needle take up just part of the yarn instead of all of it? That's known as a split stitch. Your needle may be hitting the yarn at the wrong angle as you make a stitch. Some fibers tend to split more than others. Try working from the other end of the ball. This will reverse the angle that your needle makes with the yarn and may prevent split stitches.

- Beginners should not be ashamed of constantly checking their work. Sure, experienced knitters can speed along while watching television and never seem to miss anything on the screen, but that comes from years of experience. It's all too easy to drop, pick up, or split a stitch when you aren't paying attention to what you're doing. Check your knitting every couple of inches. It is easier to fix mistakes after only a few rows.

    Unfortunately, tension doesn't always stay constant. Periodically check your gauge as you are knitting a garment. Sometimes your tension can vary and you'll need to correct any tendency to get too loose or too tight. Keep your hands, arms, and shoulders relaxed as you knit. That will help you keep the tension of your stitches consistent.

Fixing Dropped Stitches

Dropped stitches happen if you are working too close to the needle-tips, knitting very loosely, or if you are using needles made of a very polished, slippery material. Most often, stitches drop if you put your knitting down in the middle of a row. Sometimes you won't even notice it's happened until later, when you find a small hole or count stitches and realize you have too few.

ESSENTIALS — A dropped stitch can quickly unravel its way right down to the casting on. Try to catch it as soon as possible. A safety pin is perfect for securing the stitch to keep it from running farther.

When working in stockinette or garter stitch, the easiest way to fix a run caused by a dropped stitch is with a crochet hook. Catch the escaped stitch and work it up the ladder of yarn that formed when it was dropped. Do this by inserting the crochet hook through the dropped stitch, then catching the straight thread in the row above it and pulling it through the dropped stitch. (You might have to experiment to see whether you are pulling it through in the right direction for a knit or purl stitch. If the finished stitch is the wrong type, drop it again and draw the yarn through the loop from the other direction.) Repeat this for each straight thread in each row that the stitch has dropped through. Return the stitch to the row where it was and put it back in place on the needle. Make sure it is facing the right way and not twisted.

Picking up
dropped
stitches

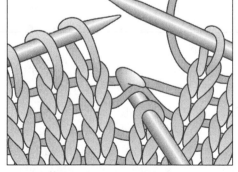

You can also do this with a small spare knitting needle if you don't have a crochet hook handy.

The tendency of dropped stitches to make ladders can be used to your advantage, too. If you've made a mistake a few rows down—twisted a stitch, made a split stitch, or gone off your pattern—you can easily correct it without unraveling rows (that is, without taking the stitches off the needle and pulling *all* the knitting out).

Just keep knitting until the last stitch before the mistake (only several rows higher). Drop the next stitch from the left needle and let it run down to the error. Now, using a crochet hook, use the same technique described earlier to correct the mistake and restore the stitch.

This technique only works for garter and stockinette fabric. Be sure you are at the right stitch—otherwise, you'll have to correct the run twice.

Unraveling Your Knitting

If you have to unravel just one row, the best way is to unpick stitch by stitch. This very time-consuming—but safe—method takes your work back a little way. Insert the left needle into the stitch below the one you've just made, transferring it back to the left needle and at the same time carefully pulling the yarn so that the last stitch comes undone. Continue in this way until you have unpicked the required number of stitches.

If there are many rows to unravel, you may have no choice but to take the work off the needles and pull the yarn.

QUESTIONS?

What is *frogging*?
Frogging is knitters' slang for unraveling knitting on purpose, either because they don't like the garment that's developing or because they made a mistake. Why frogging? Crrrr-rippit! Crrrr-rippit!

Pulling the yarn until you get to the place where the mistake was made is the easy part. Picking up all those loose stitches—that can so easily become dropped—is a nightmare. So whenever you are tempted to pull the yarn off your needles, stop!

First, take a needle of about the same length, but two or three sizes smaller, and weave it through the stitches along a knitted row below the mistake. Be careful to stay within one row; it can be easy to go higher or lower by mistake. Then you can safely extract the working needle and unravel back to where the thin needle is without losing stitches. (This will work with stockinette and simpler stitches—more complicated stitch patterns may be too intricate to pick up this way.)

If you've made a mistake in a very complicated or lacy stitch and there's no alternative but to pull the yarn, unravel to the row above the one you want to get to. Use a small size needle to pick up the stitches after pulling the knitting undone—stitches seem to shrink suddenly when they're off the needle, and a thinner needle will pick them up much more easily. Take the work back to the previous row, carefully unpicking each stitch and putting it on to a regular needle. If the yarn was knitted up for only a short time before you unraveled it, you can simply wind it up (loosely, so as not to stretch it) and start using it again.

Recycling Yarn

It's entirely possible to reuse yarn from an old or abandoned project. Although it will take a little bit of your time, good yarns and wools are expensive. Get the most for your money by reusing what you can. The following methods will help you make kinked or crimped yarn knittable again.

Rewinding Loose Yarn

To wind yarn properly, start by holding your left hand with fingers spread. Wrap the yarn around your thumb and little finger in a figure eight. When you have made a small hank this way, take it off your hand. Roll the rest of the yarn around this hank and a couple of your fingers. When you take your fingers out, the yarn can relax and won't be wound too tightly. Every now and then change the direction you wind in. Aim to make a round ball.

ALERT

Try not to pull and stretch the yarn either while you pull the knitted piece undone, or when you're rewinding it. Be especially careful with very fluffy, hairy yarns like mohair. They can easily tangle and will need to be eased apart.

If yarn has been knitted up to make a sweater and has stayed that way for weeks or more, it will become kinked and dented, especially if the finished piece was blocked or washed. But woolen yarn, in particular, has wonderful bounce-back properties. It can probably be straightened out to use again.

Refreshing Used Yarn

To reclaim the yarn from a sweater, first you need to take it apart. Snip the seams of the garment, being careful not to cut any of the yarn in the knitted fabric itself. Unpick the last binding off stitch from where the piece of fabric was cast off. (Don't start at the cast-on end, which won't unravel easily.) Start pulling the yarn across, row after row. At this stage you can just cast the yarn on the floor or wind it loosely around something large, like the bottom of a laundry basket. It won't tangle if you leave it where it lies. If you reach places that cannot be unraveled, you will have to cut the yarn.

Matching hat and mittens

knitted by Ann MacLaughlin

The next step is to find some kind of flexible, open, frame on which to wind the yarn. A wire coat hanger bent into a rectangular shape works well, as does an old lampshade frame. Wind the unraveled yarn around the frame, spreading it out as much as you can. Hang the frame in a hot and steamy place, such as over a boiling kettle on the kitchen stove, or in a just-used shower stall. When the yarn is moist, take it away from the steam and leave it on the frame to dry overnight. Then roll up the yarn using the method you just learned.

If you'd prefer to wash the yarn, wash a sample first to check that it will take washing. Then wind it into hanks by circling it around a frame, anything that you will be able to lift the hank of yarn off later. Secure the yarn at three or four places by tying it with another color of yarn or another sort of thread that will be easy to find when you go to remove it.

Wash the yarn as you would a woolen sweater. Use mild soap, in lukewarm water, without subjecting the yarn to extremes of water temperature. Squeeze the yarn gently in the sudsy water, and rinse it without stretching, wringing, or letting it hang sopping wet. After rinsing, roll the skein in a towel to remove excess water. Hang the yarn to dry, pulling it as straight as possible.

CHAPTER 12

Circular Knitting

I f you want to make gloves, mittens, socks, and turtleneck sweaters, you'll need to know the technique of knitting in the round. It may seem complicated at first glance, but circular knitting has several advantages over straight knitting and it's not difficult. In fact, some people prefer knitting in the round and would never knit any other way.

Knitting in the Round

Knitting in the round was the first type of knitting that became popular for making garments. It makes sense. After all, the body is round, and tubes of fabric are just right for covering it. Only at the end of the nineteenth century were flat pieces of knitting made, shaped, and sewn together to make tailored garments.

Many knitters consider that the most worthwhile advantage of knitting in the round is its elimination of a lot of sewing. They often find, too, that they achieve very even tension when they can just keep going, without having to stop and turn at the end of each row. Those who tend to purl more tightly than knit will probably find that circular knitting evens out their tension.

Also, when you knit only on the right side, you are always working on the surface you will see on the finished garment. This makes it much easier to keep track when you are creating a texture or color design.

Needles for Knitting in the Round

There are two different types of needles used for circular knitting. Circular needles are the easiest to use, but you won't be able to use them for everything. Similarly, double-pointed needles are ideal for small work but not for all projects.

Circular Needles

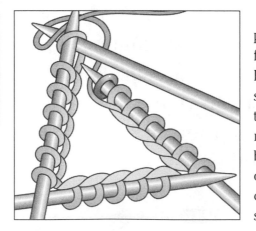

Marker indicating where the round comes together

A circular needle consists of two pointed metal needles joined by a flexible nylon tube (see page 30). Before you buy circular needles, you should know the circumference of the tubular piece you will be making. This measurement should be at least an inch larger than that of the circular needle so the stitches can fit around the needle without stretching. If the circular needles are too long for your piece, it will be impossible to achieve good tension. For this reason, a circular needle cannot make really narrow tubular fabric. A very small tube must be knitted on double-pointed needles.

When using circular needles, you cast on stitches as you would with two straight needles. The most important thing to remember when casting on is that your stitches must not twist around the needle. Be absolutely certain of this before you knit into the first stitch you cast on, which will complete the first circular row and make a continuous round.

ALERT

When casting on with circular or double-pointed needles, check carefully that none of your stitches are twisted. If they are, you will knit a Mobius strip instead of a tube.

Use a marker that will slip from one needle to the next, mark the place where you knit into the first stitch you cast on. Each time you slip the marker, it means you are beginning a new row. The marker makes it easy to keep track of each round as you work it. Slip the marker over from the left to the right needle as you come to it at the beginning of each round.

When you're making a sweater in the round, mark the stitch that's halfway around the circle as well as the one at the beginning of each round. The markers indicate where the side seams will fall, and you'll know where to start the underarm shaping.

Double-Pointed Needles

When knitting with a set of double-pointed needles, you divide the stitches among all but one of your needles. Each needle in turn holds the stitches, and the empty needle becomes the right needle, for knitting. Be sure to buy the right size of needles so the stitches do not slide off the wrong ends. (You can use small rubber bands or point protectors to keep the stitches on the needles, if necessary.)

You'll feel awkward when you first try double-pointed needles. But if you keep practicing, you'll soon be able to hold them so that they aren't poking your palms. Just hold the two working needles as usual, letting the others hang when not in use.

To cast on with double-pointed needles, divide your stitches equally over the needles. Remember that one is to work with. If you're using a set of four needles, for example, divide the number of stitches by three, and put that number on each of three needles.

Although double-pointed needles (*dpns*) are sold in sets of four or five, there's no law that says you can't use more needles if you'd prefer. More needles can make a lot of stitches easier to manage.

You may find it easier to first cast on all the stitches with two regular straight needles and work one row. Then transfer the stitches to the double-pointed needles by knitting a third of the stitches onto each one in turn. It is much easier to manipulate the double-pointed needles when there's a bit of knitting hanging from them. This also helps you avoid twisting the stitches before you join them up. (Just remember to sew up the little bit of seam that you'll have at the beginning of the work.)

To close up the circle and complete the first round, use the spare needle and the working yarn from the last stitch to work the first stitch you cast on. Keep your last and first needle as close together as possible as you work this stitch, and pull firmly on the yarn, to avoid leaving any gap at the join. Knit the rest of the stitches on that needle. When it becomes empty, it is then used as the working needle for the next set of stitches.

Once the stitches are on the double-pointed needles, and you're ready to join them so they form a round, place the three needles down in a triangle with the bottom edges of all the stitches facing the center. This will help you see that they are not twisted around the needles (see figure on page 128).

Child's mittens

knitted by Catherine Collins

One of the disadvantages of circular knitting is the little "jog" where each round doesn't quite match up with the next one. When you are knitting in the round you are actually knitting an endless spiral, which means that stripes will never join up. The way to prevent this is covered later in the section on making socks.

If you knit the first stitch that joins a round together using both the working yarn and the tail of your cast-on stitches, you eliminate the little step or "jog" that happens otherwise. Make sure that when you knit the next stitches, you continue to use the working yarn and not the beginning tail.

Differences Between Double-Pointed and Circular Needles

You'll probably need both double-pointed and circular needles as you do more and more knitting. But how do you know which needles to use when?

Circular needles, usually either 24 or 29 inches long, are generally for knitting the body of a garment. A set of double-pointed needles is better when picking up stitches for a neckline or sleeve, or when making small tubes, such as fingers for gloves.

What governs the choice is the amount of stitches you have to be worked. Too many stitches, and they'll fall off the ends of double-pointed needles; too few and they won't reach round the circumference of circular needles. Check the number of stitches you start with, and finish a piece before choosing a needle length.

Think about what and how you'll be knitting, too. If you are using many colored yarns, such as in Fair Isle designs, you may need the extra length of a circular needle to be sure your floats aren't too short and distort the fabric. And remember you can always switch between circular and double-pointed needles as you work a piece of knitting. You may start a sleeve on double-pointed needles and then switch to a circular needle when, with increasing, the stitches have grown in number.

Personal preference is a factor in the choice between circulars and double-pointed needles. Some people actually prefer a crowded needle so that the stitches come up quickly.

Hints

One disadvantage with double-pointed needles is the tendency of a visible line of loose stitches to form up the side of the fabric. These are sometimes called "ladders." They look like you've dropped a stitch, although you haven't. Ladders happen because it is difficult to keep the tension of the stitches constant at the beginning and end of the needles, where the yarn has to stretch over to its neighboring stitch on an adjacent needle. These loose stitches mark the changeover points between needles. You can prevent ladders from forming by regularly moving the changeover point by shifting 1 or 2 stitches on to the next needle. Always move them in the same direction and by the same number of stitches, or your work will become unequally divided between the needles. It may help to use markers to designate the "real" beginning of each row, especially if you are using a complicated pattern and have to take increases and decreases into account.

Where do you join in a new ball of yarn when there are no rows and, therefore, no ends of rows? It doesn't really matter when you're knitting in the round. But lumps from darning in the ends will be less noticeable if you choose the area where the side seam would be.

Knit the first 1 or 2 stitches on each new needle tighter than usual. Knitting with more needles can help, too, because that will make the angle at the beginning and end of each row less acute, placing less stress on the stitches at these points. Circular needles will eliminate ladders, and if you use the shortest ones available you can make narrow tubes with them.

Circular Patterns

In knitting patterns for garments made with double-pointed needles, you may see references to needle 1, needle 2, and needle 3 (abbreviated ndl 1, ndl 2, ndl 3). These refer to the order in which you work the fabric on the needles. If you want to use the pattern but with circular needles, put a marker where the stitches would be divided if you were working with double-pointed needles.

Patterns for circular knitting refer to rounds (abbreviated *rnd)* instead of rows. A round is worked when you've completed all the stitches around a circular needle or from all of the double-pointed needles, putting you back where you started.

Sock-Knitting Techniques

Socks have a reputation for being difficult to knit. If you follow the directions on a beginner's pattern and you take care with the tricky part—turning the heel—you shouldn't have any trouble. Sock knitters rave about the softness and comfort of hand knit socks. It's something worth trying for yourself, and they make great gifts. Most people are thrilled to get a piece of clothing you took time to make yourself. Socks can be made much more quickly than a sweater, and you can easily adapt them to appeal to the wearer's sense of style by using unique colors and patterns.

ESSENTIALS

To start off your sock-making experience on the right foot, as it were, choose a thick yarn and use these socks for wearing around the house. Big toes and long heels may be uncomfortable inside shoes.

If you're a beginner and intimidated by complex sock patterns, start out making tube socks. Because they don't have heels, there are no complicated heel-turning instructions. Tube socks are ideal for kids: there's no need to worry about getting the heel-to-toe length right, and they won't be outgrown in a few months. Even toddlers can put on tube socks by themselves.

If you've never knitted on double-pointed needles, find some made of wood. Their rough texture helps keep stitches from slipping off the wrong ends, making them easier to use. Or begin the sock on the smallest size circular needles you can find, transferring the stitches to double-pointed needles when the circumference gets too small to work on circulars.

Cast on loosely, perhaps on larger needles if you tend to cast on tightly. The cast-on edge will be the top of the sock. You want it to be stretchy so it won't bind the calf. Use the double strand or long-tail method of casting on rather than the firmer cable or knit-on cast on.

Problems and Frustrations When Knitting Socks

As noted above, colored stripes will never join up in circular knitting. Because you are making a continual spiral, rather than knitting in rows as you do with straight needles, they create a "jog" at the starting point. (If you don't change colors this won't be a problem. It's only when you make stripes that you'll notice that the end of the stripe finishes one row higher up than the beginning.)

A quick way to eliminate "jog" in stripes knitted in the round is to simply slip the first stitch of the second round instead of knitting it, to lift it up to the round you are working on.

You can prevent this with a simple method. When you come back to the first stitch of a round you just knitted with a new color, pick up the final stitch of the last color from the previous row. Place it on the left

Thick, warm hiking socks

knitted by Mary Morrison

needle, and knit that stitch together with the first stitch of the new color. This will make a large, stretched stitch. Tighten the thread from the first stitch in the color you don't want to see, and you will avoid that obvious joining. Continue knitting around with the new color.

An easy way to knit in stripes when circular knitting is to cast on each third of the stitches in a different color, on a different double-pointed needle. For example, the first third might be red, the second third blue, and the final third white. When you have cast on these stitches, join up the round. Start working from the needle containing the first third of stitches—the red ones. However, use white as your working yarn until you get to the end of the red stitches. Then take up the red as your working yarn. Continue to change your working yarn as you make the rounds. Each stripe will spiral around the leg with no join to worry about.

After your first attempts at tube socks, or after you've had experience with purely decorative socks to wear around the house, you are ready to start making regular socks to be worn with shoes for everyday wear. For these, you'll need to think about what kind of shoes the socks will be worn with and how much wear the socks will get. Choose a tightly spun yarn of sport weight or finer. The yarn should be machine washable with nylon added for longer wear. It should be an elastic fiber, like wool, so the sock will grip the calf snugly, but not too tightly. Knit in a tight gauge, for a dense, longwearing fabric.

QUESTIONS?

What yarn is best for knitting socks that will stay up?
Use a yarn that is elastic, like wool, and knit several inches of ribbing at the top of the socks. If you use a yarn that has little or no grip, such as cotton, and have stockinette at the cuff, you'll end up with droopy socks.

For smooth, bump-free socks, keep any patterning to the leg part of the sock, not the foot, where a pretty stitch can translate into a lumpy and uncomfortable experience for the foot. If you're making a multi-colored pair of socks, you should also remember to be especially careful darning in all those ends. Never make knots to join yarn—a knot in a sock will feel like a huge lump inside a shoe.

Take accurate measurements to ensure your sock fits properly. The wearer needs to be able to get the sock over the widest part of the foot, the heel. The sock should also be long enough not to rub against the toes, and yet not so big that it droops and looks floppy.

CHAPTER 13

Cable and Crossed Stitches

Cable stitches are yet another creation born of necessity. They made sturdy, warm sweaters for people who worked outdoors in bitter weather on windswept islands. The stitches are as complicated as they look, and some knitters find Aran designs a challenge to make. Cables take dexterity and a loose tension, but the result is a sweater with classic good looks and fashion appeal.

All About Aran Sweaters

Today, the phrase *Aran sweater* can describe a cabled sweater or sometimes any sweater made from off-white colored wool.

Few people stop to think how ingenious the Aran sweater technique really is—it's a method of crossing sections of stitches that doubles the warmth of a garment while keeping the ease of movement that characterizes a knit. The Aran cables, the textured stitches, and the intricate designs all evolved to make sturdy, warm sweaters that would afford the Irish fishermen protection from the elements.

FACTS

The style of knitting called Aran takes its name from a technique that evolved on the three Aran islands—Inisheer, Inishmann, and the largest, Inishmore—which lie off the western coast of Ireland, guarding the entrance to Galway Bay.

Knitting has long been part of Irish culture. It was probably first introduced by invaders as early as the 1600s and 1700s. But the style we know as "Aran" may be a recent development, according to some historians. At any rate, the distinctive style of the Aran sweater became internationally popular only in the late 1940s and early 1950s, when finished sweaters were exported and patterns published.

QUESTIONS?

What inspired Aran style?
There is general agreement that the distinctive signature of Aran knitting, the cable designs themselves, are based on the ancient art forms of Celtic imagery, echoing the cables, interlacing knots, and lattice work designs that the ancient Celts carved out of stone and metal.

Intricate cable-work and natural, off-white color characterize the traditional Aran sweater. The lighter-weight fisherman's guernseys and jerseys knitted in the round developed around the coastal regions of

Scotland and Britain probably influenced Irish knitters, but they developed their own local style.

Just as with Fair Isle designs, there are numerous legends and stories about the origins of Aran knitting. The stitches are supposedly rich in symbolism and meaning and full of religious and cultural references. Heinze Kiewe, who "discovered" the Aran sweater in 1936 and was the first to collect different styles and publish books of patterns, was sure that the stitch patterns had deep religious significance. He named many of the patterns and stitches, and said that Holy Trinity Stitch, for example, symbolized God in three parts (Father, Son, and Holy Ghost).

Knitting Cable Stitches

A cable results from crossing one group of stitches over another, altering the order in which they are worked. Essentially, the knitter changes the positions of the stitches on the needle. A cable needle (a small double-pointed needle) is used to hold the first stitches while the next group is worked. The held stitches are then transferred from the cable needle back to the main needle to be knitted. Holding stitches to the front produces a cable that moves to the left; holding them to the back makes the cable move to the right.

ESSENTIALS When making cables, tension should be kept fairly loose so as not to pull or stretch the yarn. Allow for lots of ease in a cabled sweater, too. The thick cables make a heavy fabric, and it's not comfortable to have a heavy fabric fitted too close to the body.

Every cable, no matter how intricate, is simply a combination of these front-and-back stitch movements. The differences in design come from variations in the width of the cables, the number of rows between crossings, the order of right and left crossings, and the number of background stitches between cables.

Generally, cables are made up of an even number of stitches that are divided into two equal groups and crossed in different ways.

Rope cables consist of two sections of stitches twisted around each other alternately. They are the most basic type of cable and can vary in width from 2 to 12 stitches. (If any more stitches are transposed, they will be stretched too far across one another, pulling the fabric and distorting it.)

FACTS

Traditional Aran styles have backs and sleeves that are plainer than the front. The central panel is like a large, square "canvas" to showcase the cable designs. The sleeves traditionally have a saddle shoulder.

To make the distinction between the cable and the background more prominent, the raised portion of a cable is usually worked in stockinette. The stitches on each side are purled. If the background is worked in stockinette, a few stitches in reverse stockinette are often worked on either side of the cable to give it greater visibility. Many Aran designs also use moss or seed stitch at the edges and the underarm of the sleeve to further set off the elaborate cabled center panels.

On traditional Aran sweaters, the cables on each side are usually mirror images of each other. The large central panel is surrounded by textured background stitches and smaller cables.

Tips for Knitting Cabled Designs

You'll be better prepared to attempt an Aran sweater once you've made several regular sweaters first. It will help to know a few other things, too, before you start a cabled sweater project.

- The Aran yarn produced today is slightly heavier than worsted, the usual weight of yarn used for sweaters. Bear in mind that this yarn, when combined with the thickening effects of cables, will produce a very heavy sweater.
- Making cables means doubling the fabric in places. Cabled sweaters therefore use a lot more yarn than plain patterns. If you're making an

Aran sweater with cables on the back and front, you'll need about a third more yarn than for a regular sweater.

- For those who become entranced with Aran, a software program called Aran Paint can help create and design Aran stitches and patterns.

- Do you have trouble with the loose stitches on the edges of cables or ribs? It happens because most knitters lose tension when switching between knit and purl stitches. Some types of yarn increase the tendency. Try moving your stitches closer to the tips of the needles so you make smaller, tighter stitches, and pull the yarn extra tight at the changeover point.

- When knitting Aran sweaters, take advantage of stitch markers. They will help you count the rows between crossings and will keep the various parts of the pattern separated and easier to follow.

- Some people don't use cable needles at all. They just put the stitches back on the main needle after they are crossed. This method is difficult when you are working with a large number of stitches. Other knitters have found what they consider to be better alternatives to cable needles. Large size hairpins, safety-pin shaped stitch holders, a spare double-pointed needle, or a small crochet hook will all work. Anything too heavy, though, will pull the stitches out of shape and make them difficult to handle.

ALERT

Stitches tend to slip from cable needles if they're thinner than the needles you are using for the rest off the knitting. Cable needles that have a slight bend in the middle help keep the needle from falling out of the stitches.

For your first cable project, try making a pillow cover. Use various Aran stitches to make up the front, and remember to keep your multiples in mind if you're creating your own pattern. You can use anything for the back—a simple fabric knitted from the same wool in stockinette, or a rich color velvet that will set off the detail of the stitch work on the front.

Cable Stitches

When there is a number used with the instructions, it indicates the total number of entwined stitches. The abbreviation C6, for example, indicates two bunches of three stitches entwined around each other.

ABBREVIATIONS FOR COMMON CABLES		
c4b	**Cable 4 back.**	Slip the next 2 stitches onto a cable needle, and leave it at the back of the work. Knit the next 2 stitches, then knit the 2 stitches from the cable needle.
c4f	**Cable 4 front.**	Slip the next 2 stitches onto a cable needle, and leave it at the front of the work. Knit the next 2 stitches, then knit the 2 stitches from the cable needle.
T2B	**Twist 2 back.**	Skip the first stitch, and knit into the front of the second stitch. Do not drop the stitch off the needle. Bring the yarn to the front and purl the skipped stitch through the front of the stitch. Drop both stitches off the left needle together.
T2F	**Twist 2 front.**	Skip the first stitch, and purl into the back of the second stitch. Do not drop the stitch off the needle. Take the yarn to the back, and knit the skipped stitch through the front. Drop both stitches off the left needle together.

ESSENTIALS

It's essential to do gauge swatches before starting any Aran design. Because the twisting of the stitches draws the fabric together, the tension of a cabled piece of knitting will always be much tighter than a flat one. If more than one cable pattern will be used, each panel must be separately measured.

Simple Cable Patterns

Here are some of the cables used most often in cable and Aran sweater patterns. Try making swatch samples of them before you attempt a full-scale garment to make sure you're comfortable with the style.

SIMPLE LEFT-TWIST CABLE

This makes a cable of 6 knit stitches against a background of garter stitch. Cast on a multiple of 24 stitches.

1st row (right side): P9, K6, P9.
2nd row: K9, P6, K9.
3rd row: P9, K6, P9.
4th row: K9, P6, K9.
5th row: P9, K6, P9.
6th row: K9, P6, K9.
7th row: P9, C6F, P9.
8th row: K9, P6, K9.

Note to row 7: The abbreviation C6F signifies the following: Slip the next 3 stitches onto a cable needle and hold them at the front of the work. With the right needle knit the next 3 stitches from the left needle, then knit the 3 stitches from the cable needle.

These 8 rows form the repeat of the pattern. Repeat at least three times to see the pattern emerge.

Using a cable hook

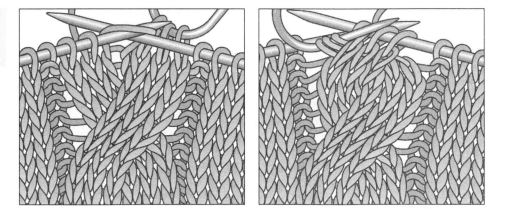

SIMPLE RIGHT-TWIST CABLE

This makes a cable of 6 knit stitches against a background of garter stitch. Cast on a multiple of 24 stitches.

1st row (right side): P9, K6, P9.
2nd row: K9, P6, K9.
3rd row: P9, K6, P9.
4th row: K9, P6, K9.
5th row: P9, K6, P9.
6th row: K9, P6, K9.
7th row: P9, C6B, P9.
8th row: K9, P6, K9.

Note to row 7: The abbreviation C6B signifies the following: Slip the next 3 stitches onto a cable needle and hold them at the back of the work. With the right needle knit the next 3 stitches from the left needle, then knit the 3 stitches from the cable needle. These 8 rows form the repeat of the pattern. Repeat at least three times to see the pattern emerge.

HONEYCOMB STITCH

Cast on a multiple of 8 stitches.

1st row: (right side) K to end of row.
2nd row: (wrong side) P to end of row.
3rd row: (right side) K to end of row.
4th row: (wrong side) P to end of row.
5th row: * C4B, C4F. Repeat from * to end of row.
6th row: (wrong side) P to end of row.
7th row: (right side) K to end of row.
8th row: (wrong side) P to end of row.
9th row: * C4F, C4B. Repeat from * to the end of the row.

Note to rows 5 and 9: The abbreviation C4F signifies the following: Slip the next 2 stitches to the cable needle and hold to the front of the work.

Knit the next 2 stitches from the left needle, then knit 2 stitches from the cable needle. The abbreviation C4B signifies the same sequence, except that the cable needle holding the 2 stitches is held at the back of the work, rather than the front.

The 8 rows from the second to the ninth row form the pattern. Repeat them at least three times to see the honeycomb design emerge.

Making Bobbles

Bobbles are raised stitches that can vary in size from a little knot to a large cluster of knitted rows. They are one of the traditional ways of adding texture to Aran sweaters.

The basic method of making a bobble is to cast on several stitches and then to cast them off again almost immediately, but there are several ways to make them. This results in a cluster of stitches that bunch together to form a little ball. The larger the increase, the larger the bobble.

A pattern will generally describe the bobble stitch to be used and thereafter use the abbreviation *MB* (make bobble), but you can add them anywhere on a plain sweater. (Keep in mind that they take up extra yarn if you add a lot of them to a pattern, and allow for the extra.)

SMALL BOBBLES

Here is a simple stitch for a small, smooth bobble. At the place you want the bobble, knit 1 stitch on the right side of the fabric. Knit 1 in back of same stitch, then knit 1 again. Slip these 3 stitches back to the left needle and knit them. Slip stitches back to left needle. Slip 1, knit 2 together, pass slipped stitch over. Resume knitting normally.

MEDIUM BOBBLES

For a medium-sized bobble, try this stitch. With the right side facing, and using a two-needle method of casting on, cast on 3 stitches in a stitch where you want the bobble, working into the same stitch each time. (You now have an extra 4 stitches on the left needle.) Purl these stitches. They will now be on the right needle and can be cast off. Slip the second stitch over the first, then the other 2, 1 at a time. Resume knitting normally.

LARGE BOBBLES

Here is the pattern for a large, 4-stitch bobble. On the right side of the fabric, work knit one, purl 1 twice, all into the same stitch, at the place where you want the bobble. The 4 new stitches will be on your right needle. You will now work 3 rows of stockinette on these 4 stitches: Turn the knitting so its wrong side faces you, and purl the 4 stitches. Turn the work again and knit the 4 stitches. Turn again and purl the 4 stitches. Turn the work (the right side should now be facing you) and slip the first 2 stitches on to the right needle. Knit the next 2 stitches together, then pass the 2 slipped stitches over the first stitch. Resume knitting normally. You should have exactly the same number of stitches on the row that you started with.

Bobbles can even be made separately and sewn on, but it's easier to work the bobble while you are knitting. Bobbles make good, small, unobtrusive buttons, too.

The main problem with bobbles is keeping them on the right side of the work. To keep them from migrating to the back, knit the stitches before and after the bobble very tightly. Also, on the row after the bobble, on the wrong side of the fabric, pick up the bottom of the bobble stitch and work it together with the stitch on the needle on the wrong side. This connects the top and the bottom of the bobble from the back so it can't move.

Bobbles are also sometimes known as "popcorns." A fabric that has even rows of bobbles throughout is worked in popcorn stitch. Here are two such patterns.

POPCORN STITCH

This pattern has a medium-sized bobble. You can vary the spacing between the bobbles by increasing or decreasing the number of purl and knit rows between them. You can also increase or decrease the number of knit stitches worked between each bobble on a row.

Cast on a number of stitches that is a multiple of 6, plus 3.

1st row (right side): K to end of row.

2nd row: P to end of row.

3rd row: K1 * make bobble in next stitch [(K front and back of loop) twice, then slip the second, third, and fourth stitches over the first], K5. Repeat from * to last stitch, K1

4th row: P to end of row.

5th row: K to end of row.

6th row: P to end of row.

7th row: K4, *make bobble, K5. repeat from * to last 4 stitches, K4.

8th row: P to end of row.

These 8 rows form the pattern.

BLACKBERRY (OR TRINITY) STITCH

The trinity stitch, often used in Aran patterns, makes a smaller, denser bobble-covered fabric. After knitting row 2 of this pattern, you will have 2 fewer stitches than the number you cast on. You will get them back by the end of row 4.

Cast on a number of stitches that is a multiple of 4, plus 3.

1st row (right side): P to end of row.

2nd row: *P3 together, Knit, purl, then knit again into next stitch, repeat from * to end of row, P3 together.

3rd row: P to end of row.

4th row: *Knit, purl, then knit again into first stitch, Purl 3 together, repeat from * to end of row. Knit, purl, then knit again into last stitch.

These 4 rows form the pattern.

1 Basket-weave pattern; page 76 • knitted by Christel Shea
2 Double seed stitch; page 75 • knitted by Christel Shea
3 Small bobble stitch; page 145 • knitted by Christel Shea
4 Lace stitch #3; page 176 • knitted by Christel Shea
5 Diamond pattern; page 78 • knitted by Christel Shea
6 Ridge pattern; page 78 • knitted by Christel Shea
7 Cross stitch 2 LK; page 151 • knitted by Christel Shea
8 Broken rib stitch; page 76 • knitted by Christel Shea
9 Ridge pattern in baby weight yarn; page 78 • knitted by Christel Shea
10 Three afghans knitted in worsted weight yarn.
   Top: Spotted blanket • knitted by Ann MacLaughlin
   Middle: Blue blanket • knitted by Lillian Silverberg
   Bottom: Cream blanket • knitted by Christel Shea
11 Off-white basket stitch afghan (Chapter 11) • knitted by Christel Shea
12 Blue afghan in seed stitch and simple cable patterned panels with fringe accents
   • knitted by Lillian Silverberg
13 Top: A ribbed cap knitted in worsted weight variegated yarn • knitted by Sophie Cathro
   Middle 1: Sand tracks light green scarf (Chapter 18) knitted in sport weight
   3-ply yarn • knitted by Christel Shea
   Middle 2: Ribbed taupe scarf knitted in basic 1 x 1 (knit 1, purl 1) pattern
   • knitted by Janet G. Bisaillon
   Middle 3: White scarf knitted in modified basket stitch with seed stitch border
   and fringe accents • knitted by Lorraine Cunningham
   Bottom: Stockinette multi-colored scarf in worsted weight variegated yarn
   • knitted by Sophie Cathro
14 The knitting basket: straight and circular needles (Chapter 3)
   Worsted weight and bouclé yarn (Chapter 2)
   Scarf knitted in worsted weight variegated yarn • knitted by Daria Perreault
15 Stockinette multicolored scarf (left) • knitted by Sophie Cathro
   Bottom: Light green sand track scarf • knitted by Christel Shea
16 Use of contrasting colors emphasizes detail of entrelac technique (Chapter 13)
   • knitted by Judith MacInnes
17 Ribbed cap in 2 x 3 pattern, stockinette scarf, and cardigan. Open work detail on
   cardigan uses a slip 1, knit 1, pass slipped stitch over technique (Chapter 15).
   Hat • knitted by Sophie Cathro
   Scarf • knitted by Colleen Cunningham
   Sweater • knitted by Alice Cathro

13

14

15

16

17

18

19

20

21

22

23

24

25

26

27

28

29

30

31

32

33

34

35

36

37

38

39

Color Photograph Reference

18 Purl stitches form relief pattern on stockinette background • knitted by Judith MacInnes

19 The versatile basket stitch adds both texture and weight to a sweater appropriate for men and women. • knitted by Ann MacLaughlin

20 Neck and buttonhole detail of a classic cardigan (Chapter 18) knitted in worsted weight variegated yarn • knitted by Ann MacLaughlin

21 Roomy crewneck with interlocking chain cables, and basket stitch scarf
Sweater • knitted by Lillian Silverberg
Scarf • knitted by Lorraine Cunningham

22 Pullover in stockinette stitch with loose ribbed cuffs and waistband, with three-button band at neck • knitted Ann MacLaughlin

23 Child's sweater with bunny motif at cuffs and waistband (Chapter 19) • knitted by Judith MacInnes

24 Children's cardigans knitted using the Fair Isle method (Chapter 14) • Both articles knitted by Catherine Collins

25 The wide block of seed stitch down the center of this afghan creates texture and warmth • knitted by Lillian Silverberg

26 Use double-pointed needles to create a knitted tube (eliminating seams) for items like these hiking socks (Chapter 12) • knitted by Mary Morrison

27 Reversible blue and white blanket with pattern • knitted by Judith MacInnes

28 Items in garter stitch, like this scarf, are perfect for beginning knitters • knitted by Colleen Cunningham

29 Scarves in ribbed and stockinette patterns are fast and easy projects for those who have mastered (or need to practice!) knit and purl stitches
Left: Taupe scarf • knitted by Janet G. Bisaillon
Right: Multicolored scarf • knitted by Sophie Cathro

30 Detail of interlocking chain cables • knitted by Lillian Silverberg

31 Cable left pattern; page 143 • knitted by Christel Shea

32 Elongated lace pattern; page 178 • knitted by Sharon Shea

33 Cable right pattern; page 144 • knitted by Christel Shea

34 Seed stitch; page 75 • knitted by Christel Shea

35 Honeycomb pattern; page 144 • knitted by Christel Shea

36 Zigzag pattern; page 77 • knitted by Christel Shea

37 Crochet stitch • knitted by Catherine Collins

38 Charted pattern sample; page 246–7 • knitted by Christel Shea

39 Crochet stitch • knitted by Catherine Collins

Traveling or Crossed Stitches

A traveling stitch is like a miniature cable stitch. It seems to move in a diagonal line across the surface of a fabric. This can be seen in diagonal lattice effects, like that created in the basket-weave stitch, resembling woven fabric. Sometimes crossed stitches make patterns that create criss-cross and zigzag lines against a plain background fabric. Traveling stitches are usually made with a knit stitch on a reverse stockinette ground.

Like cables, these patterns are made by switching the order in which a group of stitches is worked. This pulls them diagonally, producing the design. With crossed-stitch patterns, only 1 or 2 stitches are worked out of order at a time. When single stitches are crossed, they cover the next stitch. The two regular left and right needles are all that's necessary to make these simple traveling stitches. To cross 2 stitches, you work the second stitch on the left needle, skipping the first stitch, then you go back to the first one, slipping both stitches off the needle together.

E ALERT

If three or more stitches are moved across another group of stitches, the pattern is a cable pattern and a cable needle should be used. Only experienced knitters should attempt cable stitches without using cable needles.

Another way of making traveling stitches is to twist them by working into the back of the stitch. This is abbreviated as *tbl*. When twisting 2 stitches by working them in the wrong order, the abbreviation is *tw2*.

Another difference between cables and traveling stitches is that cables are worked every few rows, with the ropes climbing up for a space. Crossed stitches are most often worked every row, making a continuous line of diagonal stitches.

The direction of these crossed stitches, as with cable stitches, depends on the way the stitches were worked, whether they were held at the front or the back.

ABBREVIATIONS FOR COMMON CROSSED STITCHES

cross 2 RK	**Cross 2 stitches right, knit.**	Knit into the second stitch on the left needle. Do not drop the stitch off the needle, but knit into the front of the first stitch (the one you skipped). Drop both stitches off the left needle together.
cross 2 RP	**Cross 2 stitches right, purl.**	Purl into the second stitch on the left needle. Do not drop the stitch off the needle, but purl into the front of the first stitch (the one you skipped). Drop both stitches off the left needle together.
cross 2 LK	**Cross 2 stitches left, knit.**	Knit into the back of the second stitch on the left needle. Do not drop the stitch off the needle, but knit into the back of the first stitch (the one you skipped). Drop both stitches off the left needle together.
cross 2 LP	**Cross 2 stitches left, purl.**	Purl into the back of the second stitch on the left needle. Do not drop the stitch off the needle, but purl into the back of the first stitch (the one you skipped). Drop both stitches off the left needle together.
cross through 2 RK	**Cross through 2 stitches right, knit.**	Knit 2 stitches together through the front, but don't drop the stitch. Knit through the first stitch again, then drop both stitches off the left needle together.
cross through 2 LK	**Cross through 2 stitches left, knit.**	Knit 2 stitches together through the back, but don't drop the stitch. Knit through the first stitch again from the front, then drop both stitches off the left needle together.
cross through 2 RP	**Cross through 2 stitches right, purl.**	Purl 2 stitches together through the front, but don't drop the stitch. Purl through the first stitch again, then drop both stitches off the left needle together.
cross through 2 LP	**Cross through 2 stitches left, purl.**	Purl 2 stitches together through the front, but don't drop the stitch. Purl through the first stitch again from the back, then drop both stitches off the left needle together.

Crossed
stitches:
2RK 2LK

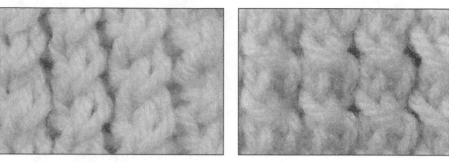

Entrelac Knitting

Entrelac is a type of knitting that looks like a very wide cable because the stitches seem to weave in front and behind each other. It is made with a technique that incorporates short rows and picked up stitches.

FACTS

The word entrelac means "interlaced" or "entwined" in French. A piece of knitting done in entrelac looks as if it has been woven. It is patterned of squares knit at right angles to each other, like a large basket weave pattern. Entrelac is knitted in one piece.

Entrelac
sweater

knitted by Judith MacInnes

Entrelac is done by knitting triangles to begin with, then picking up stitches at their sides to make rectangles. In the rectangles, the stitches are at an angle to the direction of the stitches in the triangles. You keep adding squares by picking up stitches from the sides of the completed squares.

It may sound complicated, but entrelac is not too difficult to actually create. The woven effect can be made more obvious by using different colors for the different squares. When you become proficient, you can add cables or other stitch patterns to the blocks for an even more intricate design.

CHAPTER 14
Knitting in Color

Color is probably one of the most compelling reasons to get hooked on knitting. Yarn's texture seems to intensify its colors, and a good yarn store is like an Aladdin's cave of gorgeous, glorious shades. The wider the choice, the harder it can be to choose—and you don't have to! Do as lots of knitters do and collect a stash of different yarns for upcoming projects.

Two Methods of Knitting in Color

When you knit in two or more colors, you have to use two or more balls of yarn, which are trickier to manipulate than just one. Vertical stripes twist the yarn a certain way, while horizontal stripes twist it in another. Borders, motifs, and yoke patterns each require different techniques.

Usually, the pattern calls for you to use one color yarn for a while and then to switch to another before you take up the first color again. The main problem in color knitting—and the more colors, the more of a problem it is—is what to do with the yarns waiting to be used. This is a problem both while you are working with the yarns and in the knitted fabric itself. As you are working with the alternate skeins, they get tangled. In the fabric itself, the colored yarns need to be integrated with each other neatly.

The word *intarsia* comes from the Italian word for inlay work. It originally referred to a mosaic technique using wood, ivory or metal. The word "jacquard" was originally used to describe a type of loom designed to make a patterned fabric. It was named after its inventor.

The two main methods of working in color represent two different solutions to this last problem. Intarsia is a method of working with colored yarns that keeps each different color separate, in blocks or stripes. Fair Isle, or jacquard, is a way of working in smaller areas of color where the spare colors are carried along the back of the knitting, creating what are called "floats."

Intarsia Knitting

Intarsia means knitting in solid blocks of color. Each yarn is worked in turn to supply a patch of color. It is kept hanging, or is broken off, when not needed. When one color is abandoned for the next, the yarns must be twisted around each other to keep a hole from forming.

When you first start knitting with several different balls of colored yarns, you may conclude that more time is spent untangling yarn than actually knitting. Over the years, knitters have found a number of ways to keep order, and some of their solutions are outlined here. Not all methods are useful for every project or every person—organize your yarn the way that makes sense to you.

ESSENTIALS

The key to keeping the yarns untangled is to keep the distance from the ball to your work as short as possible. If you take time to unsnarl the strands at the end of each row when you are turning the fabric around, and to keep the colors separate, you'll lessen the chance of tangles or knots.

For work that involves just two colors, place one on the right and one on your left, keeping each in a separate shopping bag or cardboard box. Every time you turn your work to begin a new row, switch the boxes around, too.

If you only need enough yarn for very small area of color, simply measure out one or two yards of yarn and let it hang free. When it tangles you can easily pull it loose.

If you need several yards of yarn, make a *butterfly twist* or finger skein of it. Start with the end of the yarn in the palm of your hand, held in place with your index finger. Keeping your other fingers stretched out, wind the yarn in a figure-eight motion around your thumb and little finger. Fasten the end of the yarn by wrapping it around the center of the butterfly, and secure. If you work from the loose end at the beginning, the yarn pulls from the center of the skein and should unravel just a little at a time. Because there is only a short length of loose yarn from the ball to the needles when you use a bobbin or butterfly twist, is the yarn has less chance to get tangled.

Clipping a small amount of yarn to the knitting itself also means that you can unravel a little at a time, leaving not much distance for the different threads to tangle. Knitter's bobbins of lightweight plastic shaped like a capital H are available at yarn shops, but some knitters improvise their own bobbins by cutting the same shape out of cardboard. Choose light cardboard, though—the bobbins should not be so heavy that they pull down the knitting and affect your tension. Some people use wooden clothespins, the kind with a metal spring. Wind a length of yarn around the middle of it and use the gripping part to attach it to your knitting.

FACTS

If you only need a few stitches in another color, to add detail to a design, why not embroider them on later? Duplicate stitch, or Swiss darning, appears to have been knitted in, but it is much easier to do on small areas. It doesn't leave holes or areas of loose tension the way changing colors can. See Chapter 19 for an explanation of how to work in duplicate stitch.

To use whole balls of yarn in several different colors, you can keep the threads from getting tangled if you keep each ball in a separate jar, bowl, or box. You can also put each ball in its own zip-closure bag. Zip the bags up most of the way with just a small opening for the yarn to get out. Whatever containers you choose, collect all these containers close to you so there is less distance for them to get tangled.

Stripes

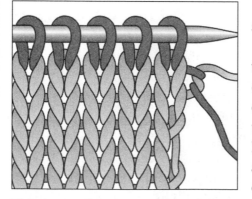

Twisting yarn to change colors at the end of a row

The simplest intarsia design is stripes.

Horizontal stripes are very easy to do: Make them simply by dropping the color you are working on at the end of a row and picking up the new yarn in the new color, leaving a 5- to 6-inch tail end. After a few stitches, tie the old and new ends in a temporary loose knot. This keeps the tension taut and makes it easier to work the stitches at the ends of the rows. You can untie and then weave these ends into the fabric later, or you can sew them up with the seams.

If you are working thick stripes of an inch or more, take up a strand of the abandoned yarn at the edge of the fabric. Knit it together with the current yarn into the first or last stitch of every alternate row. This will keep the unused yarn from tightening the side of the work when you use it again. If the stripes are so thick that they are more like squares or blocks than stripes, it is better to cut the old yarn and join in new yarn.

FACTS

If you are knitting very thin stripes (an inch or less), you can carry the yarn loosely at the edge of the fabric. You don't need to break it off. When you are ready to use a new color, twist it around the last color you used so that the yarns are intertwined.

In stockinette, if you change color at the beginning of a knit row, you get a neat, even line of color on the right side of the fabric. On the purl side, or in reverse stockinette, you get broken lines of color where the purl stitches interlock the old color with the new. (A similar effect happens when working stripes in garter stitch.) For clean lines of color in stockinette, work an even number of rows in each color. The dotted-line effect of the wrong side isn't a bad look, necessarily—you can make it part of the pattern.

Blocks of Color

Changing colors within a row

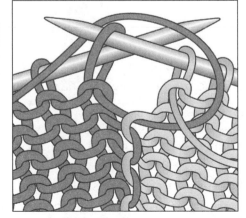

For a tartan or checkerboard design, or for a "picture knit" (a motif created in stitches of different colors), each block of color needs its own ball of yarn. Each ball must be secured to the last color when you change from one to the other.

The strands of yarn must be crossed around each other properly where you change colors. Drop the old color on the wrong side of the work (at the back, if working the knit side in stockinette, or at the front if working on the purl in stockinette).

Insert the needle into the next stitch where the new color is going. Before you take up the next color, lay the strand of the yarn from the old color over the strand you are about to pick up. As you work the stitch, the new strand catches up the dropped strand of the old color and keeps it caught.

When changing from one color to another in the middle of a row, you must always cross the strands as you drop one color and pick up the next. If you don't twist the yarns around each other, you'll end up with a hole and two completely separate strips of knitting.

Maintain an even gauge when wrapping your yarn. If it's too loose, you'll get gaps and holes; if it's too tight, the stitches will pucker. Aim for completely even tension at the point where the color changes. Immediately after changing colors it will be impossible to do this, because the old yarn has nothing to draw taut against. But as you work the piece and take up the old color again, pay attention to the tension where the colors join. Pull both strands to make sure the stitches involved in the join aren't loose. If the stitches at the joins look distorted after you've finished the whole piece of knitting, take a blunt embroidery needle and pull at the stitches on the right side of the work. Coax them into position until they look more even.

Making Stripes

The following pattern demonstrates how to wrap the yarn when creating blocks of color. Once you understand the principle, you can create stripes of any width or color.

To work a wide stripe, using a separate ball of yarn for each color.

*Cast on 6 stitches in blue, 6 in white, then repeat from * for a total of 24 stitches.

First row: (right side) * Using white, knit 6 stitches. Hold the white yarn to the left at the back of work. Take up the blue and bring it forward to the right side, at the back of work and under the white yarn.

knitted by Ann MacLaughlin

You can also knit in different colors by using multi-colored yarn

Knit 6 stitches in blue. Hold the blue yarn to the left at the back of work. Take up the white and bring it forward to the right side, at the back of work and under the blue yarn.

Repeat from * to end of row. End with 6 knit stitches in blue.

Second row: (wrong side)* Using blue, purl 6 stitches. Hold the blue yarn to the left at the front of work. Take up the white and bring it towards the right, at the front of work and over the blue yarn.

Purl 6 stitches in white. Hold the white yarn to the left at the front of work. Take up the blue and bring it towards the right, at the front of work and over the white yarn.

Repeat from * to end of row. End with 6 purl stitches in white.

These 2 rows form the repeat of the pattern.

Weaving in Ends

In complicated intarsia knitting, lots of different colors are involved. Using a separate piece of yarn for each area of color would leave so many ends dangling that the fabric would end up positively furry. Weaving in all those ends can turn into a real darning marathon.

ALERT

If the prospect of darning in a multitude of loose ends is daunting, try doing it a bit at a time. Work about a third of a piece and weave in the ends before you continue. Remember, you need only darn in the ends in the middle of the piece of fabric. Anything at the edges can be hidden in the seams.

As with managing multiple balls of yarn, there are various ways of dealing with loose ends. You can choose the way you like best.

Needle and Thread

The usual way to weave in ends is with a blunt-ended tapestry or embroidery needle. Thread it with one of the hanging ends. Insert the needle vertically into an adjacent stitch and pull the yarn. Don't pull too tight: aim to keep the tension consistent with the rest of the stitches. Some knitters advocate splitting the stitches you darn into for a more secure darn that also hides the tail better.

Darning in the ends as you go

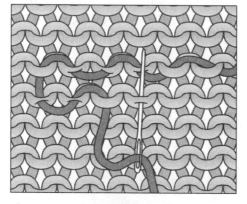

Pull the tail through 3 or 4 stitches, go diagonally in two directions, then backward. Cut off the excess yarn, leaving about a half-inch tail. This will prevent the woven yarn from escaping while the sweater is being worn or washed.

When you are weaving in the ends and have a needle at hand, it's also a good time to catch any stitches that are pulling away from each other and creating holes.

An embroidery needle isn't the only solution to loose ends. Some people find it easier to use a crochet hook or rug hook to weave them in. You can also braid ends together if they have no place else to go, although this makes a thick tail that could show through as a lump on the right side of the work when working with thin yarns. Secure the end of the braid by tying.

Knitting Right In

Perhaps the best solution to loose ends is to knit them into the fabric as they occur. In his book *Glorious Knitting*, Kaffe Fassett recommends using just short lengths of yarn of about 2 or 3 feet, tying on more as you need it and knitting in the ends as you work. Knitting in the ends is probably quicker than darning them in later.

With this method, yarn not being used is looped over or under the working yarn on the wrong side of the work at every stitch, or every other stitch. This method works in much the same way as entwining two different colors when changing from one to another. Insert the right needle into the stitch in the normal way. Lay the idle end of yarn over the working yarn, then knit the stitch in the usual way. If you have done this the right way and not knitted with it by mistake, the idle yarn is now carried by the working stitch.

Knitting in can create a very heavy fabric, and you must take care that the wrong color does not show through to the right side. The technique works with lots of color changes more or less evenly distributed over the piece of fabric.

Fair Isle and Stranded Color Knitting

Stranding colors

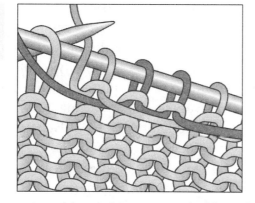

The island of Fair Isle, to the northeast off the mainland of Scotland, is only about 3 miles long and 1 mile wide. But its name is known worldwide, thanks to the unique style of knitting that developed there.

The term Fair Isle is used to describe a way of knitting with two or more colors. The strands of nonworking colors are carried loosely along the wrong side of the knitted fabric, behind the worked stitches. The technique gives the fabric's back a characteristic streaky look from all the gathered horizontal strands of yarn. This technique is also called stranding, or stranded knitting, and sometimes jacquard, two-color, or double knitting. It results in a dense, thick fabric, because of all the extra yarn padding the back. The loops of carried yarn are known as floats. They are usually stranded (left loose) if they are carried for only a few stitches. If the floats were longer, the back of the garment would be a mess of long, drooping loops sagging and catching on things. Therefore, nonworking yarn across 5 stitches or more is usually knitted in with the working stitches, in the manner described above for knitting in ends.

Traditional Fair Isle sweaters are worked in the round on four 14-inch needles. Because knitting was a cottage industry for many years on the island, the people who earned their living from it developed techniques to make the process as quick and easy as possible. Thus, original Fair Isle sweaters are interesting examples of decorative knitwear made with great economy of effort.

ESSENTIALS

For designs with only one or two large blocks of color, knitting in the ends will leave noticeable lumps. In this case, leave the ends loose, about 2 or 3 inches long, and darn them in later.

Knitting in the round means that the right side always faces the knitter, making it easy to keep track of the pattern being worked. Because only knit stitch is worked, it's easier to achieve a good tension and faster speeds. Stranding the yarns means that the different colors are always at hand. In traditional Fair Isle patterns, only two colors are used at once in a row, the background color and the pattern color. The knitter gets the maximum color variation by changing these colors with each row. (That's why one gets the impression that Fair Isle sweaters are made of hundreds of colors, whereas authentic styles use only a few.) By keeping the degree of contrast between the background color and pattern color as constant as possible, no matter how frequently the colors change there is a unity to the overall color tone of the garment.

The original Fair Isle knitters also combined Continental and English styles of knitting by holding one color in their right hand and the other in their left, another time-saving maneuver. Although it will feel awkward at first, see if you can teach yourself to knit this way—you will find it a quick and easy method of working with two colors. Alternatively, you can try looping one color over the first finger of the hand you usually throw the yarn with, and the second color over the middle finger of the same hand.

The decorative patterns on authentic Fair Isle patterns are small, symmetrical, and geometric, worked on bands of four or eight similar motifs. Each band from hem to shoulder features a different motif. When you realize that Fair Isle is closer to Norway than it is to Scotland, you can understand the influence of Scandinavian design motifs on the geometric patterns used in the characteristic patterns. The traditional colors were red, blue, brown, yellow, and white, but in the 1920s Fair Isle sweaters knitted in the natural wool colors of brown, gray, fawn, and white became highly fashionable. Older Fair Isle patterns have an unusual rib, called a corrugated rib: a knit two, purl two pattern that uses one color for the knit stitches and another for the purl.

Working with Multicolored Yarns

Variegated yarn scarf

knitted by Colleen Cunningham

Variegated yarns—painted, ombre, or space-dyed—are dyed so that the colors change over the length of the yardage. They can look very tempting in the store, so it may be an unpleasant shock to learn that there can be difficulties in knitting them up. Often, the difficulties won't show up when you make a normal, small gauge swatch, but they will be glaringly obvious when you make a sweater.

Suitable Projects

You won't have a problem if you are making something simple like a pillow cover, where both back and front panels are formed by squares of the same dimensions. But in a project that uses pieces of fabric with varying widths, such as the typical sweater, you will find that the way the color is distributed can change dramatically. The sleeves can have wide pools of some colors while in the body of the garment the same color will be flattened out to wispy strands, making it look as if you ran out of yarn.

ESSENTIALS Not all variegated yarns have this problem. It depends on the length of the color patches, how often they recur, and how these intervals interact with your fabric width, stitch pattern, and shaping changes.

It's always wise to see if the yarn store has a sample knitted up of the yarn you want to use. Even if they provide only a small square, it will give you a better idea than the skein of what a finished garment will look like. However, the only true way to know what is going to happen when you knit the yarn is to do a swatch that is as wide as each piece you are going to make, or actually start a few inches of each piece of the garment. This is a nuisance, but you'll know sooner, rather than later, how the color changes are going to fall.

Mending Colors

There are several ways of dealing with bad color effects, depending on how much they bother you.

If you do decide to use a multicolored yarn for a whole sweater, you can avoid mismatched striping by choosing a pattern that is simply constructed. Look for a sweater pattern, for example, where the pattern diagram shows the design to be made up of two squares for the front and back, with no shaping, and drop sleeves that are also made up of squares.

QUESTIONS?

How can I use multicolored yarn that doesn't work in my pattern?
If you really hate the way a variegated yarn knits up, consider using it mainly for accents. Use it for the cuffs and collar of a sweater, pom-poms, tassels, or a decorative cord. Or use for squares in a patchwork afghan.

Another way around the problem is to use two different balls of yarn and alternate them every two or four rows. This makes for much more choppy color changes, but at least they will be uniform throughout the piece. Try beginning alternate skeins from the outside or changing your stitch so the colors come in different places on each row. (Remember, though, that using a different stitch could mean that you need more yarn to complete the project.)

You can make sleeves look similar by knitting them both at the same time, on the same needle but with separate balls of yarn. This way you can begin new balls of yarn at the same time and change to new ones if the colors aren't making desirable patterns.

Children's cardigans with large buttons for little hands

knitted by Catherine Collins

Charts for Colored Patterns

Most Fair Isle and jacquard patterns are shown as graphs or charts. When you get used to them you will find they are easier to work than a line-by-line pattern, especially for colored designs, because you can see the whole pattern at a glance. What you are aiming toward and where you are in the pattern are clearly defined. You just have to look at the front of your work and compare it with what's shown on the chart.

ESSENTIALS

The best charts for colored patterns are printed in color. A chart in black and white with symbols to represent a colored pattern takes a bit more figuring out. You can make it easier to decipher the pattern by using colored pencils or highlighters to mark the pattern before you begin knitting.

Charts are printed on a squared grid. Each horizontal row of squares, which should be numbered at the side, represents a row of knitting. You start at the bottom and read from right to left for a knit row, from left to right for a purl row. If you are working from a chart designed for circular needles, all rounds are read from right to left.

Each square represents a stitch. A symbol in any of the squares represents the kind of stitch to be worked.

When working from a chart, check that you are at the right place by checking that the colors you are working on the current row line up properly with the colors on the previous row. Picture knits are easy to check this way—you will quickly notice if the picture is not developing properly just by comparing the fabric to the chart.

In Chapter 19 you will learn how to transfer your own motif to a chart so you can knit these designs into your work.

CHAPTER 15
Lacy Stitch Patterns

Lace stitches use open areas—holes—to form a pattern. There are so many laces to choose from! Each type of lace varies, based upon the stitch combinations that form the holes, their size, how close they are, and how the stitches surrounding them are interlocked. Although lace stitches are slightly more complicated, they make elegant fabric and are worth learning.

About Lace

Lace made by knitting is not the same as regular lace. Lace is now machine-made, but it was traditionally made either by needlepoint or through manipulating bobbins. Knitted lace has its own history. It has been made since the fifteenth century in Europe. Bobbin lace, which was being made earlier, didn't have the elasticity necessary for the contoured stockings fashionable—for men as well as women—in Elizabethan times. Later, in the eighteenth century, when quality, thin cotton was imported from the east, knitted lace became very popular as a genteel handicraft. It was known as "white knitting."

FACTS

Some knitting historians differentiate between lace knitting and knitted lace. They describe lace knitting as fabric where rows of stockinette or another plain stitch are incorporated into the pattern. Knitted lace is fabric where holes are created in every row. Of the two types, knitted lace looks more like "real" handmade lace.

Whereas cables and slipped stitches make knitted fabric narrower, the openwork stitches used in lace patterns make fabric wider and airier. If you tend to knit tightly, you may find lace easier to knit than other stitches. Not only does lacy fabric look lovely, but it knits up quickly due to the holes in the pattern!

Tips for Knitting Lace

The main headache when knitting lace stitches comes from losing your place in a pattern. Most patterns require working several rows to create each repeat. Knitters who often make lacy stitches agree that it helps a lot to use markers generously and often. Have a large selection of different colored markers available as you work to designate different divisions. Anything will work that stays in place between the stitches (even next to yarn-overs, which tend to slide around) and that stands out from the rest of the knitting.

On Your Mark

Use the markers in a way that makes sense to you and the pattern you are using. For example, you could add a marker to the needle every 10 stitches, and slip it over to the next needle every time you come to it. This will make it easier to see at a glance whether you are keeping a constant number of stitches along the row. Or you could use a marker between each multiple of the stitch pattern. If one of the multiples has the wrong number of stitches or looks different from the others, you'll notice it before you go too far along with the instructions. Mark each row where a new repeat begins, too, or use a row counter (see Chapter 3).

ALERT

Use lots of markers when doing lace stitches. Even different colored yarn cut into short lengths and tied in a knot to make a small loop will do if nothing else is available.

The fabric might look the same on both sides, but to follow the pattern accurately you will need to keep in mind which side is the right side. If you have trouble remembering which is the right side of the work, find a way to mark that, too.

If you are using very fine yarns to knit lace, you will have to experiment to find the ideal needle. Wooden needles can catch the thread. That's good if you're using a slippery yarn, like silk, but it may be a nuisance otherwise. On the other hand, stitches can slip off metal needles too easily, especially yarn-over stitches. Many knitters find plastic needles work well for making lace.

Lace Patterns

Stitch patterns for lace fabric stitches can be either written line by line or displayed in chart format. As with other stitch charts, they're printed on a squared grid where each horizontal line of squares—which should be numbered at the side where you begin—represents a row of knitting. Each square represents a stitch, and a symbol in any of the squares represents the kind of stitch to be worked. You start at the bottom and read from right to left for knit rows, from left to right for purl rows. On charts designed for circular needles, all rounds are read from right to left.

ESSENTIALS

On a stitch pattern chart, heavy black lines indicate the edges of multiples and repeats, the same way asterisks and brackets do in line-by-line patterns. Not all pattern makers use the same symbols, so be sure you know what each one means before you begin. The pattern should provide a key.

It always helps to make your pattern user-friendly, but that's especially true with lace patterns. Enlarge chart patterns by photocopying and enlarging them. Then use a highlighter to pick out repeated multiples of stitches. This way you'll see the whole sequence at a glance. Or highlight each row when you've finished it. You'll know where you are in the pattern, but you'll also be able to read back to previous instructions if you need to.

ALERT

When working lace patterns, avoid putting down your work in the middle of a row. It's all too easy to lose track of where you are in the increasing and decreasing sequence of a stitch multiple.

When choosing a lace stitch to use with a garment pattern, keep in mind that lacy fabric is much more fragile than solid knitted fabric, especially when knitted with fine yarns. It's also more elastic and can stretch out of shape easily. Keep very open patterns for shawls and throws where this tendency doesn't matter so much, and work sweaters in closer, denser stitch patterns. If the garment pattern allows, work a narrow border of a firmer stitch, such as garter stitch when making a lacy garment. This will make it much easier to sew up.

For smaller items like gloves and socks, choose a small, compact pattern with a short multiple and repeat. A pattern with large holes will be too open and loose for small areas of knitting. Socks, in particular, need to be made in a dense lacy pattern, especially if they are going to be subject to lots of wear. Again, you could combine stitch styles. Use stockinette for the main part of the sock that covers the foot and thus needs to be made of tough, durable fabric. Use a lacy stitch to make a decorative cuff around the ankle.

Yarn for Knitting Lace

What kinds of yarn work best with lace patterns? That depends on the look you want. Lace can be knitted with any weight of yarn, with different effects depending on the yarn you choose. To get the hang of lacy stitches, practice with a medium-weight yarn that will hold the stitches firmly and let you see the pattern soon.

To highlight the stitches, choose a yarn that is tightly spun, with a firm twist. Don't write off fancy yarns completely, though—a hairy yarn like mohair can work well with large needles and a pattern that creates big holes. As usual, it's a good idea to make up test swatches. Textured, nubbly yarns have bumps and slubs that tend to end up on the purl side of the fabric and will make a very bumpy fabric if the pattern has a lot of purl stitches.

ESSENTIALS

Cotton yarns can make fabrics that will stretch and drop out of shape if knitted in lacy patterns on large needles: as always, work a sample to see the effect before making up a whole garment.

With lace stitches it's very important to do swatches, mainly to see the effect of the combination of needle and yarn you've chosen. Even stockinette can look quite different depending on whether it's made up with large needles and thin yarn or fine needles and worsted. Large needles can give just about any pattern a lacy look. Gauge matters when making clothes, of course, but not so much when you are making a shawl or tablecloth. If these items turn out a bit bigger or smaller than you were expecting, it's not a disaster.

Making Lace Shawls

Lacy bits of fabric for throwing over your shoulders or snuggling under on the sofa are rewarding to make and quick with large needles. You can make rectangular, triangular, round, or square shawls of any size, but keep in mind that the larger the shawl, the more stitches you'll need to cope with. Long circular needles are often the best solution. Another option is to make a long tube, casting on twice the number of stitches you'd need for a single width scarf. This shape ensures neat edges and the warmth of double fabric.

Perhaps the easiest shawl shape to make is triangular—think of the shape as that of a pyramid, and start at one side rather than with the widest, bottom edge. This way, you immediately start decreasing and the stitches stay at a manageable number. Sew two triangles together to make a square shawl.

One of the most tiresome chores is dealing with a yarn that sheds over everything in your wardrobe. Pick a yarn that won't shed. (If you suspect that it may, pick a color that won't matter! A white shawl that leaves lint can't be worn over a dark coat but is fine with a white jacket.) Also be sure to test whether the yarn will irritate the skin by placing a ball of it next to your neck for a few minutes. A scratchy scarf is one you won't wear.

On a lacy shawl there is no wrong side—and therefore nowhere to hide loose ends by darning them in. This is one time to join yarn by splicing. Splicing makes a thick area of yarn where the two ends are joined, but when knitted up it's not very noticeable.

ESSENTIALS
Keep two things in mind when choosing yarn for a shawl or scarf: find out whether it sheds, and be sure to test it against the skin.

Your casting on must be loose and stretchy for the lace fabric of a shawl. A puckered edge ruins the look. If you know you tend to cast on tightly, cast on with an extra-large needle to make sure the edge of the lacy fabric doesn't draw in. Or you can try holding two needles together. When you've cast on the required number of stitches, simply extract one of the needles. You're ready to begin knitting with the regular size needle.

FACTS

Many lace stitches look fine without blocking or pressing. That means they work well with synthetic yarns, which are usually very light—ideal for making delicate shawls.

Yarn Over and Other Lace-Making Stitches

The usual way of making holes in lace fabrics is to increase 1 stitch by taking the yarn over the needle. The new loops that are made this way are worked as normal stitches on the following row. A stitch is also decreased at some point to keep the total number of stitches in the fabric constant.

As you saw in Chapter 8, yarn-over-the-needle increases can be indicated in patterns by several different abbreviations. Be sure to read the pattern to understand the terminology it uses.

Yarn Forward or Back

When you work a yarn-over-needle increase, you must be sure that the extra loop is made correctly around the needle. On a knit row, where your yarn is at the back, bring it forward, over, and then under the needle and to the back of the work again. On a purl row, where your yarn is at the front, take it over the right needle, and then bring it back under the needle so it is again at the front, ready to make the next purl stitch. For a rib pattern, where you work a knit stitch and then make a yarn over before the purl stitch, bring the yarn forward between the needles. Then take it back over the right needle and forward again, under it, so the yarn is in the right position to make the next purl stitch.

Sometimes the pattern will call for you to make several consecutive stitches with the yarn-over method. (Yarn over twice is abbreviated *yo2.*) When you do this, you should work the made stitches on the following row as knit and purl alternately, unless the pattern instructs otherwise.

Tips for Making Yarn Overs

This way of making a new stitch—by simply putting a loop of yarn over the needle—is an easy technique, but it's also easy to get wrong.

Working a lacy pattern stitch requires attention. Watch what you are doing when making a yarn over! If your yarn is in the wrong position when you do a yarn over the needle, you may lose the stitch or twist the stitches—and therefore close the holes instead of making them. This, of course, would mean that you lost the lacy effect of the pattern.

With all the increasing and decreasing that you must do when working lace stitches, it's all too easy to end up with the wrong number of stitches on your needle. Count stitches often. And remember lace stitches are usually worked in pairs when you increase a stitch, you later decrease it.

Pay attention to what happens to the yarn after you've put it over the needle. It can easily move to the wrong place. You may need to put a finger on the yarn after you drape it over the needle to keep it in place until you make the next stitch. When you come to work the yarn over as a stitch, keep your finger on that thread until you make the stitch. If you work the stitch before the yarn over without watching what you're doing, you can lose the loop of the yarn over. It also helps to work close to the tips of the needles. That way you don't pull the yarn over off the needle by mistake the way you might when you have to drag each stitch a long way down the needle.

Other Common Techniques for Making Lace Stitches

To keep a constant number of stitches in your lace pattern, you must decrease the same number of stitches that you increase. Several methods are commonly used in lace pattern stitches.

Knit 2 stitches together (*K2 tog*). Insert the right needle through 2 stitches instead of 1, then knit them together as 1 stitch. This makes 1 stitch out of 2. The "purl two together" instruction is the same, except that you purl the 2 stitches together instead of knitting them.

Pass slipped stitch over (*psso*). Take the stitch you have just slipped from the left needle to the right. Lift it over the stitch just before it, as if you were binding off.

Slip one, knit two together, pass slipped stitch over (S1*K2tog, psso*). Slip the first stitch, knit the next 2 stitches together, and then bring the slipped stitch over the knitted stitch as you would if you were binding off.

If you need to review decreasing methods, you can also refer to Chapter 8. Remember that it's important to increase and decrease as the pattern indicates to ensure that your fabric maintains its intended shape.

A Collection of Lace Stitches

If you don't have a specific pattern in mind, you may want to try some of the following patterns. Experiment with both the yarns and needles you use until you get a feel for what style you enjoy most.

These patterns are not abbreviated to make them easier for the beginner to understand.

LACE STITCH #1

Cast on an even number of stitches.
1st row: Purl 1 stitch, * yarn round needle, purl 2 stitches together; Repeat from * to last stitch, knit 1 stitch.
2nd row: * Purl 1 stitch, purl 1 stitch through back of the loop (thus twisting the stitch); Repeat from * to the end of the row.
3rd row: Knit to the end of the row.
4th row: Purl to the end of the row.
5th row: Purl 1 stitch, * purl 2 stitches together, yarn round needle; Repeat from * to the last stitch, purl 1 stitch.
6th row: * Purl 1 stitch through back of the loop (thus twisting the stitch), purl 1 stitch; Repeat from * to the end of the row.
7th row: Knit to the end of the row.
8th row: Purl to the end of the row.
These 8 rows form the repeat of the pattern.

The abbreviated form of the pattern above would be as follows:

 LACE STITCH #1

Cast on an even number of stitches.
1st row: P1, * yon, P2 tog.; Rep from * to last stitch, K1.
2nd row: * P1, P1 tbl; Rep from * to end of row.
3rd row: K to end of row.
4th row: P to end of row.
5th row: P1, * P2 tog., yon; Rep from * to last stitch, P1.
6th row: * P1 tbl, P1; Rep from * to end of row.
7th row: K to end of row.
8th row: P to end of row.
These 8 rows form the repeat of the pattern.

LACE STITCH #2

Cast on a multiple of 3 stitches.
1st row: (right side) Purl.
2nd row: K2, * yf, sl1, K2 tog. * Repeat from * to * across row. End with K1.
3rd row: P to end of row.
4th row: K to end of row.
5th row: P to end of row.
6th row: K1, * Sl1, K2 tog., yf. * Repeat from * to * across row. End with K2.
7th row: P to end of row.
8th row: K to end of row.
These 8 rows form the repeat of the pattern.

LACE STITCH #3

Cast on a multiple of 5 stitches, plus 3.
1st row: P2, * K2 tog., yf, K1, yf, sl1, K1 psso. * Repeat from * to * across row. End with P1.

2nd row: K2, * P5, K2. Repeat from * to end of row.
3rd row: P2, * K5, P2. Repeat from * to end of row.
4th row: K2, * P5, K2. Repeat from * to end of row.
These 4 rows form the repeat of the pattern.

LACE STITCH #4

Cast on a multiple of 6 stitches, plus 2.
1st row: K1, * yf, K3 tog. tbl, yf, K3. Repeat from * to end.
2nd row: P to end of the row.
3rd row: K1, * K3, yf, K3 tog. tbl, yf. Repeat from * to the last stitch, K1.
4th row: P to end of row.
These 4 rows form the repeat of the pattern.

LACE STITCH #5

Cast on a multiple of 6 stitches plus 3.
1st row: (right side) K2, * yrn, sl1, K1, psso, K1, K2 tog, yrn, K1. Repeat from * to the last stitch, K1.
2nd row: P to end of row.
3rd row: K3, * yrn, sl1, K2 tog. psso, yrn, K3. Repeat from * to end of row.
4th row: P to end of row.
5th row: K2, * K2 tog, yrn, K1, yrn, sl1, K1 psso, K1. Repeat from * to the last stitch, K1.
6th row: P to end of row.
7th row: K1, K2 tog., * yrn, K3, yrn, sl1, K2 tog, psso. Repeat from * to last 6 stitches, yrn, K3, yrn, sl1, K1, psso, K1.
8th row: P to end of row.
These 8 rows form the repeat of the pattern.

Other Ways of Making Lace Stitches

Another way of making lacy fabric is to elongate the stitches. This makes a long, thin opening and a slightly different type of lacy look. You elongate stitches by wrapping the yarn around the needle more than the usual once. When you come to the wrapped stitch on the next row, you unwrap it and treat it as 1 stitch, or you work just the first wrap and drop the other loops. All the extra yarn creates a very long stitch. The more times you wrap the yarn around the needle, the longer the stitch. You must take care when working this stitch to unwrap the elongated stitches and not knit them as extra stitches by mistake.

If you want a whole row of elongated stitches, another way to get the same effect is to use a much thicker needle. You can also create the stitches with the regular needle, and then slip them onto an object like a ruler as a holding needle.

The following stitch pattern is an example of elongated lacy stitches.

ELONGATED STITCH LACE

Cast on a multiple of 6 stitches, plus 7.

1st row: (right side) K2, * (K1, winding the yarn three times around the needle as you do so) three times, K3; Repeat from * to the last 5 stitches, (K1, winding the yarn three times around the needle as you do so) three times, K2.

2nd row: K2, slip the next 3 stitches on to the right needle dropping the extra loops to make 3 long stitches, then slip these 3 long stitches back onto the left needle, yrn, P3 tog., yrn, * K3, slip the next 3 stitches on to the right needle dropping the extra loops to make 3 long stitches, then slip these 3 long stitches back onto the left needle, yrn, P3 tog. yrn. Repeat from * to the last 2 stitches, knit 2 stitches.

3rd row: K5, *(K1 winding the yarn three times around the needle as you do so) three times, K3. Repeat from * to the last 2 stitches, K2.

4th row: K5, * slip next 3 stitches on to right needle, dropping the extra loops to make 3 long stitches, then slip these 3 long stitches back onto the left needle, yrn, P3 tog., yrn, K3. Repeat from * to the last 2 stitches, K2. These 4 rows form the repeat of the pattern.

CHAPTER 16

Developing Your Own Patterns

O ne of the best reasons to knit is the opportunity it gives you to create your own personal designs—in fabric *and* fashion. As you get more proficient, and after you've made several garments by following printed patterns, you'll want to try ideas of your own. After all, if you just wanted a plain sweater, you could buy one!

Easy-to-Make Pattern Changes

Is ignoring the printed instructions asking for trouble? Is it ever a good idea to change anything from what the pattern tells you? Sometimes. Once you know what you are doing—and you will after just a few projects—you'll know what's within your capabilities. It's not a good idea to make changes in yarn or needle size without thinking them out carefully and doing tests with gauge swatches, but sometimes you learn more from your mistakes. Experiment with smaller projects at first—that way, you can see the effects of your changes without making a sweater that no one can wear.

ESSENTIALS

You can make unique knitted garments without changing patterns. Although you may not be a designer, you have imagination and personal preferences. Take this opportunity to express them!

Even a new knitter can usually adjust sleeve and body length on a plain, one-color garment pattern with no problems. Just add or subtract the extra length from a part of the pattern where there is no increasing or decreasing. For example, after the initial ribbing and shaping at the bottom of sweater, the instructions will usually read "work in pattern until length measures 15 inches," or words to that effect. This is where you can add or subtract inches. Look at the schematic drawing to work out how many. For the front of a sweater, the measurement is from under the arm to the hem. Measure that same area on a sweater you already own, or measure yourself, and make the necessary adjustments.

Remember, of course, that you must duplicate any changes you make to the length of the front on the back of the piece as well.

Changing the selvage stitch is not too great a change. If the pattern gives a selvage stitch you don't want to use, omit it. On the other hand, if you would prefer to use one in a pattern that doesn't specify it, go ahead.

When making toys for children, pay attention to potential safety hazards. Change the pattern if it calls for beads or buttons for eyes, or anything that could cause choking if it works loose and is swallowed.

Embroider instead. When knitting baby clothes, use Velcro strips instead of buttons, or knit in soft bobbles for the buttons. Never put drawstrings in children's clothing, especially around the neck or on hoods. And because of the danger from smothering, babies should not wear garments made from a fluffy yarn like mohair, or have mohair blankets.

ALERT

If stitch or color pattern repeats have to be taken into account, changing length might be trickier—but it's not too difficult if you can increase or decrease your pattern by one complete repeat.

And here's a slight change that can make life easier. When you are knitting sleeves, the matching halves of the front of a cardigan, or anything in two pieces, consider knitting them both at the same time. You can put the two pieces on one long needle and work them with two separate balls of yarn, doing first a row of one piece, and then the same row of the twin piece.

There are several advantages to this method. You will be sure both pieces are exactly the same length, and you can match what you are doing on both pieces simultaneously. If you are working bands for a cardigan, for example, when you make buttonholes on one band you can mark the button position on the other. If you are knitting sleeves, you'll be sure the shaping is exactly the same on each. You simply reverse what you are doing for the second sleeve.

ESSENTIALS

Another way to keep the two pieces equal is to attach some sort of marker, such as a safety pin, to every tenth row. This makes it easy to match up two pieces of knitting and see instantly whether they are the same length.

When you're knitting two pieces at once, be careful to always knit the current row of both pieces before putting down your work. Otherwise it can be easy to forget where you were and begin knitting on the last sleeve you worked on, giving it 2 rows more than the other.

Making a Pattern Larger or Smaller

Suppose your sweater pattern comes in sizes 8, 10, and 12, but you want to make it in size 14. How can you make it larger? There's a way of adjusting the size if you are prepared to do the math. Look at the number of stitches the pattern asks to be cast on for each size. The instructions might say, "Using size 7 needles cast on 55 [60, 65] stitches." From this you can see that the difference between each size is 5 stitches. To get the number of stitches to cast on for a size 14, add 5 to the number of stitches to be cast on for size 12.

You will have to go right through the pattern, altering the numbers given for shaping the armhole, neck, shoulder, and so on. In every case, find the difference in the number of stitches for sizes given by subtracting the smallest size from the medium size and the medium size from the largest size. Then add that difference to the largest size given. To make the pattern smaller, work the opposite way, subtracting the difference from the smallest size given.

It takes time, but this method will give you the figures you need.

QUESTIONS?

To make a pattern a size larger, can you simply use a heavier yarn than the one the pattern calls for?
You can change the yarn or use larger needles to produce a larger garment. But unless you check your gauge, you can't be sure how much bigger it's going to be.

To try making a larger sweater just by changing your yarn, make a gauge swatch with the heavier yarn. Say you get 4 stitches to the inch with the new, heavy yarn. Look at the measurement at the most important part of the pattern for fitting. In a sweater, that's around the bust or chest. See how many stitches are used there—say it's 100. Divide that number of stitches by 4, the number of stitches you get to the inch, to get the width in inches. Does that figure represent the necessary number of inches to cover the chest? If not, keep doing gauge swatches until you get the right measurements.

Be sure that the fabric you create is suitable for the garment you're making. In an effort to get the right gauge, your yarn and needle-size combination might make a fabric that is very thick and stiff, or full of holes and sloppy. If you are still new to knitting, it may be wiser to seek out a pattern that fits without having to go through this lengthy trial and error process.

Creative Changes to a Pattern

You can get creative even when you are still learning to knit. Take a basic scarf pattern and work it using different stitch patterns. Use any one of the stitch patterns in Chapter 7 (or Chapters 13 or 15) that looks interesting. The only thing you have to check is whether you'll be able to fit enough multiples into the width of your fabric. Make sure that the stitch multiple divides into the number of stitches you use for your scarf. For example, a stitch pattern that has a multiple of two, such as a basic knit 1, purl 1 rib, can be used for any pattern that calls for an even number of stitches. Most other decorative stitches are more complex and have larger multiples, but the principle is the same.

Basic scarves
using
different
stitch
patterns

knitted by Sophie Cathro (l); knitted by Janet G. Bisaillon (r)

Another relatively simple way to exercise your creativity is to experiment with a plain, simple sweater pattern in a size that fits well. Make it in different yarns, perhaps, or with random stripes or blocks of color. Look through all sorts of patterns—from kids' clothes and toys to couture knits—to get design ideas. If you see a detail that appeals to you, an unusual stripe or decorative pattern on the front, you can probably adapt that one detail to your basic sweater pattern.

Another great way of personalizing a simple sweater is to design your own picture motif for the front—the details are in Chapter 19.

Designing Your Own Pattern

If you can use and have access to, or own a computer, you can buy knitwear design software programs to help you design your own sweaters. You simply make your choices from the lists of options available and the program generates a custom-made pattern for you, complete with schematic diagrams, charts, text directions, and estimated yardage required.

FACTS

Computers have revolutionized pattern design. The easy way to design your own knitwear is to buy one of the special software programs available, such as Sweater Wizard 2001, Garment Styler, or Knitware Sweater Design.

First you select the intended owner of the garment, a man, woman or child. You choose the chest size, a fabric weight, and the amount of ease you wish to incorporate in the pattern, from very close to oversized. You can choose whether to knit the piece on straight needles, circular needles, or from the top down. And there's an array of design options for the shape of the sleeve and neckline, too. You can even program the software to work with your own particular knitting gauge. When you're finished designing, the printout provides you with an easy-to-follow pattern.

CHAPTER 17
Detail Work

The look of a well made garment comes as much from the details as from the quality of the fabric itself. Hems, buttonholes, and pockets that are saggy, crooked, or lumpy will ruin the entire effect of your efforts. Although these details seem minor compared to the amount of knitting you're doing, they are critical to the overall success of your project.

Buttonholes:
Eyelet, Vertical, and Horizontal

For a cardigan, you need to think about buttons at the beginning of the project, not the end. You may find that the pattern instructs you to knit in a buttonhole but doesn't tell you how. That's because the size of the buttonhole depends on the size of the buttons you choose.

So which buttons should you choose? Naturally, color is the first consideration. But you should also think about where you'll be wearing the cardigan. For a casual garment, or a children's sweater, you can choose fun buttons. There's also the weight of the knitted fabric to take into account. Heavy buttons weigh down a lightweight sweater. The fabric and button textures should be compatible, too. Buttons with a rough surface may catch on an angora sweater. If you don't want buttons to stand out, have them match the color of the knitting. But a match that isn't quite right is far worse than using a contrasting color.

ESSENTIALS

Avoid cheap plastic buttons. There are so many beautiful buttons available! Search out a shop with a wide selection, and take your knitting swatch to hold the buttons up against.

Covered buttons are a possibility, too. They're the most unobtrusive choice. You can buy the frames at a notions shop. The fabric you knit to cover the buttons must be thin, though, so if you are using a thick yarn you might have to unravel some of it and split the ply to have enough fine yarn to knit into little circles with which to cover the buttons. Knit with very small needles to make a dense fabric that will not reveal what is behind it. If you have a collection of old buttons, you might find some suitable for covering. Baste in a drawstring hem around the circle of covering fabric, and pull it in tight at the back.

Neck edges and bands for buttons and buttonholes are usually worked after the main part of the garment has been sewn up. Sometimes they are worked separately and sewn on, and sometimes stitches are picked up from the rest of the knitting. These bands are usually done in rib, garter, or moss stitch to keep them from curling.

When picking up stitches, it's important to get the right number and to space them evenly. Too many, and the band will create a frill; too few, and the band will pull in and pucker the garment. (See Chapter 8 for a description of how to pick up stitches.)

The buttonholes on men's clothes are on the left side of the garment; for women's garments, they go on the right. (The way to remember this is that "a woman's clothes close over the heart.")

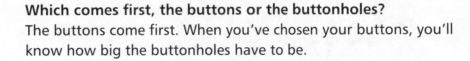

Which comes first, the buttons or the buttonholes?
The buttons come first. When you've chosen your buttons, you'll know how big the buttonholes have to be.

Where do you place the buttonholes? Usually the top one goes at the neck and the last goes at the bottom. But don't place either too close to the garment edges—the button should not overlap the edge. There should also be a button at the fullest part of the bust. The others are spaced out evenly between these.

Eyelet Buttonholes

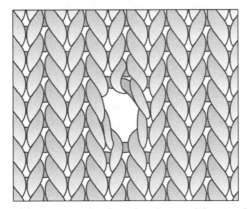
An eyelet buttonhole

If you want to use small buttons, make an eyelet buttonhole. The way to do it is to bring the yarn forward (making a stitch), then knit the next 2 stitches together. Work the next row normally, including the stitch you made. Make this sequence on the right side of the fabric wherever you need a little round hole.

For a bigger button, you'll need either a vertical or horizontal buttonhole, depending on the width of the buttonhole band. Horizontal buttonholes tend to look neater than vertical ones, which can stretch and gap if the sweater pulls tightly across the chest or back.

The Basic Two-Row Horizontal Buttonhole

Basic two-row horizontal buttonhole

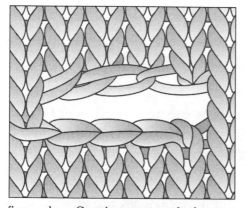

The usual method of making a horizontal buttonhole is over 2 rows, binding off on the first row and then replacing the stitches on the next row above. Bind off either 3 or 4 stitches (depending on the size of the button and the thickness of your yarn) on the right side of the fabric where you want the hole. Work tightly to give the buttonhole a firm edge. Continue to work the rest of the row. When you are back to the cast off stitches on the next row, on the wrong side of the fabric, cast on the same number of stitches you bound off, twisting the stitches as you make them.

Binding off is not the best way to make buttonholes if you are using large buttons. It creates a hole with weak sides that will stretch. It's better to use a two-needle method of casting on. For that, you need to turn your work immediately after casting off and work back over the gap. This is called a "self-reinforcing" buttonhole.

Self-Reinforcing Horizontal Buttonhole

This method makes an unobtrusive, firm buttonhole. It does not have a lot of elasticity, though, so test that your button fits through after you've done one.

Work to the place for the buttonhole on the right side of the fabric.

Slip 1 stitch purlwise from the left- to the right-hand needle. Bring your yarn to front of your work. Slip the next stitch purlwise, and pass the previous stitch over it to bind off. Repeat twice. Slip the last cast-off stitch back onto the left needle.

Turn your work so the wrong side is now facing. Bring the yarn forward between the needles. Cast on 3 stitches. Cast on another stitch but bring the yarn forward before placing it on the needle.

Turn the work so you are on the right side. Slip 1 stitch knitwise, and pass the last cast-on stitch over it to bind off.

Vertical Buttonholes

Vertical buttonhole

A button that is appropriate for the yarn will usually fit a 3-row vertical buttonhole. For this method you'll divide the work, meaning you'll need an extra ball of yarn.

When you get to the place the buttonhole should be, turn your work. Leaving the other stitches for the time being, work 3 rows. (You can either find another needle of the same size, or leave the stitches you are not working at the end of the needle you are using.) Then leave those stitches and turn your attention to the other side of the fabric, and knit 3 rows on the other side, joining in new yarn to do it.

FACTS

When sewing on buttons, wrap the thread around under the button four or five times to make them stand up a little from the knitted fabric.

When both sides are equal again, work the next row work all the way across with one ball of yarn and continue as normal.

When you've finished, thread the ends of your yarn onto an embroidery needle, and sew a few stitches at either end to strengthen the corners of the buttonhole.

After you've made the first buttonhole on a project, check to see if the button will pass through it. It is usually better to make the holes a little snug than too loose. If you find later that the holes are too big, you can always thread a needle and make them smaller with a few stitches at the end.

Beyond Ribbing

The usual edging for knitting, ribbing, is done to help the garment retain its shape. But there are other stitches that also do this without the pulling-in effect that ribbing has. You can work borders in garter or moss stitch, both of which create a firm, edge that won't curl. Either pick up stitches or sew them on if they are not worked with the main part of the garment. Crocheting on a decorative edging after you've finished knitting the garment is also an option. For starters, try one of the following alternatives.

Picot Hem Edging

Picot hem edging

To make a picot edge, cast on an odd number of stitches with smaller needles than you are planning to use for the rest of the garment. Work in stockinette for an inch or so, or however deep you want the hem to be, and end on a purl row.

To make the eyelet holes *Knit 1 stitch, bring the yarn forward, knit 2 stitches together, then repeat from * to the end of the row.

Continue working in stockinette with regular-sized needles to make the rest of the piece. When you are done, turn up the hem at the eyelets to leave a scalloped edge. Use a needle and thread to secure the hem in place.

Rouleaux Hems and Edgings

Stockinette has a natural tendency to curl unless you use one of the traditional edging stitches, such as rib. This tendency is called a rouleaux edge. It looks good when it makes a mock turtleneck, where the right side of the stocking stitch curls back to show the reverse stocking stitch.

There's no law that says you have to have ribbing at the bottom of a sweater. Patterns for baby's clothes often substitute a pretty picot hem. You can do this on any garment, although because the hem turns up, it may be too bulky with a thick yarn.

Hems can also be done this way. Remember to use needles a size or two smaller than for the body of the garment and to add 1–2 inches to the length. The best part of a rouleaux edge is that you don't have to do anything to achieve it! It will happen naturally if there are enough stitches for the fabric to roll back on itself.

Making Yarn Cords

Cords made from yarn have many uses. Make them from the same yarn you used for your knitted garment to create professional-looking piping, tie fastenings, or drawstrings. You can also twist the cord into shapes and sew them in place. A simple project for children is to make a length of cord, then coil and sew it to make a round mat. Cord also looks good used as a decorative ribbon sewn onto a knitted garment. You can jazz up a plain sweater by swirling a length of I-cord all over a finished garment and sewing it in place. You can also use I-cord or finger crochet to make "frog" fastenings, those elaborately coiled buttonhole loops and buttons often seen on silk kimono-type jackets.

Why does I-cord go by so many names in different countries?
It's also known as bobbin knitting, spool knitting, or French knitting. No one knows the answer.

Finger Crochet

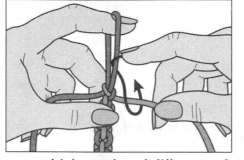

Making
finger
crochet cord

For a skinny, flat cord, you can crochet three lengths of single chain and plait them together. (See Chapter 20 for more information on crochet techniques.)

Or try doing "finger crochet" which makes a square cord.

For this you'll need two balls of yarn, which can be of different colors. Knot the two ends together and hold this knot between the thumb and middle finger of your left hand. With the first finger of the left hand, hold up one strand of yarn to make a loop. With your right hand, drape the other strand of yarn also over your left forefinger and pass the first strand over the second. Take the first strand of yarn and drape it over the forefinger again. Pass the strand already there over this new strand. Continue in this manner, alternating strands, to form the cord.

Twisted Cord

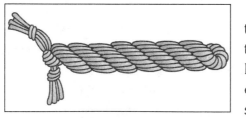

Twisted
yarn cord

It's easy to make a simple, twisted yarn cord. Just remember to start with yarn three times the length that you want the finished cord to be. If you start with two strands, you'll end up with a cord four strands thick and less than half the length of the original.

ESSENTIALS

The tighter you twist the yarn as you're making twisted cord, the firmer the finished cord will be. Extra twisting means that the cord will be shorter.

To make a twisted yarn cord, take the number of strands you've chosen for the thickness you want. Knot them at each end. Attach one end to something stable, like a drawer handle. Skewer a knitting needle through the knot at the other end.

Turn the knitting needle round and round until the yarn is twisted enough to fold back on itself. Grasp the cord in the middle and allow it to continue twisting around itself, making sure it doesn't tangle. Knot each finished end and trim off the loose ends.

Regular buttons and buttonholes are not your only options for closures. You can use ties made of cord, "frog" closings, beads, or Velcro strips. Or you can consider using unusual small decorative items, such as small shells with holes drilled through them.

Knitting Pockets in Garments

Pockets can be both decorative and functional. On a knitted garment they won't hold a whole lot without sagging. So think of them as decoration, and put them in unusual places: a tiny pocket in a knitted glove for a subway token, for example. A pocket could hold an embroidered frog, be a flowerpot for an appliquéd daisy, or home to a teddy-bear pin. And think about adding pockets as squares—or triangles—of color. Pockets don't have to be square! Consider making a child the perfectly pocketed jacket to accommodate his or her small toy collection—pockets just the right size and just where they're needed!

There are two things to know about pockets in knits. You should plan them in advance, and you should be sure to use yarn strong and thick enough to support the pockets.

Pocket Options

Cardigan with knitted-in pockets

knitted by Alice Cathro

Pockets in knits are of two types. Either they're added to a garment after it's made, like patch pockets or pockets let into seams, or they're knitted in as part of the garment itself. Patch pockets are the easiest to plan because you can decide where they go after you've finished. But they're also the hardest to make look neat and professional. Unless the sides of the knitted patch are really tidy, you'll need to turn them under before attaching them, which makes bulky edges. In fact, because pockets are so visible, all the sewing connected with them should be done very neatly, using a whipstitch seam. Remember, too, that the edges of a pocket will get a lot of stress and should be sewn securely.

To figure out pocket positioning and size, it may be helpful to cut out a fabric or paper pocket before you begin knitting and safety pin it to a garment similar to the one you are making. This helps you to work out its placement on the pattern diagram.

Of course, you can make patch pockets in a way that leaves a naturally tidy edge: You could crochet a square or make a circular pocket from a length of I-cord wound into a circle. These pockets could be sewn onto the right side of the knitted garment without turning the edge under.

If you have dressmaking experience, you'll need to rethink pockets in terms of the way you add them to garments. The type of pocket most suitable to knitting is the kind you knit in to the garment and plan in advance.

How to Make Horizontal Knitted-in Pockets

The basic method of making a knitted-in pocket is to bind off stitches for its opening, then replace them with lining stitches. Start knitting the front of the sweater. Put markers at the stitches where you want the pocket to begin and end. Work to about an inch before the row where you want the pocket to open. Continue knitting across each row, but work the stitches between the markers in a rib.

After an inch of ribbing, cast off the pocket stitches loosely on a right side row. It's very important to get the tension of this binding off right. Too tight a binding will pull the garment out of shape, and too loose will make the pocket droopy. Then finish working to the end of the row.

Horizontal knitted-in pockets

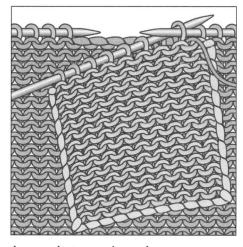

The next step is to knit the lining of the pocket separately. Take a spare pair of needles, and cast on the same number of stitches you just bound off for the opening of the pocket.

Work in stockinette for about 4 inches or to the depth you want the pocket to be. End with a knit row. Now, going back to the main garment, take up the needles and work the purl row until you get to the pocket opening where you cast off the stitches. Pick up the needle with the pocket lining fabric on it, and purl those lining stitches until you're back to the main garment. Continue to purl the stitches on the other side of the pocket. The pocket lining is now incorporated into the fabric!

ESSENTIALS

Work the inside of the pocket in stockinette. It makes the thinnest fabric, and you don't want lumpy pockets. Make a border at the edge of the pocket in rib or another stitch that won't curl. With a very heavy yarn, try making the linings in a matching yarn of a finer ply, and adjust your gauge accordingly.

When you finish knitting the whole front of the garment, whipstitch the three sides of the pocket lining to the wrong side of the fabric. Take care that you sew it flat. If it bulges or pulls, you'll notice wrinkles at the front.

CHAPTER 18
Patterns to Try

The following patterns represent items of varying degrees of difficulty. A classic cardigan in stockinette stitch lets you get comfortable with increasing and decreasing, while the scarf and pillow cover let you practice more intricate stitches in simple, oblong fabric. If you feel really adventuresome, use these patterns as basic templates, and create your own designs using stitches you learned earlier.

Basket Stitch Afghan

Perfect for beginners who want a substantial project, this simple afghan is alternating squares of stockinette and reverse stockinette, with a garter stitch border. Variegated yarns hide uneven stitches for new knitters, and consistent knitters can use solid colors to emphasize the stitch pattern. More daring knitters can modify the pattern to use either a contrasting or complementary color for the garter stitch border.

MATERIALS: Worsted weight yarn, 4-ply: 36 oz. (for two colors, use 27 oz. MC, 9 oz. CC)
Size 10 needles (26-inch circular, or 14-inch straight)

GAUGE: In stockinette, 3 sts = 1";
5 rows = 1"
Finished size is approximately 58" × 64" (19 squares by 21 squares); fits twin or double bed.

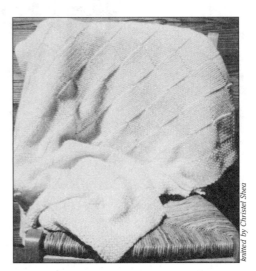

knitted by Christel Shea

INSTRUCTIONS: Cast on 172 sts.
Row 1–20: Knit in garter stitch.
Row 21: K10; *P8, K8; repeat * 8 times; P8; K10.
Row 22: K18; *P8, K8; repeat * 8 times; K10.
Repeat rows 23–32 in pattern (completes first square: 8 sts by 12 rows).
Row 33: K18; *P8, K8; repeat * 8 times; K10.
Row 34: K10; *P8, K8; repeat * 8 times; P8; K10.
Repeat rows 35–44 in pattern (completes second row of squares: 8 sts by 12 rows).
Repeat rows 21–44 in pattern through row 272 (completes twenty-first row of squares).
Rows 273–292: K in garter stitch.
Bind off.

INSTRUCTIONS: Finishing
Weave in loose ends, wash, and block.

Classic Cardigan

The beauty of this sweater is that you can follow the pattern, or you can vary it to your own preferences. Instead of ribbing the bottom hem, do straight stockinette and turn it under. Make the body longer for a tunic-style sweater. Work from your own measurements (refer to the body diagram on page 92), and create a custom made garment. Note that this pattern is for a woman's sweater.

MATERIALS: Worsted weight 4-ply: 22 oz, or 1,230 yards, for a medium sized sweater (17" across back of shoulders; 24" from collar to waistband).
Sizes 6, 8 straight needles
Stitch markers, stitch holders, safety pins, buttons (7), sewing and tapestry needles

GAUGE: In stockinette, 4½ sts = 1"; 6 rows = 1". Adjust needles as necessary to obtain gauge.

INSTRUCTIONS: Sleeves (2)
Using smaller needles, cast on 40 sts.
Work in 1 x 1 rib (K1, P1) for 2½". In last row of ribbing, increase 4 sts, evenly spaced. (Recommend K5, inc 1, *K10, inc 1; repeat from * across.)
Row 1 (right side): Change to larger needles, knit.
Rows 2–4: Continue in stockinette.
Row 5 (inc): K1, inc 1, knit to last 2 sts, inc, K1. You should have 46 sts. Continue in stockinette, increasing in pattern in rows 11, 17, 23, 29, 35, 41, 47, 55, 63, 71, 79. Increasing at each end of these rows, you should have a total of 68 sts.
Work until sleeve measures desired length from wrist to underarm (see page 92), ending with a purl row.
To begin shaping the shoulder, bind off 6 sts at the beginning of the next 2 rows and work across, leaving 56 sts.
Row 3 (dec): K1, sl1 K-wise, K1, psso, knit to last 3 sts, K2 tog, K1.

Row 4: Purl.

Repeat rows 3 and 4, 13 times, leaving 28 sts.

Bind off 3 sts at the beginning of the next 6 rows, working across, leaving you with 10 sts.

Bind off last 10 sts in pattern.

QUESTIONS?

Can you customize a pattern to specific measurements?
Using simple math, you can adjust almost any pattern to fit custom measurements. It's simply a matter of taking your body measurements, multiplying the length or width by the gauge, and adjusting the rest of the pattern accordingly.

INSTRUCTIONS: Back

Using smaller needles, cast on 88 sts.

Work in 1 x 1 rib for 2 inches.

Row 1 (right side): Change to larger size needles, knit across.

Continue in stockinette until back measures approximately 16 inches from cast on edge. (This part of the pattern is where you would make any length adjustments.) End on a purl row.

To begin shaping the armhole, bind off 6 sts at the beginning of the next 2 rows and work across, leaving 76 sts.

Row 3 (dec): K1, sl1 K-wise, K1, psso, knit across to last 3 sts, K2 tog, K1.

Row 4: Purl.

Repeat rows 3 and 4 six times, leaving 62 sts.

Work even until armholes measure approximately 8¾ inches, ending with a knit row.

To begin shaping the shoulder, bind off 5 sts at the beginning of the next 2 rows and work across, leaving 52 sts.

Rows 3 and 4: Bind off 6 sts at the beginning of the next 2 rows and work across.

Rows 5 and 6: Bind off 6 sts at the beginning of the next 2 rows and work across.

Slip remaining 28 sts onto stitch holder.

INSTRUCTIONS: Left Front

Using smaller needles, cast on 53 sts.

Row 1 (wrong side): P11, place marker (to set off front band), begin 1 x 1 rib across.

Row 2: Continue rib in pattern to marker, K5, sl1 P-wise, knit to end.

Repeat rows 1 and 2 for 2 inches, ending with wrong side row.

Change to larger needles, and knit across to marker, K5, sl1 p-wise, knit to end.

Purl across, and continue in pattern until front measures approximately 16¼ inches from cast on edge, ending on a purl row.

To begin armhole shaping, bind off 6 sts, knit across.

Row 2: Purl.

Row 3 (dec): K1, sl1 K-wise, K1, psso, knit to end.

Repeat rows 2 and 3 six times, leaving 40 sts.

Work even until armhole measures approximately 6 inches, ending with a knit row.

To begin neck shaping, P17, and slip purled sts onto a stitch holder; continue purl to end.

Row 2 (dec): Knit to last 2 sts, K2 tog.

Row 3 (dec): P2 tog, purl.

Row 4 (dec): Knit across to last 2 sts, K2 tog.

Row 5: Purl.

Repeat rows 4 and 5, 3 times, leaving 17 sts.

Work until Left Front measures approximately 25 inches from cast on edge, ending with a purl row.

To begin shoulder shaping, bind off 5 sts, knit across, leaving 12 sts.

Row 2: Purl.

Row 3: Bind off 6 sts, knit across.

Row 4: Purl.

Bind off last 6 sts in pattern.

INSTRUCTIONS: Right Front

Using smaller needles, cast on 53 sts.

Row 1 (wrong side): 1 x 1 rib (start with purl stitch) to last 11 sts, place marker, and purl across.

Row 2: K5 sts, sl1 P-wise. Knit to marker, continue in rib pattern across. Continue in pattern for 3 more rows.

Row 6 (begin buttonhole): Knit 1 st, bind off next 2 sts, K1, sl1 P-wise, K2 bind off next 2 sts, knit to marker, continue rib in pattern.

Row 7 (finish buttonhole): Rib in pattern to marker, P1, turn work and cast on 2 sts in two-needle cast on method (see page 44). Turn work again; new sts should be on right needle. P5, cast on 2 sts, purl to end.

Row 8: Repeat row 2.

Continue in pattern (repeating rows 1 and 2) for 2 inches, ending on wrong side row.

ESSENTIALS

When placing your buttons, remember that one is located on the waistband, and one on the neckband. The remaining five will be spaced evenly along the vertical band of the left front. Count the rows between the buttons, and knit in corresponding buttonholes on the right front.

Change to larger needles, K5, sl1 P-wise, knit across.

Purl across, and continue in pattern until Right Front measures approximately 16¼ inches from cast on edge, ending with a knit row.

To begin armhole shaping, bind off 6 sts, purl.

Row 2: Knit.

Row 3 (dec): P1, P2 tog, purl across, leaving 46 sts.

Repeat rows 2 and 3 six times, leaving 40 sts.

Work even until armhole measures approximately 6 inches, ending with a knit row.

To begin neck shaping, purl across to last 17 sts, slip remaining sts onto stitch holder.

Row 2 (dec): Sl1 k-wise, K1, psso, knit across, leaving 22 sts.

Row 3 (dec): Purl across to last 2 sts, P2 tog.

Row 4 (dec): Sl1 k-wise, K1, psso, knit across. You should have 20 sts on the needle.

Row 5: Purl.

Repeat rows 4 and 5 three times, leaving 17 sts.

Work until Right Front measures approximately 25 inches from cast on edge, ending with a knit row.

To begin shoulder shaping, bind off 5 sts, purl to end, leaving 12 sts.

Row 2: Knit.

Row 3: Bind off 6 sts, purl.

Row 4: Knit.

Bind off remaining 6 sts.

Check your measurements and your gauge regularly as you work each piece. Your sleeves should match each other, the two front panels should be symmetrical, and the front and the back should be the same length.

INSTRUCTIONS: Finishing

Congratulations! You're in the home stretch. Only assembling, finishing the neckband, and blocking are left. Depending upon how even your pieces are, blocking can go one of two ways. One option is to block the pieces individually to help mold and shape them as needed. They may also be easier to work with at this stage because they're flat.

Your second option is to finish the sweater, and block it as a complete garment. The advantage to this choice is that blocking will work out any easing or adjustments you made while sewing up the seams or insetting the sleeves (see Chapter 10).

Sew shoulder seams together using a backstitch seam (page 107). To begin the neckband, use the smaller needles to K5 from the stitch holder, sl1 P-wise, and knit remaining sts from holder.

Pick up 22 sts from right neck edge, knit on 30 sts from back stitch holder, pick up 22 sts from left neck edge.

Slip last 17 sts from stitch holder the empty needle. K11, sl1 P-wise, knit to end. You should have 108 sts on your needle.

Row 1: P11, place marker, *K1, P1, repeat from * to last 11 sts, place marker, P11.

Row 2: K5, sl1 P-wise, knit to marker, continue in 1 x 1 rib to second marker, K5 sl1 P-wise, knit to end.

Row 3: P11, 1 x 1 rib to second marker, P11.

Repeat rows 2 and 3 for half an inch. Knit buttonhole in right front band (see Chapter 17 [Row 6 (begin buttonhole):]).

Continue in pattern until neckband is 1".

Bind off in pattern.

ESSENTIALS

Casting on and binding off should maintain the gauge of the entire fabric. This is especially important with ribbed bands. Ribbing provides elasticity—don't lose that by having edges that are too tight.

Sew the last button onto the neckband.

Set in sleeves along the shoulder, and attach using a backstitch seam.

Close up the side seams (you may be able to use yarn ends for this if they are long enough) and sleeve seams at one time. Flat seems work best on ribbing (see Chapter 6), so use that at the waistband and cuffs. For the rest of the body and sleeve, use a mattress stitch (see Chapter 10) to create an invisible seam.

To finish the front, fold the two front bands back along the line of slipped stitches. Use a neat whipstitch to sew in place on the wrong side of the fabric. The buttonholes also need to be finished. Use embroidery floss, matching thread, or even two strands of your 4-ply yarn to stitch around the inside of each buttonhole. Be sure to go through both thicknesses of the band. The extra effort you put into the front band now will strengthen both the buttons and the buttonholes, and will help your garment retain its shape.

Sand Tracks Scarf

This scarf is excellent for learning to use a cable needle. The moss stitch border and garter stitch selvage set off the sand tracks throughout the body of the scarf. The scarf's length is entirely up to you, and the preference of the wearer.

MATERIALS: Sport weight 3-ply, or "soft" worsted-weight 4-ply: 10 oz.
Size 7 needles
Cable hook, markers

GAUGE: 5 sts = 1 inch; 6 rows = 1 inch

INSTRUCTIONS:
Cast on 52 sts.
Row 1: K1, *K1, P1; repeat * 24 times; K1.
Row 2: K1, *P1, K1; repeat * 24 times; K1.
Row 3: K1, *P1, K1; repeat * 24 times; K1.
Row 4: K1, *K1, P1; repeat * 24 times; K1.
Repeat rows 1–4.
Row 9: K1, *K1, P1; repeat * 3 times; K38; *K1, P1; repeat * 3 times; K1.
Row 10: K1, *P1, K1; repeat * 3 times; P38; *P1, K1; repeat * 3 times; K1.
Row 11: K1, *P1, K1; repeat * 3 times; K1; * sl 3 sts to cable needle, leave at front, K3, K3 sts from cable needle, K6; repeat * 3 times; K1; *P1, K1; repeat * 3 times; K1.
Row 12: K1, *K1, P1; repeat * 3 times; P38; *K1, P1; repeat * 3 times; K1.
Row 13: K1, *K1, P1; repeat * 3 times; K38; *K1, P1; repeat * 3 times; K1.
Row 14: K1, *P1, K1; repeat * 3 times; P38; *P1, K1; repeat * 3 times; K1.
Row 15: K1, *P1, K1; repeat * 3 times; K1; *K6, sl 3 sts to cable needle and move to back, K3, K3 sts from cable needle; repeat * 3 times; K1; *P1, K1; repeat * 3 times; K1.
Row 16: K1, *K1, P1; repeat * 3 times; P38; *K1, P1; repeat * 3 times; K1.
Repeat rows 9–16 in pattern to desired length (approximately 58–60 inches).
Last 8 rows repeat rows 1–8 in moss stitch.
Bind off in pattern.
INSTRUCTIONS: Finishing
    Weave in loose ends and block.

Knitted by Christel Shea

Aran Stitch Sampler Pillow

Learning any new skill begins with mastering individual elements, then combining them. Aran sweaters, themselves, require an understanding of sweater basics: necklines, sleeves, increasing, and decreasing. They also call for a series of moderately complicated stitches with varying multiples and repeats. Think of this sampler pillow as an functional swatch—with a purpose!

knitted by Christel Shea

MATERIALS: Worsted weight 4-ply: 10 oz. (Light, solid colors are easy to work with, and show off intricate stitches.)
Size 9 needles. (Size 9 needles produce a fabric loose enough to work complicated stitches easily, yet tight enough for the fabric to hold its shape.)
Cable hook, markers
14–16 inch pillow form, or fiber fill (washable)
½ yard muslin as backing for knitted fabric. If you make your own pillow form, remember to allow additional fabric for the pillow casing.
½ yard fabric of your choosing for pillow backing. Consider a richly textured fabric, such as corduroy or velvet.

GAUGE: 4½ sts = 1 inch; 5 rows = 1 inch. It's important to know whether you knit to gauge, but this project is an opportunity to learn and practice new stitches. For now, concentrate on keeping your fabric even and consistent; make gauge adjustments later.

KEY: Chapter 13 explains each of these stitches in detail. Refer back for specific instructions on how to use the cable hook, how to do crossed stitches without a cable hook, and how to create bobbles.

- b (small): Small bobbles are easy, and will get you used to working 1 stitch several times.
- C4B, C4F and C4F, C4B: Together this series of stitches forms a honeycomb pattern. The order in which the cables are worked keeps

them from actually crossing each other, in contrast to cables, which always twist the same way.

- C6B: Right-twist cable.
- C6F: Left-twist cable.
- Cross 2 LK: Cross 2 to the left (knit) produces delicate mini-cables without using a cable hook.
- Cross 2 RK: Cross 2 to the right is a mirror image of cross 2LK. Most Aran knits use stitch patterns that mirror each other.

INSTRUCTIONS:

Cast on 92 sts.

Row 1 (wrong side): Purl.

Row 2: Sl1 K-wise K2; *cross 2RK (5 times); K11; P2, K6, P2; K24; P2, K6, P2; K11; *cross 2LK (5 times); K3.

Row 3: Sl1 P-wise (to form slip-stitch selvage); work across as presented (P purled stitches, K knit stitches).

Row 4: Sl1 K-wise, K2; *cross 2RK (5 times); K2, b, K5, b, K2; P2, K6, P2; K24; P2, K6, P2; K2, b, K5, b, K2; *cross 2LK (5 times); K3.

Row 5 (and every odd row): Repeat Row 3.

Row 6: Sl1 K-wise, K2; *cross 2RK (5 times); K11; P2, C6F, P2; *C4B, C4F (3 times); P2, C6B, P2; K11; *cross 2LK (5 times); K3.

Row 8: Sl1 K-wise, K2; *cross 2RK (5 times); K5, b, K5; P2, K6, P2; K24; P2, K6, P2; K5, b, K5; *cross 2LK (5 times); K3.

Row 10: Sl1 K-wise K2; *cross 2RK (5 times); K11; P2, K6, P2; *C4F, C4B (3 times); P2, K6, P2; K11; *cross 2LK (5 times); K3.

Rows 3–10 form the repeat of the pattern. Work in pattern to approximately 15 inches (or until fabric is square), ending on a Row 3 of the pattern.

Knit across last row, and bind off in pattern.

INSTRUCTIONS: Finishing

If you have used light-colored yarn, you will probably need to wash the fabric even before you block it. Refer to the washing instructions on the yarn label. As the fabric dries, block it, paying special attention to uneven stitches that might need to be adjusted. Also make sure none of the bobbles have migrated to the back side.

Muslin will provide a sturdy backing for the knitted pillow-front. The backing will help both the pillow and the knitting hold their shapes. First, sew the knitting to the muslin backing. You may find it helpful sew tiny stitches near the bobbles to tack the two fabrics together. That will prevent the fabric from getting pulled and stretched out of shape over time.

Next, with right sides facing, sew the pillow backing to the knit-muslin on three edges only. Turn the pocket right side out—you now have the pillow cover. All that's left is to insert the pillow form, tuck in any raw edges on the fourth side, and whipstitch the last seam together.

As you get more adventuresome, try similar projects with other stitches. Even just practicing is fun when it's productive, too!

CHAPTER 19

Decorating Knitted Garments

I t can be more fun to decorate your sweaters than it is to knit them! Knitting with beads can turn plain yarn into a sparkly, bejeweled fabric. Personally designed motifs—either knitted or embroidered—can transform an ordinary sweater into a handcrafted work of art. The difficulty of each technique varies, so move at your own pace.

Graphing Motifs

Once you've made a sweater and know you can cope with the technicalities, you'll want to get creative and make your knits true one-of-a-kind works of art. One great way to do that is by designing your own motifs. All you need is a good, reliable sweater pattern in stockinette and a burst of creative thinking!

It really helps when designing motifs for knits if you've made a sweater in stockinette that's turned out well. You can use this as a gauge guide and visualize more easily where the motif should go.

Start with something simple—a letter sweater, for instance, with a big red letter L on a white background. The first thing to do is to make a chart on knitter's graph paper.

Charting the Design

You can use regular graph paper, which has square blocks, but knitter's graph paper is drawn to better proportions, giving you a better idea of how the finished graphic will look. If you look at a knitted stitch, you will see that it is wider than it is tall. Knitter's graph paper has "squares" shaped more like a stitch.

The knitter's graph paper used in the charted pattern and motif samples is for a stitch of medium width. Just as gauge varies depending on the stitch you work, so does the width of a stitch. To make your own graph paper, or to work out whether regular graph paper will work for your chosen stitch, first make up a swatch of fabric. Measure a 4-inch square section, and count the number of stitches and rows. Then divide the number of rows by the number of stitches. If the result is very close to one, your stitches are almost square. If the answer is closer to 1.5, you have medium-wide stitches. Any answer of 1.7 or more means a very wide stitch. With wide stitches, use regular squared graph paper but figure two squares for each stitch, in terms of width.

Figuring Placement

Look at the sweater you've made, or any sweater you own, and decide how big you want your motif to be. It makes things simpler to have the motif complete before you start the armhole shaping, but you can put it anywhere.

Suppose you want to make your red L 4 inches high and 3 inches wide. Work out the number of stitches that represents, using either the sweater you've made and are taking as a gauge guide, or using the gauge on the knitting pattern. If your gauge is 4 stitches to an inch, the L will be 12 stitches wide. If there are 6 rows to the inch, the height of the letter will be 24 rows. On your graph paper, draw a rectangle that's 12 squares wide and 24 squares high. Draw the L inside this rectangle. Once you have the general outline, fill in every square of the graph paper that's part of the design. Each filled square represents a stitch to be worked in the color you choose. (To begin, try a design that uses just one background color.)

ESSENTIALS Before you begin knitting in different colors, review Chapter 14 for a reminder on how to work with colors and to work out whether it's better to use an intarsia or Fair Isle technique for your design.

How do you know where to work the motif on the front of your sweater? Placing it exactly in the middle is easy. Look at the number of stitches the pattern asks you to cast on for the front of the garment. If it's 36 stitches, the letter can take up the middle 12, leaving 12 on each side. Note on the graph paper that when you come to the row where the letter begins, you must work 12 stitches in the background color, white, then work in red for 12 stitches. To go back to white for the last 12 stitches of the row, join in a new ball of white yarn. Don't attempt to carry the yarn behind your work.

When you use large blocks of color, as you would with a big, blocky letter, you are working in intarsia. You need to know how to link the different yarns by twisting them around each other. If you are using little bits of color here and there, as you would if you were working a small repeated motif, you will strand the colors at the back of your work in a Fair Isle technique. Try to design so you don't have to carry your yarn a long way across the back. Keep your designs simple, and don't use too many colors in a row. Consider using duplicate embroidery for small areas of color.

Advanced Designs

Ready to design a more detailed motif? Keep the shapes bold, and step the curves on the squared grid. Fill in the different areas of color with colored pencils or markers.

If you don't want to draw something yourself, look through books on needlepoint and embroidery. You'll see lots of designs, conveniently drawn up into squares and ready to use. They'll be on square grids, but you can transfer them to knitter's graph paper, or you can use them as is and get a slightly flattened version of the design.

ALERT

Simple, bold designs work best for sweater motifs. Drawings with lots of curves are not so successful—they become squared off, like pixilated images on a computer screen.

Single motifs are usually shown in the center of a chart, with repeat patterns displayed from edge to edge, although sometimes just one repeat of the pattern is given. Some charts show every repeat; some just show as many as necessary. The stitch multiples and repeats are usually bordered by heavy, bold, black lines.

Single motif

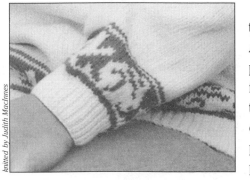

knitted by Judith MacInnes

Inspiration for motifs is all over the place, once you start to look. A photograph, a label, or a wallpaper sample can give you an idea for something you'd like to use on the front of a sweater. Kilim rugs or antique woven textiles can also provide inspiration for color and pattern.

Find a copy machine that you can easily load with your own paper so you can copy your grid onto sheets of blank tracing paper rather than blank white paper. Feed in the tracing paper and reproduce the illustration of knitter's graph paper onto it. You can slip this graphed tracing paper over any picture. Trace over an illustration in pencil, and then fill in the squares that will become stitches.

This charted motif is a beautiful accent around the bottom of a girl's sweater

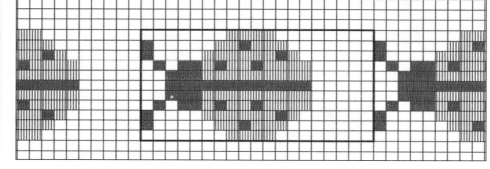

Knitters who are computer savvy can buy one of the software programs for hand knitters, such as Stitch or Motif Maker, that generate a grid with a design, ready to use. These programs can help you design your own Fair Isle designs, symbols, and motifs. You can import a scanned image or use a saved bitmap picture and turn it into a grid.

Embroidering on Knits

Embroidery can turn a plain sweater into something special. In fact, you can use it to revive any clothes in your closet that could use a lift. For a professional look, match the scale of the design you apply to the type of garment you are decorating. Small, delicate embroidery belongs on small, delicate garments; big, bold patterns work on heavier clothes.

Duplicate Stitch or Swiss Darning

Duplicate stitch embroidery

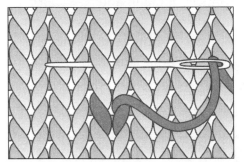

When you embroider in duplicate stitch, it feels like cheating. The result looks knitted in, as though you've carefully worked from a complicated pattern. In fact, all you've done is sewn over some of your stitches and "duplicated" them in other colors.

Duplicate stitch works best on stockinette stitch. For best results, wash and block, or at least press, the finished piece of fabric (depending on what the laundering instructions allow) so it lies flat and smooth. Use the same yarn, if possible, as the knitting yarn, but in a different color. The whole point is to mimic the stitches you've knitted. A different kind of thread will be noticeable, and a different type of fiber might present difficulties when you wash the garment.

FACTS

Duplicate stitch (also known as Swiss darning) imitates the knitted stitch, but it is actually embroidery worked on the surface of the fabric. You can also use duplicate stitch to conceal small mistakes and holes in the fabric.

Use a darning or tapestry needle with a blunt point that will glide through stitches easily. You don't want to split the yarn. Thread the needle, then bring it up from the wrong side of the fabric at the base of the stitch it is to cover. Go over one side of the stitch completely, then the other.

Keep the stitches loose so they don't pucker the fabric. Duplicate stitch is worked more loosely than embroidery on fabric. Your aim is to make the stitch look the same as the surrounding stitches. Be aware that even if you use loose stitches, the area you duplicate is not going to be as elastic as the rest of the fabric. It's a good idea to keep the decoration to an area that doesn't need to stretch too much. (Avoid it around a neckline, for example, because that needs to stretch.)

You can also embroider in regular embroidery stitches, such as a chain or satin stitch, as long as it treats the knitted fabric like any other fabric to be embroidered on. Use a sharper needle and any kind of thread, although it's a good idea to keep to the same type of fibers for ease of laundering—cotton on cotton, wool on wool. If you want to use the same sort of yarn used in the knitting but it's a bit heavy for embroidery, unravel a length and embroider with just one ply.

Chain Stitch Embroidery

You can "write" or "draw" on any knitted fabric with chain stitch embroidery. It's fun to do, and using a crochet hook makes it easy.

Insert the crochet hook through the fabric from the right side, and draw the embroidery yarn through from the wrong side. With the yarn still around the hook, put the hook through the knitted fabric, again a little farther ahead. Draw a new loop of embroidery yarn through the fabric, then through the loop already on the hook. (When you've done this, 1 loop should remain on the hook.) Repeat this method, following the line you want to make.

Try working without guidelines—if you make a mistake in direction it's simple to unpick the embroidery back to where you started to go wrong.

Knitting with Beads or Sequins

Beads can look pretty sprinkled over a sweater or cardigan. They're best kept to decorative edges and details at the top of your garment, where the beading won't drag the knit down. It can also be painful to lean or sit against a completely beaded garment!

FACTS

An easy way to get a beaded effect without a lot of work is to buy one of the novelty or designer yarns on the market with beads already spun into it.

The traditional way of knitting with beads is to thread them on the yarn before you start knitting. You can also slip beads over a whole stitch, but this nestles the beads into the fabric of the knitting, whereas stringing the beads along the yarn results in beads that sit on the surface of the fabric. The choice depends on the look you want and your patience for stringing beads.

The important thing to remember when you buy beads for knitting is that they should be light enough, and the yarn sturdy enough, to avoid having the fabric dragged down by the extra weight. The beads must also have holes large enough to be threaded onto the yarn you use. (If you really want to use beads with small holes together with a thick yarn, consider threading the beads on a finer version of the yarn you want to use, and knitting both the thin and thick yarns together as one strand.)

FACTS

Sequins can be threaded on to yarn and knitted the same way as beads, and because they are lighter, you can use more of them without risk of dragging down the fabric.

If you are knitting with beads, it's best to use a plain stitch like stockinette. Its smooth surface gives a good background for the decoration. The fabric should also be dense and firm so the beads don't slip to the wrong side of the fabric. Working with a firm tension will also help prevent the beads from migrating.

Threading Beads over a Whole Stitch

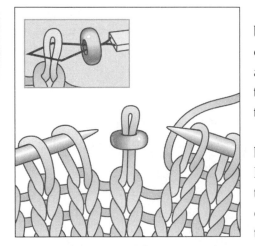

Threading beads over a whole stitch

This is the easy way to add beads to your knitting. You can decide to add any colored bead at any time, and it won't roughen up the surface of your yarn as threading beads can.

You prepare the stitch where the bead will be threaded by making it longer than normal. When you get to the row immediately below the one where you want the bead, and to the stitch you will want to use on the next row, wrap the yarn twice around the needle instead of the usual once when making the stitch.

Work to the end of the row and the beginning of the next until you are at the elongated stitch. You will now need the help of a wire needle-threader. These diamond-shaped pieces of wire are available at sewing notions counters.

Push the threader into the hole of the bead so that it comes out the other side. Remove from your knitting needle the stitch you want to put the bead on. Thread it through the needle-threader and slip the bead on to the stitch. Place the stitch back on the knitting needle, and continue knitting.

ALERT

Remember when buying beads for threading through stitches that they must have big enough holes for a double loop of yarn to be pulled through.

Making Pom-Poms, Tassels, and Fringe

The trick with these traditional decorations is to use them in an imaginative way. Don't stick with the usual—go for the outrageous. Everyone has pom-poms on their floppy caps—put yours on the backs of a pair of gloves!

There's a practical side to this whimsy, too. Tassels and other ornaments are good ways to use those spare bits and pieces of leftover yarn.

How to Make a Pom-Pom

You can make pom-poms in any size. Try lots of tiny ones in bright colors on a child's sweater, or you can make a row marching down a shoulder or around the brim of a cap. Make them with a mixture of different colored yarns for a speckled or marbled effect.

To make a pom-pom, take a piece of stiff cardboard and cut two circles, both the same size. The pom-pom will be the size of these circles. The next step is to cut identical holes in the middles to transform them into "doughnuts."

Next, wind the yarn around and around the twin cardboard "doughnuts" until no space remains in the middle hole. Your ball of yarn may be too big to go through the small hole, so unravel a few yards of yarn to start with. Hold the two cardboard rings together and pass the yarn around them. Use doubled-up yarn to work even more quickly. Don't worry if you have to keep starting with new lengths of yarn, just leave the ends hanging out. As the hole in the center gets smaller, you will need to use an embroidery needle to get the last lengths of yarn through.

When the center hole is completely filled up and you can't wind any more yarn around, sever the yarn at the edge of the outer circle with a sharp blade until you get to the cardboard rings. Place the lower point of a pair of scissors between the two pieces of cardboard and cut the yarn at the edge all the way around, keeping the scissors between the circles the whole time. When you can separate the two rings, wind a length of yarn, using a double strand, between the two circles of cardboard to gather all the strands at the waist of the pom-pom together. Wind the yarn around a few times, pull tightly, and knot to secure.

Tear the cardboard so you can pull it out of the pom-pom and discard it. Trim any uneven ends from the pom-pom, but leave one long end for sewing it to your knitwear.

Making Tassels

Making a
yarn tassel

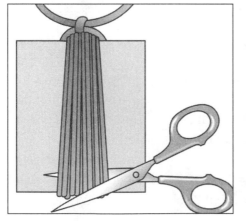

Tassels can decorate the hem of a sweater, form epaulettes on the shoulders of a jacket, or decorate the drawstring on a hood or knitted bag. Thread beads on the ends of each strand of a tassel for an exotic look.

All you need to make a tassel is a small rectangle of stiff cardboard the same length of the tassel you want. Wrap the yarn around the cardboard until the small hank is as hefty as you want your tassel to be. Thread an embroidery needle with a separate length of yarn. Slip this under the gathered yarn to secure it at the top, and tie a tight knot. Cut the tassel free of the cardboard at the bottom end. With the needle still threaded with the yarn, wind it around the top of the tassel, gathering the folded parts together ½ to ¾ of an inch from the top. Knot again, and then bring the needle up through the center of the tassel to leave a long end for sewing on.

Making Fringe

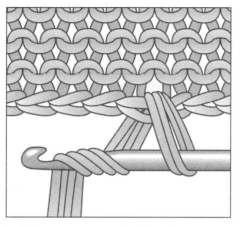

Tying fringe onto a garment edge

Fringe is simply sections of yarn drawn through the edge of a piece of knitting at even intervals. You can make fringe thick or wispy and as long as you like. Cut several lengths of yarn a bit longer than twice the length you want the finished fringe to be. Bundle these together, fold them in half and push the folded end through a gap in the knitted edge you want to decorate. It may help to use a crochet hook as you pull the cut ends through the loop at the folded end of the strands and pull to secure.

Adding the Finishing Touches

Finishing touches on a garment give it a one-of-a-kind designer look that make the hand-knits in stores so expensive—yet they are easy to do on handmade knits! Special decorations give your creations personality. They can turn even the simplest thing you've knitted into a unique gift. They can also rescue a sweater that has seen better days or been attacked by the family pet.

Whether you choose buttons, beads, odd bits and pieces from your jewelry box, tiny clay-craft objects, or dollhouse items, you can sew on anything that is small and light enough not to weigh down the fabric. You can also crochet chains or knit little flowers or squares to add embellishment.

To find stores carrying interesting bits and pieces, look up "bead suppliers," "dollhouse furniture makers," "craft supplies," or "sewing notions" in the Yellow Pages or on the Internet. Here are some ideas to spark your imagination:

- Tiny shells with holes in them can add personality to a basic summer knit.
- Anything that will fit through a buttonhole can be used as a button! All you need to do is glue a little ring to the object to enable you to sew it on the button band of a cardigan. Jeweler's supply stores are a great source of these sorts of fittings.
- Lightweight, knitted mittens in contrasting colors sewn onto the front of a sweater are perfect for kids to slip their hands in to get warm—and they won't get lost!
- Clusters of buttons, arranged to form a shape such as a circle or heart, can decorate a lapel or a sleeve.
- White yarn embroidery on a plain black sweater will give it pizzazz. Add some mock lacy white cuffs or collar. Add "angel wings" to the back. Write a word in script.

You can find countless ideas by looking through books on costume and fashion design throughout history. Your local library or museum may also be a source of inspiration. And if all else fails, trust yourself and go with what *you* like!

CHAPTER 20
Crochet

Many people find crochet easier to learn and quicker to do than knitting. It's more portable, too. Even if you decide you prefer knitting, you'll find it's handy to know the basic crochet stitches for lacy edgings or decorative cords. Crocheting is also a good way to join seams on knitted garments.

Popular Crochet

If knitting has become the latest fashionable pastime amongst actresses and models, crochet may be even more so.

Trend-tracking *People Magazine* has featured crochet in its "Style Watch" section, reporting that "such stars as Cindy Crawford and Tori Spelling have gotten hooked." The article, entitled "Loop Dreams," mentions crochet's previous period of popularity, in the 1970s, when "crochet's cachet was limited to hippies, hammocks, and hanging planters." It goes on to quote designer Vivienne Tam, who says that crochet is sexy "because it falls just right over the shape of the body."

She might have added that when you use lightweight, soft yarns, you can make delicate, lacy fabrics in crochet that are even sexier.

It's hard to know where and when people began crocheting. The craft could have originated in Arab countries and spread to Europe from there. Evidence of crocheting appears in primitive tribes in South America and in China, too. The type of crochet we do today was developed during the sixteenth century—Italian nuns of the 1500s were making crochet lace for fabrics used in churches. Today, all different types of yarn and crochet hooks, from tiny to huge, are used to make everything from jackets to baby booties.

The Differences Between Knitting and Crochet

Crochet fabric is like knitting in that it is made with a single strand of yarn worked in horizontal courses, but the loops are locked at the sides as well as up and down. This makes crochet fabric even stronger than knitted fabric. It's firmer and denser, too, depending on the yarn and stitch used. Maybe that's one reason crocheted shoulder bags continue to be a popular accessory.

Many people find crochet quicker than knitting, since the basic chain stitch is easier to master than knit and purl stitches. And once you can make a chain, more complex stitches aren't too difficult to learn.

Like knitting, crochet begins with a slipknot, but from then on you make chains rather than stitches. To make a chain, wrap your yarn around a hook and pull it through the previous loop, twisting the crochet hook slightly so as to slip the stitch through easily.

ESSENTIALS

While knitting is done on two pointed needles of the same size, crochet uses a single implement, a hook. To crochet, you simply draw one loop of yarn through another, and the dominant hand does most of the work.

In knitting, the left needle holds the finished work while the right needle creates the next row. With crochet, you can also work in rows, building each stitch on one from the previous row, turning, and working back, producing a flat piece of fabric. But because it's easy to add extra stitches in crochet, it's also easier to make three-dimensional items such as toys, hats, and baskets. Alternatively, you can crochet rounds by making a length of chain, joining it at the beginning to create a ring and then adding stitches in a circle. Some projects combine both crocheting in the round and crocheting by row.

E

FACTS

Crochet is even more portable than knitting—if you are making granny squares for an afghan, you can make one in a few minutes. No need to work out where you are in a pattern or to measure your progress.

Crochet Hooks

The word "crochet" comes from the French word for "a little hook," and that's what you make crochet with: a small rod with a hook at one end for catching loops of yarn and drawing them through stitches. Like knitting needles, crochet hooks come in different sizes and are made from different materials. You can find antique crochet hooks made from exotic materials such as whalebone, ivory, and bronze.

In Victorian times, the well appointed home displayed a wealth of crocheted fabrics: curtains on most windows; closets full of tablecloths; antimacassars to protect the backs of armchairs from the hair oil gentlemen wore; doilies that nestled in platters and under vases; and lacy collars for children and maids. These fine lacy cloth items were all made from thin, fine cotton thread and tiny, steel crochet hooks for lace, sometimes known as thread hooks. These tiny crochet hooks are still available, but now they also come in plastic. They are about 5 inches long and are sized from 00 (3.5 mm), the largest, to 14 (.75 mm), the smallest. A higher size number indicates a smaller hook size. (That's the usual range made in the United States. Some imported steel hooks come in size 16 (.60 mm) and smaller.) These hooks are used with the finest-weight cotton thread.

Now, of course, crochet is also done with heavier yarns, and larger yarn hooks are used to make items such as afghans, garments, toys, and soft furnishings. These crochet hooks are made from lightweight materials such as aluminum, wood, and plastic. Their sizing range is different than the range used for finer hooks.

ALERT

As with knitting needles, different manufacturers use a variety of numbering systems to indicate the size of their hooks. Some manufacturers size them by letter of the alphabet, some by number, and some by millimeter. In all cases, the thickest part of the hook is the part used to determine its size.

The aluminum, wood, and plastic hooks made for working with yarn are usually 6 inches long or longer. The sizing system is opposite from the one used for thread hooks—the larger the number, or further along in the alphabet, the bigger the hook. In other words, a J hook is larger than an F hook. Sizes range from B (2.25 mm), the smallest, to S (19 mm), the largest. To make things more confusing, some hooks have both letter and number classifications. A J hook can also be called a #10 hook, while an F hook is a #5. Size in millimeters can vary depending on manufacturer.

Hook Styles

There are many different styles of crochet hooks. Some hooks have a flattened place along the shaft to rest the thumb, and some are circular all the way along. Then there are the Boye and the Bates hook styles. Try both to see which helps you draw the yarn through the loop more efficiently.

ESSENTIALS Commercially made crochet hooks come in two hook designs. The Boye hook has a rounded shape that flares into a bump, while a Bates hook is made in an "inline" shape. The Bates hook is made with a cut into the shaft, making the hook part flatter than on the Boye hook.

As with knitting needles, crochet hooks are made of all sorts of materials. You can buy handmade brass hooks, or plastic, aluminum and nylon hooks. There are rosewood, tonewood, or walnut models. Each material can speed up your crocheting or slow it down. You can buy most of these types of crochet hooks over the Internet, if your local yarn shop doesn't carry them. Some people even make their own crochet hooks by whittling wooden dowels. For some projects, like afghan rugs made of granny squares, the size of each square is not crucial, as long as they are all the same. A throw or lap blanket can be a bit smaller or larger than expected with no disastrous consequences. A homemade hook would work just as well for these types of patterns as one from the store.

The hook design you choose and the material the hook is made from are matters of personal preference. You should try as many different types as you can to see whether you prefer working with plastic, metal, or wood. The important thing is that you find the hook comfortable and that it gives you an even tension.

Along with the normal single-end crochet hook, there are others with specialized shapes for special stitches. The afghan hook is used for working Tunisian crochet (also called the afghan stitch), in which the fabric formed is similar to a knit. Several loops of yarn are on the hook at one time, meaning the afghan hook is often longer than regular hooks—10 to 12 inches rather than the regular 6. It also has a knob at one end to keep stitches from sliding off.

ESSENTIALS

With the sizing system for lace-making steel crochet hooks, the higher the number, the smaller the hook size. For larger yarn hooks used with worsted weight yarns, the sizing system is the opposite way around. The larger the number, or further down the alphabet, the bigger the hook.

Another special type of crochet hook is the Jiffy or jumbo hook. Available in various sizes, these are very big and made of hollow plastic (for lightness). They can be used with rug yarn or fabric strips to make a heavy afghan or crocheted rug. Then there's the double-hook needle, also called a cro-hook, which is a special double-end crochet hook used for making double-faced fabric in two colors (a technique called cro-hooking).

FACTS

The definition of the word "afghan" can be confusing. A rug or throw made up of small crocheted or knitted squares is often called an afghan, even though it is not necessarily made from afghan stitches or with an afghan crochet hook.

Hook Size Chart

How do you know what crochet hook you should use for your project? The crochet pattern will tell you. But determine where your pattern was printed so you know whether it is specifying U.S. or European crochet hook sizes. Refer to Appendix B for a table for converting other hook sizes to U.S. standards.

When it comes to choosing the correct size hook, it's all a matter of preference. Choose a hook that feels good when you're crocheting, and try to experience as many different types of hooks as you can to see which is most comfortable for you personally.

How to Hold a Crochet Hook

There are three ways to hold a crochet hook: like a pencil, like a spoon (but with the wrist twisted vertically), or under your palm, the way a knife is usually held when eating. Try each method and decide which is the most comfortable for you.

Hold the stitches close to the hook with your thumb and middle finger.

Right-handers hold the hook in the right hand and the yarn in the left—the left hand provides tension to the yarn and holds the work that is being made. The thread from the ball of yarn usually lies over your left index finger, while the completed crochet is held between the thumb and index finger. You can wind the yarn around the little finger as well, or you can use the last three fingers to keep it taut (much as you would for knitting in the Continental method). Hold the hook and yarn in the most comfortable position and the one that provides the necessary even tension.

Left-handers can hold the position diagrams up in front of a mirror to see how to hold the hook and yarn.

Holding a crochet hook (right-handed, left-handed)

English and American Terminology

Knitting patterns are pretty much the same in every country—especially chart patterns that use symbols instead of words. European knitters seem to like charts; they provide a universal language that transcends borders. But crochet devotees in different parts of the world use completely different terminology. The terms, such as single crochet and double crochet, are similar enough that they give the beginner a false sense of familiarity, but they refer to stitches that are different enough to lead to all sorts of mistakes. For example, the stitch that North American crochet patterns call single crochet is what people in Europe, Australia and New Zealand call double crochet. Therefore, it's even more important when crocheting to know where your pattern originated than it is when knitting.

ESSENTIALS The differences in terminology between European and U.S. crochet patterns can be totally confusing. The same terms often mean different things. If you want to use a foreign pattern, it's probably best to rewrite it, substituting in the terms you know.

European terms tend to count loops on the crochet hook, while North American terms don't. The chart in Appendix A describes other differences in the two terminology systems.

Basic Chain Stitch

Crochet always begins with a foundation chain, which is the easiest stitch. When you can do this, everything else is easy—the more complicated stitches just require wrapping more yarn around the hook.

Hold the crochet hook in your right hand. You can capture the short, dangling end of yarn with your little finger to keep it out of the way, if you like.

Bring the working yarn over the hook from back to front, so it is positioned between the hook and the slipknot.

Grasp the dangling end of the yarn with your left hand. Pulling it gently, ease the slipknot over the hook, drawing the hooked yarn through the slipknot. You now have a new stitch on the hook while the original slipped stitch is dropped off. It may help to twist the crochet hook slightly as you bring it through. That way, the hook part faces downward and doesn't catch on the slipknot.

Congratulations! You've made a chain stitch. The usual abbreviation for this stitch is *ch*.

Keep repeating this procedure to make a long chain. To begin with, make very loose, big chains, just to get the hang of the technique. In actual crochet, make loops just loose enough for the hook to go through easily. As in knitting, consistency is important. Make each stitch the same size as the one before it.

In crochet, the chain on the hook is never counted as a stitch. For example, if a pattern says chain ten, you should have 10 link-like stitches, plus the one on the hook.

When you are following a crochet pattern, remember that the chain stitch does not usually count as a row. It is the foundation for the stitches that follow, but it is not part of them. Note also that in crocheting, a loop is always on the hook—that loop does not count as a stitch.

Basic crochet chain

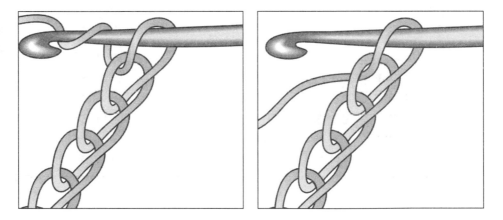

Single Crochet Stitch

If you intend to crochet any edge or finish work on your knitted projects, you'll need to know the common single and double crochet stitches. Although several variations combine these stitches for different results, we'll start with the basics.

To make the single crochet stitch, you must begin with a length of foundation chain to work from. Make a chain of 10 stitches for practice.

Count back 2 chain stitches (not counting the loop on the hook), and insert the hook into the second chain. When crocheting, unless the pattern tells you otherwise, always insert the hook into a chain or stitch from the front towards the back.

Bring the working yarn over the hook from back to front. Then, draw this yarn through the loop you just put your hook through. You should now have 2 stitches on the crochet hook. Bring the yarn over the hook from back to front again and draw it through both loops on the hook.

You have just made a single crochet stitch (abbreviated *sc*).

Single
crochet
stitch

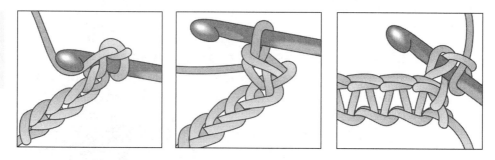

Repeat this single crochet stitch into each of the remaining chains along your length of foundation chain. Make sure you use every chain. Sometimes it is difficult to tell which is the last chain. In the sample you are working, since you started with a foundation chain of 10, you will have 9 single crochet stitches in each row, having skipped one at the beginning. If you're unsure of whether you've reached the end of a row, count the stitches. In single crochet, you will always have 1 stitch fewer than the number in your foundation chain.

FACTS

Crochet stitches are worked back and forth in rows, so the fabric is reversible. There is no right or wrong side to the fabric, which makes crochet especially nice for blankets and shawls.

After completing your first row, you are ready to turn the work and start a new row. However, before you do, you need to make a little extra length of chain to bring the level of the work up so it is high enough to make another row. These are called turning chains. On single crochet, you make just one extra stitch. On taller stitches (such as double or triple crochet), you need to make longer turning chains.

Since you are working single crochet now, you only need to make one extra chain when turning to a new row. To do this, leave the hook in the chain and turn the work so that you are looking at the back of the first row of single chain.

So begin another row, doing just as you did before, but now working into the space between the stitches of the previous row.

Double Crochet Stitch

Double crochet (abbreviated *dc*) is similar to single crochet, except that it involves a few more passes through with the crochet hook. Double crochet produces longer stitches, and it is often the primary stitch in shell or fan-like patterns.

Get used to double crochet by doing a practice swatch. To practice, start with a foundation chain of 20 stitches.

With double crochet, the first step is to bring the yarn over the hook from back to front before you insert the hook anywhere. Then count 4 chains back, not counting the loop on the crochet hook, and insert the hook into that stitch.

ALERT

At the end of each and every stitch sequence, there should only be 1 loop of yarn left on the hook. If you have more, you have made a mistake.

Bring the yarn over the hook again and draw it through the chain where you just inserted the hook (as you did in single crochet). You should now have 3 loops of yarn on the crochet hook. Bring the yarn over the hook and draw it through the first 2 loops on the hook. Two loops of yarn should be on the hook now. Bring the yarn over the hook again, and draw through the last 2 loops. You have just made 1 double crochet stitch.

Repeating these three steps, make a double crochet into each of the remaining stitches along your length of foundation chain. Make sure you use every chain.

Again, if you are not sure that you've hit every stitch on the chain, count the number of stitches of each row. If you are working just double crochet rows, and you started by inserting the hook into the fourth chain back, you will have 2 stitches fewer than the number in your foundation chain. For example, if you have a foundation chain of 20, you will have 18 double crochets in each row (the 17 you actually crocheted, plus the one at the beginning). Before you turn to make the next double crochet row, make 3 chains to get the hook up to the right height. The turning chain not only gets your hook in line; it also forms the first double crochet of that row.

Turn the work, leaving the crochet hook with its loop of yarn in place, to begin the next row.

Skip the first double crochet stitch when you start this next row, and insert the hook under the two top threads of the second stitch. Remember that when you're following a pattern, the turning chain counts as the first double crochet of that row.

Double crochet stitch

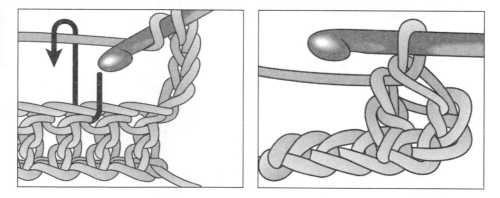

This brief introduction to the two most elementary stitches doesn't begin to cover the many facets of crochet—its stitches, uses, and versatility. A passing familiarity with single and double crochet, however, will complement your knitting experience. And it may whet your appetite just enough to learn a whole new craft once you get knitting nailed down!

The Future of Knitting and Crochet

Like many other arts and handicrafts, knitting is becoming more of a medium of individual expression and less of a discipline that follows ironclad rules.

Back in the 1930s and 1940s, people didn't have the wide variety of ready-made clothes that we have today. Knitters made their own—and their family's—underwear, swimsuits, and coats as well as sweaters. Making your own clothes saved money, too. But back then it was important to make really professional looking garments. Wearing clothes that were obviously made by loving hands at home was an acute embarrassment.

You will know if you have made too much or too little chain by examining the ends of the rows after you've made a sample piece. If there's chain billowing out, you'll know you can use fewer stitches. There should be just enough to bring the work up high enough to begin a new row.

These days, attitudes have changed. Knitwear doesn't try to copy tailored garments. Instead, it has its own identity. As quality, commercially made sweaters have become affordable, and sophisticated and artificial fibers have taken wool's place for outdoor, cold-weather wear, the emphasis has moved away from practicality to self-expression. Handcrafted knits are now a luxury item made with unusual yarns and unique trimmings—a refreshing counterpoint to mass-produced sameness.

While the knitting industry uses computerized machines to turn out garments ever more quickly and seamlessly, hand-knitting has become a craft, like handmade pottery, in which individuality has come to the fore. Knits are now truly a reflection of the people who crafted them, and the trend is toward "wearable art" that makes use of interesting yarns and clever design. Knitting patterns no longer stress speed as they did years ago. Those who knit and crochet enjoy constructing multicolored masterpieces or intricate Aran sweaters, and they don't mind spending time to make them. Most take up their hobby to produce one-of-a-kind clothing that others will admire, not in order to clothe their family cheaply.

So what's ahead for knitting and crochet? The outbreak of hoof-and-mouth disease in Europe during the first years of the century may make woolen yarns more expensive. It's also true that fewer natural fibers are being made into yarn as more man-made fibers are used for clothing. On the other hand, the Internet has given small spinning companies and home-based craftspeople a way to bring their wares to an international market. That market can only grow as computer users search for a tactile, hands-on, leisure-time activity after a day of struggling with modern technology.

Meanwhile, fashion designers such as Kaffe Fassett, Vivienne Westwood, Kim Hargreaves, and Debbie Bliss are creating vital, innovative designs that inspire home knitters to be adventurous and creative.

For centuries, people have been taking up knitting needles or crochet hooks for practical reasons. Today, although there is no real need for anyone in developed countries to continue the practice, they still do so. Obviously, the craft would have died out if there was not something magic about the process: the magic of taking a single strand of yarn in your hands and turning it into something wonderful.

Appendix A

Common Abbreviations

Most knitting patterns include a key to the abbreviations they use. Be sure to read the pattern thoroughly before you begin knitting. Your pattern might use abbreviations that are slightly different from what you've seen before, but reading the key will familiarize you with the terminology. If you are at a knitting shop, someone should be able to explain any terms you don't understand.

3-needle bind-off: Method of casting off two pieces of knitting together and joining them at the same time.

AC: alternate color (also *CC,* for contrasting color)

alt: alternate(ly) Means every other, and usually refers to rows. For example, the instruction "Dec. 2 stitches at the beginning of the next 10 alt. rows" means "decrease 2 stitches at the beginning of every other row of the next ten."

altog: altogether

approx: approximate(ly)

b: bobble

bc: back cable or back cross

beg M: beginning marker

beg: begin(ning)

bet: between

bh: buttonhole (also *but*)

BLO: back loop only

blw: below

bo: can mean bobble, in some British patterns. The British term for "bind off" is "cast off," or CO.

BO: bind off

BO in pattern: bind off in pattern. As you bind off, keep doing whatever stitch pattern you were doing before you started binding off.

BO in ribbing: bind off in ribbing. Work in ribbing as you bind off (knit the knit stitches, purl the purl stitches).

but: buttonhole (also *bh*)

C: cable

C3B: cable 3 back. See Chapter 13 for fuller explanation of these stitches.

C3F: cable three front

C4B: cable four back

C4F: cable four front

CB: cable back

CC: contrasting color (also *AC,* for alternate color)

CF: cable front

ch(s): chain(s) (crochet term)

cl: cluster

cm: centimeter

cn: cable needle

CO: cast on

cont: continue(ing)

cr b (or cross b): cross back

cr f (or cross f): cross front

Cr: cross

Cr L: cross to the left

Cr R: cross to the right

cross 2LK: cross 2 stitches to the left, knitting

cross 2LP: cross 2 stitches to the left, purling

cross 2RK: cross 2 stitches to the right, knitting

cross 2RP: cross 2 stitches to the right, purling

dbl dec: double decrease

dc: double crochet (crochet term)

dec 1st: decrease 1 stitch. On a knit row, knit 2 stitches together either through the front or the back of the stitches. On a purl row, purl 2 stitches together.

dec: decrease(ing) The two most common decrease methods are to knit stitches together (*tog*) or to slip 1 stitch, knit the next, and pass the slipped stitch over (*psso*)

diag: diagonal

diam: diameter

dir: directions

dk: dark

DK: double-knitting weight yarn (worsted)

DP or dpn: double-pointed needle(s)

dtr: double treble (crochet term)

E: every

ea: each

eon: end of needle

EOR: every other row

ER: every row

est: established

ext: exterior

FC: front cable or front cross

fig: figure

fin: finished

foll: follows, following

fr: front side (the side facing knitter)

fwd: forward

g: gram(s) [General note: "g" is the only correct abbreviation for gram, singular or plural]

g st: garter stitch. The pattern made by knitting every stitch on every row.

GN: gauge needle

gr: group

grp(s): groups

GS: gauge stitch or ground shade

in(s) or ": inch(es)

inc 1 st: increase 1 stitch. Knit 1 stitch in the usual way, but do not slip it off the left needle. Insert the right needle into the stitch behind the left needle (the back of the stitch), and work another knit stitch.

inc: increase(ing) The two most common increase methods are to knit or purl twice into the same stitch (front and back), or to pick up the strand of yarn between 2 stitches with the point of your right hand needle and place it on the left hand needle. Knit into the back of this new loop, twisting it, to create an additional stitch.

incl: including or inclusive

inst: instructions

k or K: knit

k up 1: pick up and knit the stitch in the row below

k1 f&b: knit into the front and back of a stitch (increase one)

k1, s1, psso: knit one, slip one, pass slipped stitch over

K2tog: knit 2 stitches together. Insert the right needle through 2 stitches instead of 1, then knit them together as 1 stitch.

K2tbl (or k2tog tbl): knit two together through the back of loop

kb or kb1: knit into back of stitch

kbl: knit from back of loop

kfb: knit into the front and back of a stitch (increase one)

kpk: knit, purl, knit

kssb: knit slip stitch through the back

kwise or K-wise: knitwise. Insert the needle as you would to knit.

L: left (or light)

LC: left cross

lg: large

LH: left hand

lhn: left-hand needle

LN: left needle

lp(s): loop(s)

LT: left twist

lt: light

M: meter (or marker, or make)

M. St.: moss stitch. Created by alternately working 1 knit stitch and 1 purl stitch on every row. It is a kind of off-kilter rib, because the purl stitch is worked over the knit stitch on the following row.

M1: make one. Increase the number of stitches by one. Usually the pattern will describe how this should be done, but if it doesn't, make a stitch by lifting the strand between the last stitch knit and the next stitch with the tip of the left needle. Place it on the right needle and knit into the back of it.

M1P: make 1 purl stitch. Increase the number of stitches by one. Usually the pattern describes how this should be done, but if it doesn't, make a stitch by lifting the strand between the last stitch knit and the next stitch with the tip of the left needle. Place it on the right needle and purl into the front of it.

MB: make bobble

MC: main (or background) color

med: medium

mm: millimeter(s)

mult: multiple(s)

ndl(s): needle(s)

no: number

opp: opposite

oz: ounce(s)

p or P: purl

p2tog tbl or p2tog-b: purl 2 together through back of loop

P2tog: purl 2 stitches together. Insert the right needle through 2 stitches instead of 1, then purl them together as 1 stitch. This makes 1 stitch out of 2.

pat or patt(s): pattern(s)

PB1: purl into back of next stitch

pc: popcorn

pfb: purl into front and back of next stitch

pfl: purl from back of loop

pg(s): page(s)

PK: twisted or crossed purl stitch. Bring the yarn to the front of the work. Insert the right needle into the back loop of the stitch on the left needle. Wind the yarn round, and draw a loop through onto the right needle. Slip the stitch off the left needle.

pm: place marker

pnso: pass next stitch over

pr: pair

PR: previous row or round

prec: preceding

prev: previous

PRV: private side

psso: pass slipped stitch over. This is usually part of a decrease stitch. You will have just slipped from the left needle to the right without knitting it. Lift the next stitch farther down on the right needle, over the one you just slipped.

PU: pick up (stitches)

purlwise: insert the needle as though to purl

pwise or P-wise: purlwise, or as though to purl

RC: right cross

rem: remain(ing)

rep: repeat(ing). Repeat the action just done. If instructions are given in brackets, the whole operation contained within the brackets should be repeated.

ret: return

rev St st: reverse stockinette (reverse stocking stitch)

rev: reverse(d)

RGN: ribbing gauge needle

RH or rhn: right-hand needle

rib: ribbing

RN: right needle

rnd(s): round(s)

rpt: repeat

RS: right side

rsc: reverse single crochet

RT: right twist

sc: single crochet (crochet term)

sel: selvage

sk: skip

skn(s): skein(s)

skp or skpo or sl1, k1, psso: slip 1, knit 1, pass slipped stitch over. This is a decreasing stitch. Slip the first stitch, knit the next stitch, and bring the slipped stitch over the knitted stitch as though binding off.

sl 1f: Slip a stitch onto the cable needle at front of the work.

sl 1b: Slip a stitch onto the cable needle at back of the work.

sl st(s): slip stitch(es). Unworked stitches made by passing a stitch from the left-hand to the right-hand needle.

sl: slip

sl1, k2tog, psso: slip 1, knit 2 together, pass slipped stitch over. This is a decreasing stitch. It means slip the first stitch, knit the next 2 stitches together, then bring the slipped stitch over the knitted stitch as though binding off.

slip stitch knitwise: Insert the right needle into the next stitch as if to knit, but slip it on to the right needle without knitting it. (The slipped stitch becomes twisted.)

slip stitch purlwise: slip a stitch purlwise: insert the right needle into the next stitch as if to purl but slip it on to the right needle without purling it.

sm: small

SP or spn: single-pointed needles

sp(s): space(s) (or single-point needle[s])

ssk: slip, slip, knit. This is a leftward slanting decrease. Slip 1 stitch on to the right needle without knitting it. Slip the next stitch the same way. Put both stitches back onto the left needle in their new twisted positions, then knit them together.

ssp: slip 1 knitwise, slip 1 knitwise, purl 2 slip stitches together through back of loop

sssk: slip 1 knitwise, slip 1 knitwise, slip 1 knitwise, knit 3 slip stitches together through back of loop

St st: stockinette (or stocking) stitch. Created by knitting all the stitches on one row, then purling all the stitches on the next row.

st(s): stitch(es)

T3B: twist 3 back

T3F: twist 3 front

T4B: twist 4 back

T4F: twist 4 front

TB: twist back

TBL: through back of loop(s)

tch: turning chain (crochet term)

tfl: through front of loop

TK: twisted or crossed knit stitch. Insert right needle in the back loop of the left needle and knit a stitch.

tog: together

tr tr: triple treble (crochet term)

tr: treble or triple crochet (crochet term)

trn: turn

tw: twist

wb: wool back

WE: work even

wf or wft: wool front

wl: wool

won: wool over needle

work even: Continue in the normal pattern without increasing or decreasing. (The British term is "work straight.")

wrn: wool round needle

WS: wrong side

wt: weight

wyb or wyib: with yarn in back of work

wyf or wyif: with yarn in front of work

YB or yb or ybk: yarn back

yd(s): yard(s)

YF or yfwd or yfd: yarn forward to front of work yfon (yarn forward over needle) or yfrn (yarn forward and around needle) or yo (yarn over) or yon (yarn over needle): All these terms meaning the same thing: Increase to make an extra stitch. Bring the yarn forward then over the needle to form an additional loop of yarn. The loop makes a new stitch, and also leaves a small hole in the work, which is often part of a lace pattern or for the openwork increases on raglan sleeve shaping.

yo: yarn over needle

yo2: yarn over twice

yrh: yarn round hook

yrn: yarn round needle

ytb: yarn to back of work

CROCHET TERMS AND TRANSLATIONS

CANADA AND USA	UK, AUSTRALIA, AND EUROPE
skip	skip / miss
slip stitch (sl st):	single crochet (sc)
chain (ch):	chain (sl st)
single crochet (sc)	double crochet (dc)
half double crochet (hdc)	half triple crochet (h tr)
double crochet (dc)	triple or treble crochet (tr)
triple or treble crochet (tr)	double triple crochet (dtr) or double treble (dbl tr)
double treble or double triple (dtr)	triple treble crochet (tr tr)
triple treble crochet (tr tr)	quad treble (quad tr)
raised double crochet (rdc)	raised treble (rtc)

Appendix B

Needle and Hook Conversions

All patterns list the tools you'll need. They should also indicate whether they are U.K. or U.S. patterns. If your pattern is written with metric measurements or diagrams, do all your measuring in metric units. It's possible, however, to still use your U.S. needles. Refer to the following chart for correct conversions.

KNITTING NEEDLE SIZE CONVERSIONS

U.S.	METRIC	CANADA/UK	ORIGINAL BRITISH *
000	1.5 mm	n/a	n/a
00	1.75 mm	n/a	n/a
0	2 mm	14	13
1	2.25 mm	n/a	13
1	2.5 mm	n/a	n/a
2	2.75 mm	12	12
n/a	3 mm	n/a	11
3	3.25 mm	10	n/a
4	3.5 mm	n/a	9
5	3.75 mm	9	8
6	4 mm	8	n/a
7	4.5 mm	7	n/a
8	5 mm	6	n/a
9	5.5 mm	5	5
10	6 mm	4	n/a
10.5	6.5 mm	3	n/a
n/a	7 mm	2	n/a
n/a	7.5 mm	1	n/a
11	8 mm	0	n/a
12	8 mm	0	0
13	9 mm	00	n/a
15	10 mm	000	n/a
17	12 mm	n/a	n/a
18	14 mm	n/a	n/a
19	16 mm	n/a	n/a
35	19 mm	n/a	n/a
50	25 mm	n/a	n/a

* Applicable for British patterns printed before 1965.

STANDARD CROCHET HOOK SIZE CONVERSIONS

U.S.	METRIC	CANADA/UK
n/a	2.0 mm	14
B/1	2.25 mm	13
n/a	2.5 mm	12
C/2	2.75	n/a
n/a	3.0 mm	11
D/3	3.25 mm	10
E/4	3.5 mm	9
F/5	3.75 mm	n/a
G/6	4.0 mm	8
n/a	4.5 mm	7
H/8	5.0 mm	6
I/9	5.5 mm	5
J/10	6.0 mm	4
K/10½	6.5 mm	3
n/a	7 mm	2
L/11	8 mm	0
M/13	9 mm	00
N/15	10 mm	000

Appendix C
Knitting Symbols

Knitting patterns try to fit many lines of information into as small a space as possible. Line-by-line patterns use abbreviations (described in Appendix A), but charts and labels are a sea of symbols that you may need to translate before you get too far along. The following pages list the most common knitting and fabric care symbols along with their standard definitions.

Finished product for charted pattern on page 247

knitted by Christel Shea

Stitch Chart Symbols

Here are some of the basic symbols found in knitting charts. Each pattern book seems to use different symbols, but you should learn a few of the most common (see page 248).

Because a chart is a representation of the whole piece of knitting, the symbols have slightly different meanings depending whether you are on a right side or wrong side row.

Sometimes a chart won't show rows of straight purl on the wrong side of the fabric. In that case, the row numbers and pattern instructions should indicate the extra rows.

International Care Symbols

Given the amount of work you put into creating your hand-knit item, you want to be sure you care for it properly down the road. Get to know the international symbols for laundry care so you can incorporate the label information into your yarn-buying decision.

TOP

KNITTING CHART SYMBOLS

 knit

 purl

 knit into back of loop

 purl into back of loop

 knit 1 below

 knit 1, wrapping yarn twice (elongated stitch)

 slip 1 purlwise with yarn behind work

 slip 1 purlwise with yarn in front of work

 yarn over

 raised increase, left

 raised increase, right

 lifted increase, invisible

 knit 2 together

 knit 2 together into back of loop

 purl 2 together

 purl 2 together into back of loop

 slip 1, knit 1, pass the slipped stitch over

 slip 1, knit 2 together, pass the slipped stitch over

cross or cable knit stitches to the right

cross or cable knit stitches to the left

 knit, purl into 1 stitch

make bobble

no stitch

special instructions

INTERNATIONAL CARE SYMBOLS

 Washable. Signifies that the article can be washed by machine or by hand.

 The article should be washed by hand only, in water 40°C (104°F).

 Machine wash in warm water at a normal setting.

 Machine wash in hot water at a normal setting.

 Machine wash in warm water at a gentle setting.

 Machine wash in hot water at a gentle setting.

 Do not wash.

O Dry-cleanable.

Ⓐ Dry-cleanable in all solvents.

Ⓟ Dry-cleaned with perchlorethylene or white spirit, Solvent 113 and 11.

Ⓕ Dry-cleaned only with white spirit and Solvent 113.

 The garment is very sensitive to dry-cleaning.

 Do not dry-clean.

 The garment can be tumble-dried at medium to high heat.

 The garment can be tumble-dried at low heat.

 Do not tumble dry.

 The article can be bleached.

 Do not bleach.

 Hot, can be ironed up to a temperature of 210°C (392°F).

 Warm, can be ironed up to a temperature of 160°C (302°F).

 Cool, can be ironed up to a temperature of 120°C (248°F).

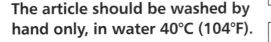 Do not iron.

 Any symbol printed in red, or with a cross through it, means "do not."

APPENDIX D
Glossary

A

acetate: A man-made fiber often blended with natural fibers such as cotton.

acrylic: A man-made fiber with a soft feel, like wool. Often blended with other fibers, both natural and man-made, to produce knitting and crochet yarn.

afghan: A crocheted or knitted blanket or coverlet, often made up of squares or triangular-shaped pieces.

alpaca: Yarn made from the hair of the animal of that name. Heavier and less elastic than wool. It wears well and when knitted it is very soft and slightly hairy. Alpaca usually comes in natural shades of beige, grays, and browns.

angora: The soft hair of the angora rabbit, used to make yarn. Rabbit hair is short and slippery, making it difficult to spin, so it's usually mixed with other fibers.

Aran: The type of wool grown on the Aran islands, off the western coast of Ireland, and a style of sweater traditionally made from it. The wool is less processed than other wool. The natural oils have not been stripped out, and it is very waterproof. Aran sweaters have distinctive patterns with cables, bobbles, and textured stitches. Aran wool, and the original sweaters of the same name, come in natural, creamy colors.

B

baby yarn (also called fingering weight): Very fine, lightweight grade of knitting yarns. In Europe they are called 3-, 4-, or 5-ply.

ball band (European term): The paper cylinder, provided by the manufacturer, which encloses a ball of commercial yarn and contains information about the knitting and washing properties of that yarn. The U.S. term is yarn wrapper.

bind off (U.S. term): A way of finishing an edge or segment so the stitches will not unravel. (U.K. term: cast off.)

blocking: The process of dampening or steaming and shaping knitted pieces to the right size and shape before they are assembled.

bobbin: A small notched pin that is used as a spool for yarn.

bobble: Raised stitches that can vary in size from a little knot to large clusters of knitted rows.

bodkin: A large needle with a blunt point and large eye, used for drawing tape or elastic through holes in knitted fabric.

butterfly twist: A hank of yarn made by winding yarn around the thumb and little finger of an outstretched hand, in a figure-eight configuration.

C

cable: A number of stitches that cross over each other, making the fabric look as if the stitches were intertwined.

cardigan: A knitted or crocheted jacket with center front closings.

cashmere: Yarn that comes from the hair of goats. Cashmere is luxuriously soft but rare and expensive. For hand-knitting, it is often spun with wool, which makes it a stronger, and cheaper, yarn.

cast off (European term): A way of finishing an edge or segment so the stitches will not unravel. The U.S. term is bind off.

cast on: To make a first, foundation row of stitches on a knitting needle so you can begin knitting.

chain: The most basic and easiest stitch in crochet. It is done by drawing a loop of yarn through another with a crochet hook. Most projects in crochet begin with a length of chain, and it is also used between other stitches to add length.

chenille: Yarns that are not spun like most yarns but made from a deep pile applied to a central core which gives them a distinctive, velvety look.

chevron: V-shaped.

chunky knit or bulky yarns: A heavy, thick grade of yarn used for outdoor garments. (European term: 12-ply.)

circular needles: Needles joined by a length of plastic cord, generally used for knitting round and round in spirals, thus producing a tubular fabric. Can also be used instead of a pair of straight needles to knit back and forth in rows.

colorway: In a knitting or crochet pattern, alternative choices of color. Multicolored yarn or thread can also come in different colorways. For example, when different versions of the yarn are manufactured, one type may have blue predominating and would be said to have a blue colorway.

Continental method: The practice of holding the working yarn in the left hand when knitting.

cotton: Fibers from the cotton plant, spun into yarn.

crew neck: A round neckline style that is close to the throat.

crochet hook: A rod similar to a knitting needle but with a hook, usually only on one end, to make crocheted fabric with.

D

darn in ends: To use a darning needle to weave any loose ends of yarn into the fabric.

darning needle: A blunt sewing needle with a large eye that will not split knitted stitches, used with yarn to do duplicate stitch embroidery or join pieces of fabric together. Similar to an embroidery needle or yarn needle.

decrease: To reduce the stitches in a row of knitting (for example, by knitting 2 stitches together).

dolman sleeves: A very deep sleeve set into a very deep armhole, which tapers in to the wrist.

Double-knitting yarn: A weight of yarn, also known as sport or DK weight, that makes lightweight adult clothes. They knit up to 5 or 6 stitches to the inch on number 6 needles. In Europe this weight is often called 8-ply. (Don't make the mistake, when you see the words "double knitting," of thinking you are being told to use two strands of yarn knitted together!) "Double knitting" can also refer to a technique that results in a double-sided or reversible fabric.

Double-pointed needles: A set of four or five straight needles with points on both ends, used for knitting round and round in spirals, thus producing tubular fabric.

drop shoulder: A sleeve style where the body of the garment provides some of the sleeve length, so the shoulder seam is located some way down the arm. There is no armhole shaping and the sleeves are short because they are an extension of the body of the sweater.

dropped stitches: Stitches that have escaped from the needle they are being worked on, usually by mistake.

duplicate stitch (also known as Swiss darning): A method of embroidery that covers existing knitted stitches.

dye lot: Yarns dyed together in the same vat that are thus exactly the same shade of a particular color.

E

ease: The difference between a person's measurements and the measurements of a piece of clothing. That is, the amount of fullness in a garment.

embroidery floss: A thread made of six-strand cotton or silk in a wide range of colors. Used for decorative embroidery done by hand.

embroidery needle: A blunt sewing needle with a large eye that will not split knitted stitches. Used with yarn to do duplicate stitch embroidery or join pieces of fabric together. Similar to a darning needle or yarn needle.

English method: The practice of holding the working yarn in the right hand when knitting.

epaulet: Shoulder trim, usually consisting of a band which lies flat across the top of the shoulder and secured by a button at the outer end.

extra bulky, super bulky or chunky: Thickest weight of wool available commercially. These yarns knit at a gauge of 2–2½ stitches to the inch on number 13 or larger needles. You can finish a garment made in extra bulky yarn in a few hours. (European term: 14-ply.)

eyelet: A small round hole in a fabric.

F

Fair Isle: A style of knitting derived from the Scottish island of the same name. Involves small repeated patterns of different colors, where the unused yarn is "stranded' in loops along the back of the fabric.

fibers: Substances, either natural, such as cotton and wool, or man-made, such as rayon and triacetate, used to make yarn.

finger crochet: A method of making a length of cord with yarn using just the fingers.

fingering weight (also called baby yarns): A very fine, lightweight grade of knitting yarn. In Europe it is called 3-, 4-, or 5-ply.

finishing: The processes that turn pieces of knitted fabric into clothes, including blocking and sewing up the seams.

fringe: An edging that is formed by loose end of yarn gathered into clusters.

frog: Decorative closing made of and looped braid or cord, coiled into curves and sewn in place. Frog closures are made in pairs, one with a loop, the other with a knot forming the button. Usually seen on Asian-styled garments. To "frog" is also a slang term for pulling undone a piece of fabric that is not right.

G

gansey: Old style English word for sweater, derived from Guernsey, one of the Channel Islands. A gansey is a pullover sweater, whose identifying characteristics are the gussets under the arms.

garter stitch: A pattern created by knitting every stitch on every row in knit stitches. Both sides of the fabric look the same.

gauge count: The number of stitches that make up a certain measure of fabric, varying depending on the size of needle or crochet hook and the weight of yarn used.

graft, grafting: To join 2 rows of knitting together by knitting (or in some cases sewing) the stitches together. Also known as kitchener stitch.

gusset: An insert of extra material, usually in the underarm area of a garment, to give it more ease and range of movement for the wearer.

I

I-cord (Idiot cord, also known as bobbin knitting, spool knitting or French knitting): A type of cord made from a primitive knitting machine made from a spool.

increase: Add stitches in a row (for example, knit in to the front and back of a stitch).

intarsia: Knitting in solid blocks of color. Each yarn is worked as it takes its turn to supply a patch of color and is kept hanging when it is not needed. When one color is abandoned for the next, the yarns must be twisted around each other to keep a hole from forming.

K

knitter's graph paper: A type of squared-off paper in the right proportion for a knitted fabric. Knitted stitches are wider than they are long.

knitting in the round: Knitting with circular of double-pointed needles to produce a tubular piece of knitting, used for making garments like socks or gloves or sweaters without side seams.

knitwise: Insert the needle into the stitch as if to knit it.

L

linen: Fabric or yarn made from natural flax fibers.

Lopi: Yarn from an Icelandic breed of sheep. It produces long, soft wool and is good for outdoor wear.

M

marker: Something to mark the place in knitting or crochet. Can be a small loop of yarn or thread, paperclip, safety pin, bobby pin or similar item, or a commercially made plastic ring.

merino: One of the best all-round varieties of wool.

mohair: A very fuzzy yarn made from the hair of angora goats. It is expensive and tangles easily but is luxurious and warm.

moss stitch: A pattern created by alternately working 1 knit stitch and 1 purl stitch. For rows 1 and 2, the pattern is K1, P1; for rows 3 and 4, the pattern is P1, K1. These 4 rows form the pattern.

multiple: The number of stitches that make up one horizontal section of a stitch pattern. A stitch pattern with a multiple of 6 means that the pattern is made up of 6 stitches that are repeated across a row. To fit complete pattern segments into the row, the segment must be made up of a number of stitches divisible by 6.

N

natural fibers: Fibers from animals or plants that are made into yarn.

no stitch: On knitting charts there are sometimes spaces left where stitches have been decreased or not yet made. Skip these spaces when working the pattern.

O

ombre: A dyeing process that produces different shades of color from light to dark along a strand of yarn.

P

picot edge: A small scalloped or semicircular edge.

pile: The raised surface of fabrics or yarns with short tufted fibers on their surface, such as velvet and fake-fur fabric or chenille yarns.

pilling: When short hairs come loose from knitted fabric and bind together to form small balls of fiber on the surface of the fabric.

place marker: Something to mark the place in knitting or crochet, such as a small loop of yarn or thread, paperclip, safety pin, bobby pin or similar item, or a commercially made plastic ring.

plain: Stockinette stitch (rows of knit stitch alternating with rows of purl) is sometimes called "plain."

ply: Number of strands woven together that make up a yarn.

polyester: A man-made fiber used to make yarn, often blended with wool or cotton.

pom-pom: Fluffy ball made up of tufts of yarn gathered together.

purl: A stitch worked with the yarn at the front of the work.

purlwise: Inserting the needle into the stitch as if to purl it.

R

raglan sleeve: A sleeve style in which the top of the sleeve forms a part of the neckline. The seam on a raglan-sleeved garment runs from the armpit to the neck.

repeat: The number of rows a stitch pattern takes to establish one complete segment of the pattern.

reverse stockinette: The "wrong" side of stockinette stitch. In other words, the purl side of a fabric made of rows of knit stitches alternating with rows of purl stitches.

reversible stitch: A knitting or crochet stitch that makes a fabric that looks the same on both side as, either side may be used as the outside.

rib or ribbing: Any stitch pattern made up of alternating knit stitches and purl stitches, producing vertical rows of similar stitches and creating a very elastic, binding fabric.

right side: The finished side of a piece of knitted fabric, which is the side that will be the outside of the garment.

row: All the stitches that make up a piece of knitted fabric from side to side. When knitting with two straight needles, after all the stitches from the left needle have been worked and transferred to the right needle, one row is said to have been completed.

S

saddle shoulder: This type of sleeve design makes a flat, square shape on top of the shoulder and is generally used only for men's sweaters.

seed stitch: A pattern created by alternately working 1 knit stitch and 1 purl stitch on every row. The purl stitch is worked over the knit stitch on the following row. The first row is K1, P1; the second row is P1, K1. These 2 rows form the pattern.

selvage stitch: Edge stitch that helps make it easier to sew seams when finishing a garment, or to pick up stitches later.

selvage: The edge of a piece of flat knitting.

set-in sleeve: This is the kind of sleeve most commonly seen in suits and shirts, where the width of the top of the sleeve is exactly the same measurement as the armhole opening it is to fit into.

setting in sleeves: The process of joining the sleeves of a garment to the main body of a garment

shaping: Changing the shape of a piece of knitted fabric by increasing or decreasing the number of stitches.

shawl collar: Neckline where collar and lapel are all one piece, forming a rolled collar where it is turned down at the back of he neck.

Shetland wool: Wool that comes from sheep on the Shetland Islands. A good fine wool for featherweight lace knitting.

short rows: A method of increasing by adding more rows to one side of a piece of fabric.

skein: A length of yarn wound in a large oval-shaped ball, ready for use in hand-knitting or crochet.

slip stitch: An unworked stitch that is passed from the left to the right needle.

space: A small opening between stitches.

sport weight yarns (also called double knit yarns, or DK weight): A midweight category of yarn that knits up to 5 or 6 stitches to the inch on number 6 needles. In Europe this weight is often called 8-ply.

steek: This Scottish term means to fasten or to close. Steeks are extra stitches that form wide ladders of yarn to mark a cutting line leaving raw edges to be sewn or otherwise kept from unraveling. These are necessary when you are working a garment completely in the round and must later cut places, at armholes for a sweater worked in the round, for example, so that the sleeve or border stitches can be knit up.

stitch pattern: A combination of stitches worked in a repeated formula to create patterned fabric.

stitch: Thread interlocked by knitting or crocheting.

stockinette (U.S. term): A pattern created by knitting all the stitches on one row and then purling all the stitches on the next row. This is one of the most common fabric stitches. It's also called plain knitting. The European term is stocking stitch.

stocking stitch (European term): A pattern created by knitting all the stitches on one row and then purling all the stitches on the next row. This is one of the most common fabric stitches. It's also called plain knitting. The U.S. term is stockinette stitch.

stranding: A method of keeping the nonworking yarn at the back of a piece of fabric when working a multicolored design such as a Fair Isle pattern.

swatch: Small sample piece of fabric, using a particular yarn and size of needles, usually knitted or crocheted for the purpose of determining gauge.

Swiss darning (also known as duplicate stitch): A method of embroidery that covers existing knitted stitches.

synthetic fibers: Man-made fibers produced from chemicals, such as acrylic, polyester, and nylon.

T

tension: The tightness or looseness with which the yarn is pulled when knitting or crocheting a piece of fabric, resulting from the degree of control a knitter has over the yarn he or she is working. The tension determines the gauge, that is, the number of stitches and rows per inch of fabric.

turn: When knitting or crocheting flat pieces of fabric, you turn your work around so the other side of the piece is facing you so you can work back across the row.

turtleneck: A type of neckline with a high collar that hugs the neck and folds down over itself.

U

unravel: When stitches in knitting or crochet disconnect from each other, and the fabric is pulled apart, either on purpose or by accident.

V

variegated yarn: Yarn that changes color along its length.

vest: A short, sleeveless jacket.

vicuna: Yarn made from the hair of the vicuna llama.

W

weight: Yarns are said to have a certain weight, giving an idea of how thick or heavy they are.

wool: Fibers from a sheep, spun into yarn. The word "wool" is often used generically to mean any yarn.

work even: Knitting or crocheting in a stitch pattern already described, without increasing or decreasing.

work in ends: Using a darning needle to weave any loose ends of yarn back into the fabric.

worsted: a weight of yarn (equivalent to the European 4-ply). Worsted weight is a good all-purpose yarn. The gauge is usually 4 stitches to the inch on a number 6 to a number 9 needle. There is also a heavy worsted weight, which is a bit thicker. (In Europe, 10-ply, or Aran weight.)

wrong side: The inside, or the side of the fabric that will not show when a garment is made up.

Y

yardage: The length of yarn in a ball or skein of yarn, or the length needed to complete a pattern.

yarn needle: A blunt sewing needle with a large eye that will not split knitted stitches. Used with yarn to do duplicate stitch embroidery or join pieces of fabric together. Similar to a darning needle or embroidery needle.

yarn wrapper (U.S. term): The paper cylinder, provided by the manufacturer, which encloses a ball of commercial yarn and contains information about the knitting and washing properties of that yarn. (In Europe, it's called a ball band.)

yarn: A long, continuous strand of any fiber long and pliable enough to be knitted or crocheted.

Index

C

THE **EVERYTHING** SERIES!

BUSINESS & PERSONAL FINANCE

Everything® Budgeting Book
Everything® Business Planning Book
Everything® Coaching and Mentoring Book
Everything® Fundraising Book
Everything® Get Out of Debt Book
Everything® Grant Writing Book
Everything® Homebuying Book, 2nd Ed.
Everything® Homeselling Book
Everything® Home-Based Business Book
Everything® Investing Book
Everything® Landlording Book
Everything® Leadership Book
Everything® Managing People Book
Everything® Negotiating Book
Everything® Online Business Book
Everything® Personal Finance Book
Everything® Personal Finance in Your 20s
        and 30s Book
Everything® Project Management Book
Everything® Real Estate Investing Book
Everything® Robert's Rules Book, $7.95
Everything® Selling Book
Everything® Start Your Own Business Book
Everything® Wills & Estate Planning Book

COOKING

Everything® Barbecue Cookbook
Everything® Bartender's Book, $9.95
Everything® Chinese Cookbook
Everything® College Cookbook
Everything® Cookbook
Everything® Diabetes Cookbook
Everything® Easy Gourmet Cookbook
Everything® Fondue Cookbook
Everything® Grilling Cookbook
Everything® Healthy Meals in Minutes
        Cookbook
Everything® Holiday Cookbook

Everything® Indian Cookbook
Everything® Low-Carb Cookbook
Everything® Low-Fat High-Flavor Cookbook
Everything® Low-Salt Cookbook
Everything® Meals for a Month Cookbook
Everything® Mediterranean Cookbook
Everything® Mexican Cookbook
Everything® One-Pot Cookbook
Everything® Pasta Cookbook
Everything® Quick Meals Cookbook
Everything® Slow Cooker Cookbook
Everything® Soup Cookbook
Everything® Thai Cookbook
Everything® Vegetarian Cookbook
Everything® Wine Book

HEALTH

Everything® Alzheimer's Book
Everything® Diabetes Book
Everything® Hypnosis Book
Everything® Low Cholesterol Book
Everything® Massage Book
Everything® Menopause Book
Everything® Nutrition Book
Everything® Reflexology Book
Everything® Stress Management Book

HISTORY

Everything® American Government Book
Everything® American History Book
Everything® Civil War Book
Everything® Irish History & Heritage Book
Everything® Middle East Book

HOBBIES & GAMES

Everything® Blackjack Strategy Book
Everything® Brain Strain Book, $9.95
Everything® Bridge Book
Everything® Candlemaking Book

Everything® Card Games Book
Everything® Cartooning Book
Everything® Casino Gambling Book, 2nd Ed.
Everything® Chess Basics Book
Everything® Crossword and Puzzle Book
Everything® Crossword Challenge Book
Everything® Cryptograms Book, $9.95
Everything® Digital Photography Book
Everything® Drawing Book
Everything® Easy Crosswords Book
Everything® Family Tree Book
Everything® Games Book, 2nd Ed.
Everything® Knitting Book
Everything® Knots Book
Everything® Motorcycle Book
Everything® Online Genealogy Book
Everything® Photography Book
Everything® Poker Strategy Book
Everything® Pool & Billiards Book
Everything® Quilting Book
Everything® Scrapbooking Book
Everything® Sewing Book
Everything® Woodworking Book
Everything® Word Games Challenge Book

HOME IMPROVEMENT

Everything® Feng Shui Book
Everything® Feng Shui Decluttering Book,
        $9.95
Everything® Fix-It Book
Everything® Homebuilding Book
Everything® Lawn Care Book
Everything® Organize Your Home Book

EVERYTHING® *KIDS'* BOOKS

All titles are $6.95
Everything® Kids' Animal Puzzle & Activity
        Book
Everything® Kids' Baseball Book, 3rd Ed.

All Everything® books are priced at $12.95 or $14.95, unless otherwise stated. Prices subject to change without notice.

Everything® Kids' Bible Trivia Book
Everything® Kids' Bugs Book
Everything® Kids' Christmas Puzzle
    & Activity Book
Everything® Kids' Cookbook
Everything® Kids' Halloween Puzzle
    & Activity Book
Everything® Kids' Hidden Pictures Book
Everything® Kids' Joke Book
Everything® Kids' Knock Knock Book
Everything® Kids' Math Puzzles Book
Everything® Kids' Mazes Book
Everything® Kids' Money Book
Everything® Kids' Monsters Book
Everything® Kids' Nature Book
Everything® Kids' Puzzle Book
Everything® Kids' Riddles & Brain Teasers Book
Everything® Kids' Science Experiments Book
Everything® Kids' Sharks Book
Everything® Kids' Soccer Book
Everything® Kids' Travel Activity Book

KIDS' STORY BOOKS

Everything® Bedtime Story Book
Everything® Fairy Tales Book

LANGUAGE

Everything® Conversational Japanese Book
    (with CD), $19.95
Everything® French Phrase Book, $9.95
Everything® French Verb Book, $9.95
Everything® Inglés Book
Everything® Learning French Book
Everything® Learning German Book
Everything® Learning Italian Book
Everything® Learning Latin Book
Everything® Learning Spanish Book
Everything® Sign Language Book
Everything® Spanish Grammar Book
Everything® Spanish Phrase Book, $9.95
Everything® Spanish Verb Book, $9.95

MUSIC

Everything® Drums Book (with CD), $19.95
Everything® Guitar Book
Everything® Home Recording Book
Everything® Playing Piano and Keyboards
    Book

Everything® Reading Music Book (with CD),
    $19.95
Everything® Rock & Blues Guitar Book
    (with CD), $19.95
Everything® Songwriting Book

NEW AGE

Everything® Astrology Book
Everything® Dreams Book, 2nd Ed.
Everything® Ghost Book
Everything® Love Signs Book, $9.95
Everything® Numerology Book
Everything® Paganism Book
Everything® Palmistry Book
Everything® Psychic Book
Everything® Reiki Book
Everything® Spells & Charms Book
Everything® Tarot Book
Everything® Wicca and Witchcraft Book

PARENTING

Everything® Baby Names Book
Everything® Baby Shower Book
Everything® Baby's First Food Book
Everything® Baby's First Year Book
Everything® Birthing Book
Everything® Breastfeeding Book
Everything® Father-to-Be Book
Everything® Father's First Year Book
Everything® Get Ready for Baby Book
Everything® Getting Pregnant Book
Everything® Homeschooling Book
Everything® Parent's Guide to Children
    with ADD/ADHD
Everything® Parent's Guide to Children
    with Asperger's Syndrome
Everything® Parent's Guide to Children
    with Autism
Everything® Parent's Guide to Children
    with Dyslexia
Everything® Parent's Guide to Positive
    Discipline
Everything® Parent's Guide to Raising a
    Successful Child
Everything® Parent's Guide to Tantrums
Everything® Parent's Guide to the Overweight
    Child
Everything® Parenting a Teenager Book
Everything® Potty Training Book, $9.95

Everything® Pregnancy Book, 2nd Ed.
Everything® Pregnancy Fitness Book
Everything® Pregnancy Nutrition Book
Everything® Pregnancy Organizer, $15.00
Everything® Toddler Book
Everything® Tween Book
Everything® Twins, Triplets, and More Book

PETS

Everything® Cat Book
Everything® Dachshund Book, $12.95
Everything® Dog Book
Everything® Dog Health Book
Everything® Dog Training and Tricks Book
Everything® Golden Retriever Book, $12.95
Everything® Horse Book
Everything® Labrador Retriever Book, $12.95
Everything® Poodle Book, $12.95
Everything® Pug Book, $12.95
Everything® Puppy Book
Everything® Rottweiler Book, $12.95
Everything® Tropical Fish Book

REFERENCE

Everything® Car Care Book
Everything® Classical Mythology Book
Everything® Computer Book
Everything® Divorce Book
Everything® Einstein Book
Everything® Etiquette Book
Everything® Mafia Book
Everything® Philosophy Book
Everything® Psychology Book
Everything® Shakespeare Book

RELIGION

Everything® Angels Book
Everything® Bible Book
Everything® Buddhism Book
Everything® Catholicism Book
Everything® Christianity Book
Everything® Jewish History & Heritage Book
Everything® Judaism Book
Everything® Koran Book
Everything® Prayer Book
Everything® Saints Book
Everything® Torah Book
Everything® Understanding Islam Book

All Everything® books are priced at $12.95 or $14.95, unless otherwise stated. Prices subject to change without notice.

Everything® World's Religions Book
Everything® Zen Book

SCHOOL & CAREERS

Everything® Alternative Careers Book
Everything® College Survival Book, 2nd Ed.
Everything® Cover Letter Book, 2nd Ed.
Everything® Get-a-Job Book
Everything® Job Interview Book
Everything® New Teacher Book
Everything® Online Job Search Book
Everything® Paying for College Book
Everything® Practice Interview Book
Everything® Resume Book, 2nd Ed.
Everything® Study Book

SELF-HELP

Everything® Great Sex Book
Everything® Kama Sutra Book
Everything® Self-Esteem Book

SPORTS & FITNESS

Everything® Fishing Book
Everything® Fly-Fishing Book
Everything® Golf Instruction Book

Everything® Pilates Book
Everything® Running Book
Everything® Total Fitness Book
Everything® Weight Training Book
Everything® Yoga Book

TRAVEL

Everything® Family Guide to Hawaii
Everything® Family Guide to New York City, 2nd Ed.
Everything® Family Guide to RV Travel & Campgrounds
Everything® Family Guide to the Walt Disney World Resort®, Universal Studios®, and Greater Orlando, 4th Ed.
Everything® Family Guide to Washington D.C., 2nd Ed.
Everything® Guide to Las Vegas
Everything® Guide to New England
Everything® Travel Guide to the Disneyland Resort®, California Adventure®, Universal Studios®, and the Anaheim Area

WEDDINGS

Everything® Bachelorette Party Book, $9.95
Everything® Bridesmaid Book, $9.95

Everything® Elopement Book, $9.95
Everything® Father of the Bride Book, $9.95
Everything® Groom Book, $9.95
Everything® Mother of the Bride Book, $9.95
Everything® Wedding Book, 3rd Ed.
Everything® Wedding Checklist, $9.95
Everything® Wedding Etiquette Book, $7.95
Everything® Wedding Organizer, $15.00
Everything® Wedding Shower Book, $7.95
Everything® Wedding Vows Book, $7.95
Everything® Weddings on a Budget Book, $9.95

WRITING

Everything® Creative Writing Book
Everything® Get Published Book
Everything® Grammar and Style Book
Everything® Guide to Writing a Book Proposal
Everything® Guide to Writing a Novel
Everything® Guide to Writing Children's Books
Everything® Screenwriting Book
Everything® Writing Poetry Book
Everything® Writing Well Book

. . . .

We have Everything® for the beginner crafter!
All titles are $14.95

Everything® Crafts—Baby Scrapbooking
1-59337-225-6

Everything® Crafts—Bead Your Own Jewelry
1-59337-142-X

Everything® Crafts—Create Your Own Greeting Cards
1-59337-226-4

Everything® Crafts—Easy Projects
1-59337-298-1

Everything® Crafts—Polymer Clay for Beginners
1-59337-230-2

Everything® Crafts—Rubber Stamping Made Easy
1-59337-229-9

Everything® Crafts—Wedding Decorations and Keepsakes
1-59337-227-2

Available wherever books are sold!
To order, call 800-872-5627, or visit us at *www.everything.com*
Everything® and everything.com® are registered trademarks of F+W Publications, Inc.